COMMUNITY WORK

Theory into Practice

Karen McArdle, Sue Briggs,
Kirsty Forrester and Ed Garrett

First published in Great Britain in 2024 by

Policy Press, an imprint of
Bristol University Press
University of Bristol
1–9 Old Park Hill
Bristol
BS2 8BB
UK
t: +44 (0)117 374 6645
e: bup-info@bristol.ac.uk

Details of international sales and distribution partners are available at
policy.bristoluniversitypress.co.uk

© Bristol University Press 2024

British Library Cataloguing in Publication Data
A catalogue record for this book is available from the British Library

ISBN 978-1-4473-6532-7 paperback
ISBN 978-1-4473-6533-4 ePub
ISBN 978-1-4473-6534-1 ePdf

The right of Karen McArdle, Sue Briggs, Kirsty Forrester and Ed Garrett to be identified as authors of this work has been asserted by them in accordance with the Copyright, Designs and Patents Act 1988.

All rights reserved: no part of this publication may be reproduced, stored in a retrieval system, or transmitted in any form or by any means, electronic, mechanical, photocopying, recording, or otherwise without the prior permission of Bristol University Press.

Every reasonable effort has been made to obtain permission to reproduce copyrighted material. If, however, anyone knows of an oversight, please contact the publisher.

The statements and opinions contained within this publication are solely those of the authors and not of the University of Bristol or Bristol University Press. The University of Bristol and Bristol University Press disclaim responsibility for any injury to persons or property resulting from any material published in this publication.

Bristol University Press and Policy Press work to counter discrimination on grounds of gender, race, disability, age and sexuality.

Cover design: Robin Hawes
Front cover image: iStock/malerapaso

Contents

List of figures and tables   v
Grateful acknowledgements   vi

Introduction   1
Karen McArdle, Sue Briggs, Ed Garrett and Kirsty Forrester

1   Professional learning   5
     Sue Briggs and Karen McArdle

2   Social justice   17
     Karen McArdle

3   Equality and inclusion   30
     Kirsty Forrester and Karen McArdle

4   Impact, change and making a difference   48
     Karen McArdle

5   Participation   61
     Karen McArdle

6   Working with communities   77
     Karen McArdle

7   Community engagement   90
     Ed Garrett and Karen McArdle

8   Networking and partnership   106
     Kirsty Forrester

9   Health and well-being   121
     Ed Garrett and Karen McArdle

10	Youth work *Kirsty Forrester and Karen McArdle*	138
11	Adult learning *Kirsty Forrester*	157
12	Employability *Kirsty Forrester*	179
13	The environment *Ed Garrett and Karen McArdle*	198
14	Community arts *Sue Briggs and Karen McArdle*	210
15	Digital community work *Kirsty Forester*	225
16	Community research *Karen McArdle*	242
17	Leadership in community work *Kirsty Forrester and Sue Briggs*	256

Conclusion and celebration   275
Karen McArdle, Sue Briggs, Ed Garrett and Kirsty Forrester

Index   278

List of figures and tables

Figure

4.1　The evidence continuum　55

Tables

1.1　Professional reflections on theory tool　14
11.1　Epistemologies of adult learning　166
16.1　Community based participatory research:　252
　　　a guide to principles and practice

Grateful acknowledgements

Our thanks to the community workers and other key thinkers with whom we spoke when preparing this book:

Janine Adams (England)
Marion Allison (Scotland)
Sarah Boath (Scotland)
Sheila Brown (Scotland)
Richard Bryce (Scotland)
Francesca Calo (England)
Jess Carnegie (Scotland)
Lynn Clark (USA)
Lada Copic (Scotland)
Kevin Ditcham (Scotland)
Matthew Evans (Scotland)
Stuart Fairweather (Scotland)
Sonia Garcha (India)
Darran Gillan (Scotland)
Belona Greenwood (England)
Alan Gunn (Scotland)
Clare Harper (Scotland)
Joan Harrison (Canada)
Ian Hunter (Scotland)
Susan Hunter (Scotland)
Kathleen Johnston (Scotland)
Martin Kasprowicz (Scotland)
Mark Kelly (Ireland)
Michael Kengmana (USA)
Fran Kennedy (Ireland)
Jo Kirby (Scotland)
Elaine Lawson (Scotland)
Margaret Ledwith (England)

Grateful acknowledgements

Suzanne MacAuley (Scotland)
Alan Mackie (Scotland)
Connor Maxwell (Scotland)
Paul McCurdy (Scotland)
Sibongiseni Mdladla (South Africa)
Jennifer Miller (Scotland)
Ken Milroy (Scotland)
Jane Mitchell (Scotland)
Paul Nelis (Scotland)
Kimiko Petsche (USA)
Pauline Rettie (Scotland)
Mark Richardson (Scotland)
Charis Robertson (Scotland)
Iain Shaw (Scotland)
Nadia Stuart (Scotland)
Kelly Tang (Hong Kong)
Dawn Tuckwood (Scotland)
Alison Urie (Scotland)
Nat Wealleans-Turner (England)
Ross Weatherby (Scotland)
Charlie West (Scotland)
Aine Whelan (Ireland)

Thanks especially to Catherine McKay for final comments and proof-reading.

Introduction

*Karen McArdle, Sue Briggs,
Ed Garrett and Kirsty Forrester*

This book is intended for community workers – professionals working in many different disciplines; working, for example, in practice linked to adult learning, youth work and community development, in the disciplines of health, social work, planning, environment and education. It is intended for people at all stages of practice, be they students, more experienced colleagues or leaders in their field. We do, however, assume a practice context, as each chapter contains not just theory but also principles for practice and challenge questions about the reader's own practice.

We have chosen to produce a wide-ranging text to introduce theory across a broad scope and field of practice. Our purpose is to stimulate interest across the profession in using theory and linking it to practice. Individual chapters may seem more relevant to the reader, but we hope you will read the whole book, as the chapters are highly interrelated. This attention to a field of practice has resulted in a choice of theorists to include in this book, which is somewhat idiosyncratic. We have selected largely ideas to discuss rather than theorists to present and have tried to choose authors who we consider to be or who are becoming significant to the field. This was a difficult task and we are aware of many seminal thinkers who have not appeared in this text. We have chapters on youth work and adult learning, for example, and cannot hope to include all the important thinkers, as even one aspect of these practice areas could fill a whole book. Instead, we have chosen to focus on current discussions and arguments in practice and, as practitioners ourselves, have taken a particular standpoint.

Each chapter is ascribed to an author(s), but it is true that the book is written by all of us. We have tried to preserve some individuality at the same time as acknowledging that this has been a process of collaboration by practitioners writing a book, in the spirit of community work. Not all of us agree with all the content, but the content is a product of discussion and, in some cases, compromise. The named author(s) for each chapter have ownership of the content and took the lead writing role. This is important to us, as we believe ideas are not owned by anyone and are improved though collaboration.

Our hopes for the book are that community workers will capture the excitement that goes with the theory of our work. We hope that, after reading, you will take the initiative and follow up ideas or find ideas of your own which underpin what you do and which make your practice robust through being underpinned by theory and substantiated in practice. It is our intention that the book should be used, so we have included a note at the end of each chapter of the 'Principles in practice' of the knowledge we have presented. We have also included 'Challenge questions' for individual or shared reflection.

We could not have written this book without assistance from people from across the world. We considered that our knowledge was not sufficient for a book about ideas, so wanted to use the lived experience, ideas and knowledge of others, including those who we hope would be the audience of the text. Accordingly, we conducted focus groups and interviews to explore ideas. This has made the book up to date with contemporary practice. We quote from academic texts but also include the voices of people deeply embedded in practice. We harnessed our networks, established over a long period of time and cannot thank enough the participants who gave so freely of their time, knowledge and expertise.

The book opens with an important chapter on the professional learning journey and the links between theory and practice, illuminating our take on this subject. Chapter 2 is also highly significant, as it describes social justice and the values that underpin what we do. It considers neoliberalism, which we

Introduction

consider to be important as a feature of the context in which our work takes place. Chapter 3 develops the ideas of Chapter 2 and looks at equality and inclusion. We have chosen to look at these concepts from the perspective of work with people with protected characteristics, covered by national and international equality or human rights legislation. These people are the usual participants of our work. Chapter 4 explores the idea of impact, as this is what we all are trying to achieve with our work. It considers change and how we can work towards this and show evidence of change occurring.

Chapters 5 to 8 focus on dimensions of community development. Chapter 5 looks at participation by populations in our work and links closely with Chapter 7 on community engagement. Chapter 6 concerns working with communities, focusing on connectedness and values of community work. Chapter 8 concerns one of the key contributors to our effectiveness, networking and partnership.

Chapters 9 to 15 concern different disciplines and activities within the domain of community work. We could not cover all disciplines which make up community work, and so we have selected those that are most common to our shared practice. Chapter 9 considers understandings of health and the role of community workers in health education. Chapter 10 considers youth work and the inherent difficulties in defining exactly who youth are and the difficulties of ensuring that youth work is valued as an educational practice. Chapter 11 looks at adult learning and we have chosen to explore what is distinct about the community-based adult learning that takes place in community settings, focusing in particular on basic skills education for adults. Chapter 12 focuses on employability. We look at whether employment is necessarily the best focus and outcome for some programmes. The chapter on environment, Chapter 13, tackles a huge topic with a consideration of social justice and the environment. Chapter 14 considers community arts with a particular focus on health and well-being.

Chapters 15, 16 and 17 concern ways of working in the community work profession. Chapter 15 concerns the use of digital technology in community work practice and the need for everyone to work with this, as it is embedded in our culture and has an impact on social justice. Chapter 16 considers community research and selects two methods, narrative inquiry and action research, for further attention because of their perceived relevance to the value base of community work. Chapter 17 concerns leadership in a community work context. Once again, the value base of community work is significant. We ask who and where are the leaders? Our final chapter is a conclusion and celebration of learning.

1

Professional learning

Sue Briggs and Karen McArdle

Introduction

We, the authors, Ed, Kirsty and Sue, are a group of community work practitioners based in Scotland. Karen makes an academic contribution to this group, also founded on her practical experience. We have tried to make this book as relevant to practice as possible and so have consulted others through interviews and focus groups to broaden the knowledge base both locally and internationally. You will find quotations from practitioners as well as the academic community. We have gathered case studies to illustrate how theory links to practice. You will find, at the end of each chapter, that we have suggested the key principles for practice that have emerged from the theory; and we have posed challenge questions to help you reflect on your own, or with others, about the theory we have chosen.

It has been exciting writing this book together. We have learnt so much about what we and others think. We have not always agreed on the themes, interpretations or importance of key ideas, but it has been enriching working to solve these tensions together. We hope the book will help you to reflect critically on theory and how it links to your practice. The reason we decided to write this book was because we considered that theory was undervalued; once community workers leave further or higher education, they leave the books behind and perhaps wider thought provocations. We hope that by the end of this book you will see that theory and practice in community work are inseparable. We have attempted to make theory highly accessible.

One of the issues that made us think deeply and try to resolve our different understandings was what exactly constitutes theory. This chapter is the result and resolution of these differences we had. It takes a purposeful look at the role of our own learning in the course of professional pursuits. We explore theory as a catalyst in sustaining good practice and invite the reader to reflect on their own influences and sources of inspiration in keeping work in community settings relevant, fulfilling and enduring. We consider theory in the simplest of translations and take a closer look at where our inspiration, understanding and knowledge come from in our everyday working lives as practitioners in community contexts.

Lost theory in the world of community work practice

Principal places of professional learning are traditionally seen as institutional establishments, where qualification and endorsed learning are housed. This book seeks to look beyond the learning experiences initially cultivated and fuelled in colleges, universities and formal settings, and into the workplace as a learning environment itself. We acknowledge that workplace-based training and apprenticeship models harness the workplace as an important backdrop, but what we are taking a closer look at is the role of theory and learning in long-established practice. Is vital theory to support practice lost, once we are consumed by the demands and timelines of our roles in community work settings? Should our work be characterised by well-informed and skilled practice leading to positive outcomes for individuals and communities? How can we ensure that this is the case? We hope to answer these questions in this book.

Eraut (1994) takes a close look at how theory influences practice and how people use the knowledge they have already acquired, in his book Developing Professional Knowledge and Competence. He states that both of these elements, theory and practice, are central to the goal of developing professional practice.

> Learning knowledge and using knowledge are not separate processes but the same process. The process of using knowledge transforms that knowledge so that it is no longer the same knowledge. But people are so accustomed to using the word 'knowledge' to refer only to 'book knowledge' which is publicly available in codified form, that they have developed only limited awareness of the nature and extent of their personal knowledge. (Eraut, 1994, 25)

The experiential learning and skill and knowledge acquired through practice can be undervalued in workplaces, including by workers and volunteers who deliver daily in important roles, we propose. This is curious and brings us back to the earlier questions. Should our work be characterised by well-informed and skilled practice, and how can we ensure that this is the case? The case and need for evidence gathering to demonstrate impact in community settings is explored in Chapter 4 and we have explored this further in The Impact of Community Work: How to Gather Evidence (McArdle et al, 2020).

It is widely recognised that, upon leaving university or college, we are rarely completely 'workplace ready'. This then places a huge importance on learning in the workplace through shadowing and in-house professional learning; peer review, support and supervision; regular dialogue with colleagues; and access to externally offered continuing learning opportunities which stretch our thinking. Many workplaces require a set amount of professional learning through record keeping by staff. This can be seen as a positive action on behalf of an employer but can also, at times, be seen by practitioners as an imposed demand, where they feel torn between the importance of delivery and the completion of learning and learning records. This suggests a state of continuous compromise and highlights a worrying picture of inward investment in self as undervalued. This is a picture recognised by many managers and practice leaders, in our experience.

The issue of time is captured in a very practical way and with solutions by Burkeman (2021). He waves a flag for that age-old expression, 'we never have time' (p 113).

The case study presented next unravels the recall and importance placed on theory by a group of community workers with Sue, but also accentuates the need for access to fresh thinking.

Case study

During a professional learning event for community workers, practitioners were offered an opportunity by organisers to reflect on which theories were influencing their current practice. There were references to seminal pieces of work and, interestingly, some less familiar or borrowed from other fields of practice. The observation by the organisers, and Sue as a participant, was that peers were drawing on familiar work and that reference to new reading or exploring new research seemed less prevalent. Many practitioners will explain their lack of access to new research in their field as due to information being held in libraries or in journals to which they do not have access.

> Sue's immediate reflection was the need to find a space to explore theory with others. Discussion with colleagues about ideas or theory does not always happen, unless you are lucky enough to find a student or a similar-minded person. Sue was not alone in this thought, as she received a few messages immediately after her activity about theory in literature and, also, she recognised a desire among colleagues to explore further.

To our way of thinking, it is important for workplaces to offer and, indeed, encourage time and space, as well as the resources, for practitioners to engage in theoretical research and discussion with peers. To keep yourself relevant, inspired and effective, we suggest, you need to see yourself as a learner in your workplace and profession. Of course, this needs to be supported by a conscientious manager or well-intentioned employer, but the learning needs to be unlocked by the individual. Socrates is believed to have aptly described education as 'the kindling of a flame, not the filling of a vessel', inspiring many similar descriptions and shining a light on the need to inspire rather than impose.

Stages of retention of inspirational theory

The preceding case study points to the fact that connection to theory encountered when undertaking professional training can stick with us, and also highlights that this can be dated and passive, rather than actively unlocked in practice. The practitioner quote here describes the impact theory can still have on one's practice many years later:

> 'Lots of the theories that we are using are quite old. There don't seem to be new theories coming out, you know, in the last 10–15 years. But the one that influenced me most in my practice is probably Foucault and his thinking of power relationships. And I think the penny dropped altogether in our work, when I read his stuff about how every relationship, any meeting with another human, is always a power relationship and how much responsibility as community workers we have to recognise that, and put ourselves on an equal footing with our learners.' (Lada Copic, 2022, Focus Group)

Professional learning delivery needs to be engaging, purposeful and valued. The active engagement of participants is essential, for learning to be absorbed. The following quotation describes approaches to be avoided: 'Teachers and leaders report having their time wasted at professional learning events that are too theoretical, tell them what they already know or are not well matched to the context in which they work' (Robinson, 2018, 88). We also need to consider the learning which occurs as a result of an exchange of practice between peers, a practitioner and a manager, or a student and a workplace supervisor. The exposure to a skilled and inspiring colleague can leave a permanent imprint on the practice of an individual. We do, however, need to consider the importance of taking the sharing of practice forward into implementation based on our learning from that experience.

> 'I think when I was supervising placements for social work students in the Drug Addiction Service, there

was often a mismatch between people's understanding of theory and their ability to apply it in their work context. Obviously, a work placement is a great way of being able to connect those two worlds; to understand theory and connect it to the way that we work and connect it to our approach with the person in front of us or within the team.' (Nat Wealleans-Turner, 2021, Focus Group)

It is also important to remind ourselves that although new and current thinking is vital in community work settings, we cannot ignore key texts which have informed and shaped our working world over many years. Seismic influence from writers such as Paulo Freire is still felt today, even though he was writing over 50 years ago. The principles and values in good community work practice occupy similar ground, despite the time lapse.

In the following quotation, Freire is challenging stereotypes for educational delivery and is setting the scene for learning in community settings.

> Through this project we launched a new institution of popular culture, a 'culture circle' since among us a school was a traditionally passive concept. Instead of a teacher we had a co-ordinator; instead of lectures, dialogue: instead of pupils, group participants; instead of alienating syllabi, compact programs that were broken down and codified into learning units. (Freire, 1974, 38)

Keeping a theoretical grounding?

We might also ask, does reflective practice build on and secure recourse to theory in our professional work? The case study presented earlier, with its practitioner contribution, would seem to endorse this. Moon (1999) depicts the function of reflective practice in a very practical way. This sits comfortably against the backdrop of our closer look at workplace-based learning and the notion of experiential learning in situ through the relationships and experiences we are exposed to in our working lives.

Interest in reflection and reflective practice in teaching, nursing and social work is not uniform throughout different roles in these professions and there are various relationships that provide contexts for professional learning and practice. All have different involvements with professional learning and different reasons for using reflective practice. The contexts are expressed in the following interactions:
- Educators teach novice practitioners
- Novice practitioners are learners in the profession
- Practising professionals are in practice with learners, patients and clients
- Practising professionals are learners in continuing professional development
- Learners / patients / clients learn and are subject to the actions of practising professionals, which may engender a process of learning (knowledge, skills and behaviour). (Moon, 1999, 56)

It is also worth remembering that practical organisational policy in the workplace is often linked to emerging local, regional and national need or requirements, which in turn may be well informed by theory; academic advice and recommendation; and social and educational policy for practice. Theory can be found in everyday texts if we are tuned in to these texts.

Our practice compass

The UK National Occupational Standards in Community Development (Community Development and Health Network, 2009), describe the development of best practice as dependent on 'reflective practice' where the worker, manager or team constantly examine their practice and actions against the values of community development; these being social justice, self-determination, working and learning together, sustainable communities and participation. These values may be seen as an anchor, or arguably a practice compass, for the busy practitioner working in communities.

In turn, reflective practice in the Standards, is defined as:

- Identifying and reflecting on your own practice, knowledge and values;
- Reviewing your own practice, knowledge and values;
- Evaluating and developing your own practice;
- Identifying and taking action to meet your own learning and developmental needs;
- Reviewing and meeting your own learning and developmental needs.

We would say that these are timeless and essential in maintaining your practice compass.

Given ongoing crises facing global, national and local communities, practitioners are required more than ever to think on their feet in the workplace, to provide rapid responses and seek perpetual solutions. This requirement must be underpinned by professional nourishment and skill development.

Values are the glue which assure certain adherence to quality practices. The Community Learning and Development (CLD) Standards Council, in Scotland, have a set of values which inform and influence practice in Scotland and are seen as fundamental to that sector. These are:

- Self-determination
- Inclusion
- Empowerment
- Working collaboratively
- Promotion of learning as a lifelong activity.

Across the wide world of community work, the existence of either an explicit or implicit value base is apparent and upheld through active learning and development work, which in turn is heavily reflective of the contexts within which community workers operate. The International Association for Community Development (IACD, 2023) describes core values in the following way: 'We are committed to promoting participative democracy, sustainable development, rights, economic opportunity, equality, and social justice, through the organisation, education, and empowerment of people within their communities'. The learner, participant, client or community group must be, and usually is, at the forefront of purpose and delivery in these values. The following quotation shows the impact that this close work with individuals and community has on ideas.

> 'I think I've been informed and shaped a lot more by the actual practical work [than by the theory]. I feel that observing the work that other people did and then joining in, doing and later starting to do my own work and working with people day to day, I feel like I've learned a little more.'

Nadia Stuart (2021) focus group

The COVID-19 pandemic has seen resilience in the community-based workforce, which has been demonstrated and evidenced throughout the world during the pandemic. When practitioners were isolated through enforced pandemic conditions, the uptake of professional learning was enhanced through webinars and digital access to programmes in many countries. Work with learners, clients and community groups continued, despite restrictions; and creative practice emerged. This underscores the widely held view that those working in communities are fleet of foot, adaptable and flexible and can confidently embrace change. The view of the authors is that this is supported by high-quality professional learning, through theory and practice and the coaching and mentoring of learners.

Choices

We have had to make choices in this book about the theory we have included. We all, as practitioners, need to make choices about the theory we choose to use in our practice. We have chosen literature which interested us and is relevant to our perspective on our practice, and we hope it interests you. We do not make claims to its being representative of the literature in a field of practice; rather, we have selected that which has had an influence on us as practitioners in the broad field of community work. We have tried our best to make it recent, while including seminal thinkers. We urge you to make choices about what we have included and to see how it relates to your practice. To achieve this, we have included in each chapter 'Principles for practice' and 'Challenge questions', which we hope will stimulate your thinking about the theory we have presented. To make the book reflective of the ideas of a wider community work authorship, we ran focus groups and have included quotations, as you have already seen, from the people who assisted us with their ideas, motivation and inspiration. These also contribute to the knowledge base we discuss in this book and this is a source of theory you could consider for practice.

We, as community workers, take our inspiration and thinking from multiple sources; we work with an invisible blanket of knowledge and skills supporting our everyday decision making. Our contexts for operating are wide and varied, and yet there is a synthesis to the value base supporting our practice. There is, however, a danger that, unless we keep ourselves relevant and informed, we will arrive at successful outcomes in our work more by accident and less by design. We therefore offer the following principles for practice and challenge questions, to sustain the reader through the remainder of this book.

Table 1.1: Professional reflections on theory tool – Elaine Lawson (2022)

Take a few minutes to think about how and why theory assists practice. Jot down a sentence or two or a bullet list to demonstrate your thinking.
Why I use theory in my practice: • Looking for the general from the particular (sociology first!). • Helps me when observing my work to understand beyond what is immediately observable. • Expands my understanding of a setting, a time, space and the experience of others. • Can offer explanations to why and how things occur. • Allows for in-depth considerations and seeing different viewpoints to organise thinking and reach conclusions or identify need for further enquiry. • Makes me stop and think, possibly alter, or amend views about practice. • Inform decisions I make. • Build ideas on the foundations of those of others. • Back up my decisions. • When faced with a problem, look for ideas or tools that work, refresh my thinking. • Grounds for research. • Stimulation of mind. • Exploring my feelings and values in relation to practice. • Enhancing my professional competency.

In Table 1.1 we have included an exemplar of a colleague's reflections on her learning from theory.

Principles in practice

The following principles are not a checklist; rather, they are suggestions from our practice about how you can use these to influence what you do and to enrich your own learning.

1. Ensure reflection on practice is a frequent activity that you undertake.
2. Make good use of available opportunities to refresh your professional thinking.
3. Consider how you can engage constructively in dialogue with peers to extend your own learning and that of others.
4. Reflect on the fact that theory encompasses the wide world of thinking, observation and dialogue as well as important written texts.
5. Revisit any professional practice competency material.
6. Participate fully in dialogue through support and supervision to connect practice to theory.
7. Take every opportunity to read current publications which relate to your professional context.
8. Keep your practice relevant and up to date, to meet changing contexts such as digital developments.

Challenge questions

1. Consider whether your own learning to improve practice is a high priority in your professional considerations. How do you manage your learning?
2. What is the role of professional reflection in underpinning our value base in challenging workplace settings? How embedded is reflection in your practice.
3. How broadly do you see theory as an influence on your practice? Can links between theory and practice be intuitive and invisible, yet effective?
4. Consider the place that the influence of others whom you work alongside has on your own practice. Think of someone

who has made an impact on your professional development. What was the nature of this impact?
5. Do you think that time spent in professional learning is worth it, and why?
6. What do you think about Elaine Lawson's use of theory in practice as presented in Table 1.1?

References

Burkeman, O. (2021) *Four Thousand Weeks: Time and How to use it*. Penguin Random House, UK.

CLD Standards Council (2023) *Professional Learning*. Available at: https://cldstandardscouncil.org.uk (Accessed: 22 February 2023).

Community Development and Health Network (CDHN) (2009) *UK National Occupational Standards in Community Development*. Available at: www.cdhn.org/sites/default/files/FACTSHEETS%202.pdf (Accessed: 28 March 2023).

Eraut, M. (1994) *Developing Professional Knowledge and Competence*. Routledge, Taylor and Francis Group, New York.

Freire, P. (1974) *Education for Critical Consciousness*. Continuum, London and New York.

International Association for Community Development (2023) *Recalling our Core Values*. Available at: www.iacdglobal.org/2019/01/01/recalling-our-core-values/ (Accessed: 13 March 2023).

McArdle, K., Briggs, S., Forrester, K., Garrett, E. and McKay, C. (2020) *The Impact of Community Work: How to Gather Evidence*. Policy Press, Bristol.

Moon, J. (1999) *Reflection in Learning and Professional Development*. Routledge Falmer, London.

Robinson, V. (2018) *Reduce Change to Increase Improvement*. Corwin, CA.

2

Social justice

Karen McArdle

Introduction

> Justice is, by definition, about fairness. Social justice is about the social context of fairness and the fairness of the social context. That is, it is not just about individual issues in specific contexts, but, rather, how those individual issues reflect wider patterns of injustice, discrimination and oppression. (Thompson, 2017, 3)

Thinking about social justice leads inevitably to thinking about social problems and wide patterns of injustice, as mentioned in the quotation that opens this chapter, for example poverty, homelessness and crime and the interrelated nature of these problems, just as the Thompson quotation illustrates. Rawls (1999) explains that the justice of a social scheme depends fundamentally on how rights and duties are assigned, and on economic opportunities and social conditions that apply to different sectors of society. He further describes how a social idea of fairness or justice is connected with 'a conception of society, a vision of the way in which the aims and purposes of social cooperation are to be understood' (Rawls, 1999, 51).

Human rights

Human rights and community work are interlinked. Change for individuals and groups is linked to social justice. As Beck and Purcell (2020) point out, upholding the freedoms that human rights point to indicates that we have powerful reasons for action. As community development has at its heart active citizenship, to achieve social justice we need to engage in consciousness raising of the social, economic and policy context and social mobilisation. For many, in our experience, working to maintain the status quo and preparing people to better fit into an unjust society are the main purposes of what they do. We would argue that this approach to work is insufficient and community workers should be working at micro, meso and macro levels. This means working with individuals for change; working with local systems and issues that may inhibit change; and working to change wider social and economic policies that may be linked to injustice. We think this can take courage but is perfectly possible at some level for all community workers to have a lasting, sustainable impact. To think about this, we need to start at the macro level.

The core idea of a good society, argues Fleurbaey (2018), starts from the idea that everyone is entitled to full dignity, irrespective of gender, race, religion, education, talent and productive abilities. This idea of dignity includes the possibility to participate in social life on an equal footing with others and to be in control of one's own life. Neoliberalism, discussed in the next section, is closely linked to discourses of a failure of human rights.

> The real trouble about human rights, when historically correlated with market fundamentalism, is not that they promote it but that they are unambitious in theory and ineffectual in practice in the face of market fundamentalism's success. Neoliberalism has changed the world, while the human rights movement has posed no threat to it. (Moyn, 2018, 216)

It is our opinion that social justice as a concept, has become weakened by overuse and has become a safe term for community workers by being elided and equated in practice with inclusion and equality. Anderson (2004) cites Dworkin (1981) with a more radical and risky definition of equality that we find interesting and more closely associated with our conceptualisation of social justice: 'An envy-free distribution of resources' (Anderson, 2004, 154). This definition emphasises the emotional dimension of equality. Anderson (2004) argues, and we agree, that equality is not there to compensate people for undeserved bad luck, such as bad parents or being born into the wrong environment. Equality activity has lost sight of the distinctively political dimensions. Anderson says the aim of egalitarianism is not to eliminate the impact of 'brute luck' but to 'end oppression, which is socially imposed' (Anderson, 2004, 155). Its proper purpose, she says, is to create a community in which people stand in relations of equality to others. She describes equality as a relationship among people, as well as a pattern of the distribution of goods or resources. She also considers respect for citizens in a policy context. A society that permits its members to sink to the depths hardly treats them with respect.

Accordingly, we urge readers to consider if they too have elided social justice with the safe territory of equality, rather than thinking about the policy and political change that social justice implies. We intend in this chapter to suggest ways in which this challenging of policy and politics can occur.

Neoliberalism

Neoliberalism is an ideology that we consider has had in the past, and continues to have, an impact on wealthy Western nations and, through these countries' actions, an impact on poorer nations elsewhere. Neoliberalism is an ideology characterised by a belief in sustained economic growth as the means to achieve human progress, its confidence in free markets as the most efficient means of allocation of resources, its emphasis on minimal state intervention in economic and social affairs and its commitment to the freedom of trade and capital.

Neoliberalism has its origins in the 18th century with the publication of Adam Smith's *Wealth of Nations*. It is difficult to find in the literature relevant to community work, or indeed any other work, beyond economic considerations, contributions that justify neoliberalism. Yet the underpinning ideology is apparent in policy, political speeches and practice. We make no apology for our criticism of neoliberalism; it is not just an economic idea but also, as Imogen Tyler (2021) puts it, a social idea. It embraces a form of 'governance through which public consent is procured for policies and practices that effect inequalities and fundamentally corrode democracy' (Tyler, 2021, 5).

The history of neoliberalism is well described by Ledwith and Springett (2022). Essentially, in 1947 in Switzerland, a group of men came up with the ideology that Ledwith and Springett suggest 'would replace cooperation and compassion with competition and exploitation' (Ledwith and Springett, 2022, 44). It is evident in right-wing populist politics in the US and the UK. Ledwith and Springett describe how the right wing of politics postures to the poor by claiming to believe in the people, nationhood and culture, while at the same time 'reaping the harvest of the injustices of poverty, inequality and discrimination' that go with the ideology (Ledwith and Springett, 2022, 49). 'The current global dominant narrative, neoliberal capitalism, based on values of competition, status and individualism gives rise to excessive greed and consumption which inevitably creates extreme social inequalities and causes ecological destruction' (Ledwith and Springett, 2022, 198).

It is impossible to think of social justice without thinking of injustice. Dorling's (2015) five tenets of injustice, in his book called *Injustice: Why social inequality still exists*, are illustrated with statistics for the UK and US, in particular. The five tenets are reasons or justifications for a common-sense understanding of inequality, often propounded within the neoliberal ideology.

- Elitism is efficient;
- Exclusion is necessary;
- Prejudice is natural;
- Greed is good;
- Despair (for some) is inevitable.

Elitism is efficient is based on the notion that allowing certain groups to have privileges enables the economy to operate more efficiently (Thompson, 2017), and is linked to the economic concept of the trickle-down effect, where the increasing wealth of the rich trickles down to those less well-off for the good of both.

Exclusion is necessary also implies exclusion is acceptable. It is an idea based on thinking that certain groups in society are inherently superior to others. Thompson (2017) suggests that this is linked to thinking that ideas of a fairer outcome are excluded from consideration because the current arrangements in society are 'necessarily so'.

Prejudice is natural is an assumption that it is a human characteristic to be prejudiced against others, and that it is natural therefore it can be justified. Prejudice often manifests itself through stereotyping of those who are disadvantaged in this way. Thompson (2017) describes this as a pervasive and powerful, but distorted, representation of reality.

Greed is good is again linked to the trickle-down notion of the distribution of wealth in the economy. It is also assumed that greed is a good thing and is needed for the well-being of the economy, which is essential for people's well-being. It is assumed that people, as a whole, will benefit from greed, not just the individual.

Despair (for some) is inevitable is an idea that suggests those at the bottom of the heap will always be miserable. This idea suggests that it is once again necessarily so and can, therefore, be justified.

These five tenets can be viewed as assumptions about the way the world is and that they are immutable.

Tyler (2021) describes how neoliberalism has contributed to dimensions of social injustice, citing how governments have come to govern *for* the markets but *against* the people. She describes how Britain has witnessed an erosion of workers' rights, civil liberties and human rights, which are seen to block market competition. She cites Harvey (2005), who argues that neoliberalism is a class project, 'an ideology, which aims to restore and consolidate class power, under the veil of the rhetoric of individualism, choice, freedom, mobility and national security" (Harvey, 2005, 7).

The ideas of neoliberalism are closely linked to ideas of globalisation. Bauman (2007) describes how we currently live in 'liquid times' and describes the uncertainty of living that this creates. He describes, *inter alia*, the divorce of power and politics, as decisions and power are no longer just local but global. Interhuman bonds, or what we might think of as community, were once woven into a security net worthy of a continuous investment of effort but have now become frail and are admitted to being temporary, says Bauman. He also cites how the collapse of long-term thinking and planning leads to short-term projects which do not combine with ideas such as development, maturation, career or progress. Finally, in describing 'liquid times', he explains how the vexingly volatile and constantly changing circumstances are shifted onto the shoulders of individuals, who are now free choosers and bear in full the consequences of their choices. We would add to this, not only are they free choosers, but they are also designated as consumers in a neoliberal society. Liquid times lead to a sense of anomie or powerlessness, where a good life may be construed as having the best or right things. Bauman suggests that fear adds strength to desire (Bauman, 2005) and some of us attempt to spend our way out of fear.

> Those of us who can afford it fortify ourselves against all visible and invisible, present or anticipated, known or still unfamiliar, diffuse but ubiquitous dangers, through locking ourselves in behind walls, stuffing the approaches to our living quarters with TV cameras, hiring armed guards, driving armoured vehicles (such as the notorious SUVs), wearing armoured clothing (like 'big-soled shoes') or taking martial arts classes. (Bauman, 2005, 69)

Tyler (2021) argues that a major characteristic of neoliberal democracies is that they function through the generation of fear and anxiety rather than fidelity to national identity.

> The state of insecurity is continuously fuelled and orchestrated through the proliferation of fears about border controls and terror threats, as well as economic insecurity and labour precariousness. In such a climate public anxieties and hostilities are channelled towards those groups in the population, such as the unemployed, welfare recipients and irregular migrants, who are imagined to be a parasitical drain and threat to scarce national resources. (Tyler, 2021, 9)

Hegemony, power and social justice

> The basic premise of the theory of hegemony is one with which few would disagree: that man [sic] is not ruled by force alone, but also by ideas. (Gramsci, 1971)

Hegemony, as described by Gramsci, may be thought of as the dominance of one group over another through the legitimisation of dominating norms and ideas, often through public consent. Social control is maintained through persuasion, not overt force. Gramsci was born in Sardinia in 1891 and was concerned with why Marx's prediction of a proletarian revolution had not happened (Beck and Purcell, 2020). Gramsci believed that the false understandings of subordinated groups was the starting point for transformative change. Here we shall concentrate on the idea of hegemony and later in this chapter on counter-hegemony.

Hegemony for Gramsci was about the cultural and moral dimensions of the exercise of political power. Hegemony is constructed though mechanisms of political negotiation and intellectual persuasion (Hoare and Sperber, 2016). The media play an important role in the idea of hegemony, often playing to the fears and anxieties, and indeed prejudices, of people, as this sells papers and programmes. This mirroring of fear serves to reinforce these fears and often contributes, we propose, to prejudice.

Examples of hegemony in practice can be seen in Dorling's five tenets of injustice. Greed is good and despair is inevitable are messages that are presented as truths and can be accepted as truths, rather than thinking about the social, cultural, moral and economic assumptions that underpin these supposed truths.

Case study

> Saresh was a youth worker and noticed that the local paper had a habit of reporting negatively about young people and vandalism and petty crime. It always gave details of the actual crimes and the location, Castlehill, often with photographs of the damage done, which Saresh thought reinforced the fear that some people had in the same neighbourhood of young people and

gangs. He worked in Castlehill and knew that gangs, as such, did not exist, just groups of young people hanging out together, but he also knew it frightened the older people. He was aware that stereotyping young people as criminals was taking place. Yes, there was vandalism, graffiti on walls, but there was nothing else for young people in the area to do.

The first thing Saresh did was to apply successfully for a street art project for young people to decorate the underpasses that were located around the neighbourhood. It was organised so that the local community could have a say in the design the young people chose for the walls. Saresh arranged for the local paper and TV to come and see the young people at work. Saresh recognised that changing attitudes was a long-term project and that many of the challenges young people faced were in the control of politicians. He saw himself waging a long-term campaign in both the community and the town hall to change attitudes to young people and their life chances. It took considerable energy and commitment, but Saresh knew he had to do it.

Power and social justice

Power, or lack of it, is an idea closely linked to the concept of social justice. Michel Foucault (1976), a French philosopher, is very influential in thinking about power. He saw power not as being something some people have and others do not but, rather, as being in every transaction in life between people, so power is beyond systems and structures. He was preoccupied with how people can become conscious and free themselves from power structures and false consciousness (Ledwith and Springett, 2022). Power relations, according to Foucault, are embedded in discourse, or the narratives that are created around ideas, such as education, religion, criminal justice and the behaviours that discourse engenders in people. 'Power is not something that is acquired, seized or shared, something that one holds onto or allows to slip away; power is exercised from innumerable points, in the interplay of nonegalitarian and mobile relations' (Foucault, 1976, trans Hurley, 1998, 94). Foucault believed that we are always inside power, there is no escaping it. Like Freire, Foucault believed that people could overcome false consciousness, as Foucault described it. We choose to discuss this process of overcoming as critical reflection. Critical refers to the ability to be transformative, to lead to fundamental changes in perspective (Fook, 2010). Critical also implies a focus on hegemonic perspectives. Critical reflection enables an understanding of the ways in which society's systems and structures, individuals and groups may be socially restrictive. Thus it is thought to lead to empowering ideas and behaviours. Critical reflection involves, for example, how people engage with the world; how they construct a sense of identity; how they construct personal meanings (Fook, 2010). This applies to all people, to the participants as well as the community workers.

What we can do about social justice

Thinking about social justice is important, but can make the community worker feel the problems are too big or too political for them to tackle, from our experience. We suggest moving beyond equating social justice with simple equality in practice.

We propose the need for:

- Counter-hegemony and critical education;
- Sharpening up of our language and speaking truth to power;
- Amplifying and interpreting voice and stories.

Counter-hegemony sees changed thinking and changed action as part of the same process. This is important because hegemony is experienced as 'an internalised reality, which is both understood and felt, it is not just an abstract structure' (Beck and Purcell, 2020, 59). Hegemony makes people see things which may oppress them as normal, so counter-hegemony or change can challenge both feeling and thinking. Hegemony asserts control over knowledge and culture, affirming the ideas of the dominant culture and inevitably marginalising and silencing others (Ledwith and Springett, 2022). Counter-hegemony is change that reshapes the balance of social power away from ruling elites into the hands of people who are marginalised (Beck and Purcell, 2020). Changes in class consciousness are necessary for transformative change, and this change is a psychological process that Gramsci sees as cathartic (Hoare and Sperber, 2016). It comes about through actions. The most important for the community worker, we suggest, are critical thinking and collective action.

Stimulating critical thinking and reflection assists people to see that the normal balance of power may indeed be oppressive and that things could be different. The work of Freire in the 1970s is significant in focusing on critical education, raising awareness of how the norm has come to be the norm, focusing on the history, the narratives, the discourses and underpinning assumptions.

Collective action assists with overcoming the sense of loneliness or not belonging that can go with being oppressed; it also lays the foundations for action to achieve change. Beck and Purcell (2020) argue that we can assist with developing links locally, nationally and internationally, as we live in a globalised society. Most recently, political literacy or helping others learn how to be heard is one way of assisting with both critical thinking and collective action.

Sharpening up our language means telling it as we see it; and perhaps seeing things more plainly. Black Lives Matter, as a phrase, is so much stronger than speaking about racial equality. It is so easy for decision makers to hide behind the bland language of inclusion and equality, without doing very much differently. We suggest that it is the role of the community worker to speak truth to power and to discuss discrimination and injustice where it exists. Rather than speaking of food insecurity we can speak of hunger and prevent decision makers from hiding from the truth. This demands courage, as it will not be popular, but it is integral to the values that underpin the profession.

Amplifying and interpreting voice and story are crucial as a response to social justice. The voice of our participants can be amplified, placed in a context and interpreted by us for decision makers. A story of an individual having to choose whether to eat or heat the house because of poverty can be illuminating for politicians, and we can work hard to secure these stories; but we, as community workers, can explicate the context of poverty and can propose measures to tackle poverty and to target the lived experience that is being heard.

It is important to note that the impact of neoliberalism and hegemony affects us as well as our participants. Over the years, the authors have noticed an increasing reluctance among community workers to tackle difficult injustices with seniors, politicians and key decision makers. It is a version of the 'tall poppy syndrome', where people are afraid to stand out above the crowd or rock the organisational boat. We suggest the reasons for this are multilayered and complex and are linked to the factors described earlier by Zygmunt Bauman. One way of overcoming this is to have mutual support for each other so that the tall poppy syndrome does not apply. We have taken some space to describe neoliberalism, but we think it is important for the community worker to understand what we consider the origins of poverty to be among our participants, that so we can work against this.

Principles in practice

1. Consider neoliberalism and how it has an impact on your participants economically, socially, culturally and emotionally.
2. Identify hegemony and the assumptions that underpin disadvantage and vulnerability. How are your participants represented in the media and social media?
3. Identify the discourse or narrative that surrounds the places you work and the people you work with. How does this characterise your work?
4. Find ways of discussing points 1–3 with your participants and see what this means for them, seeking ways in which to turn the findings into positive empowerment in thinking and behaviour.
5. Consider how you and your profession of community work may contribute to hegemony and find ways of sharpening language to overcome this, seeking ways to amplify the voice of participants.
6. Speaking truth to power is something that we all should do. Think about how you can do this, giving and seeking support for speaking the truth to decision makers.

Challenge questions

1. Who in society experiences social injustice? Why is this so?
2. How political are you and why is this the case? How can you be stronger at this?
3. When was the last time you engaged in critical reflection with participants?
4. How do you contribute to hegemony? Why is this?
5. Can you think of examples of your own practice that are like Saresh's example in the case study?
6. What assumptions underpin the profession of community work?

References

Anderson, E.S. (2004) Against Luck Egalitarianism: What is the point of equality? In M. Clayton and A. Williams (eds) *Social Justice*. Blackwell Publishing, Malden, MA.

Bauman, Z. (2005) *Liquid Life*. Polity Press, Cambridge, UK.

Bauman, Z. (2007) *Liquid Times: Living in an age of uncertainty*. Polity Press, Cambridge, UK.

Beck, D. and Purcell, R. (2020) *Community Development for Social Change*. Routledge, New York.

Dworkin (1981) What's Equality? II equality of resources. *Philosophy and Public Affairs* 10, 283–345.

Dorling, D. (2015) *Injustice: Why social inequality still persists*. Policy Press, Bristol.

Fleurbaey, M. (2018) *A Manifesto for Social Progress: Ideas for a better society*. Cambridge University Press, Cambridge.

Fook, J. (2010) Beyond Reflective Practice: Reworking the 'critical' in critical reflection. In H. Bradbury, N. Frost, S. Kilminster and M. Zukas (eds) *Beyond Reflective Practice: New approaches to professional lifelong learning*. Routledge, Abingdon.

Foucault, M. (1998 [1976]) *The Will to Knowledge: The history of sexuality: 1*. Trans R. Hurley. Penguin Books, London.

Gramsci, A. (1971) *Selections from Prison Notebooks*. International Publishers, New York.

Harvey, D. (2005) *A Brief History of Neoliberalism*. Oxford University Press, Oxford.

Hoare, G. and Sperber, N. (2016) *An Introduction to Antonio Gramsci: His life, thought and legacy*. Bloomsbury, London.

Ledwith, M. and Springett, J. (2022) *Participatory Practice: Community-based action for transformative change*. Policy Press, Bristol.

Moyn, S. (2018) *Not Enough: Human Rights in an unequal World*. The Belknap Press of Harvard University, Cambridge, MA.

Rawls, J. (1999) On justice as fairness. In M. Clayton and A. Williams (eds) (2004) *Social Justice*. Blackwell Publishing, Malden, MA.

Smith, A. (2016 [1776]) *The Wealth of Nations*. Aegitas, Toronto.

Thompson, N. (2017) *Social Problems and Social Justice*. Springer Nature Ltd, London.

Tyler, I. (2021) *Revolting Subjects: Social abjection and resistance in neoliberal Britain*. Zed Books Bloomsbury, London.

3

Equality and inclusion

Kirsty Forrester and Karen McArdle

Introduction

Community work is, at its core, about addressing inequalities to enable the full and meaningful participation of communities and individuals in any and all aspects of their lives. While we should look to address all forms of inequality in our work, in this chapter we will explore work with people with protected characteristics covered by national and international equality or human rights legislation, including discrimination against Indigenous peoples, migrants, minorities, women, people with disabilities, racial and religious discrimination and discrimination based on sexual orientation and gender identity (United Nations, 2022). Work which seeks to address other forms of injustice, such as poverty, for example, will be discussed in other chapters.

Context

Changes to migration patterns arising from climate change; foreign conflict, or national policies such as Brexit in the UK; shrinking economies; and cuts to welfare and public services; the impact of digitisation; the role of social media in all our lives; and the impact of pandemics have meant that the profile and needs of individuals and communities continue to change and we must adapt our services in response to the resulting inequalities and divisions. Work to broker understanding and trust within communities has never been more important, as illustrated in the following quotation.

> Changes to the welfare system since 2010 have made life harder for those in poverty, and this disproportionately affects a large number of disabled people, women, and people from ethnic minorities. Spikes in hate crime and worrying levels of sexual violence and domestic abuse also give cause for concern in relation to the safety of our citizens in their personal lives and on the streets. Women are still not benefitting from equality in practice and there are increasingly large gaps between the experiences and outcomes of disabled people and some ethnic minorities and the population as a whole. The persistent disadvantages faced by certain groups raise significant concerns that some people are being forgotten or left behind. (Equality and Human Rights Commission, 2019)

It is a sad fact that many children are bullied because of their protected characteristics. Girls are more likely to be bullied than boys, disabled people more than non-disabled people, and those who identify as lesbian, gay or bisexual more so than straight people (Ditch the Label, 2020). In Britain, 84% of LGBT (lesbian, gay, bi-sexual and transgender) young people who said they had been bullied had thought about taking their own life (Equality and Human Rights Commission, 2019).

The proportion of disabled people with no qualifications is nearly three times that of non-disabled people (Papworth Trust, 2018). Work in the community is essential to enhance people's prospects and is particularly important for at-risk groups. Anti-racist, anti-discriminatory practice must, and usually does, underpin any intervention in the community.

Human rights approach

There is work to be done, in all community work contexts, to ensure that the people with whom we work understand their rights and their responsibilities. Many of these people come from communities where, because of their gender, class or disability, they are conditioned to see themselves as second-class citizens, or they come from countries where they don't have democratic rights or, because of their immigration status, they are scared to challenge injustices.

Community workers can use a human rights approach with communities to ensure that duty holders live up to their responsibilities (Scottish Human Rights Commission, 2020). For example, while in some ways women's equality has progressed significantly, full gender equality has not been achieved. Bullying and sexual harassment are widespread at work and in education, and three-quarters of new mothers have had a negative or potentially discriminatory experience at work as a result of pregnancy or maternity (Equality and Human Rights Commission, 2019). Adopting a human rights approach within a family learning context to focus on rights around family and employment could mitigate some of the experiences mentioned earlier.

Unconscious bias

We are all guilty of unconscious bias towards other people; our brains are arguably designed that way. It is what psychologists call 'heuristics' (Seighart, 2021), the categorising of our world so that we don't have to process too much information. 'Instead of treating each person as an individual, we map on to them our assumptions about what they should be like or what we expect them to be like, based on the stereotypes we've been brought up with and are surrounded by' (Seighart, 2021, 5).

While, on average, girls are as intelligent as boys, generally develop faster and do better at school, research shows that parents believe that their sons are cleverer than their daughters (Seighart, 2021). An American study found that elementary and middle school boys had eight times more classroom attention than girls. 'Teachers (regardless of gender) talk less to girls, question them less, praise, probe, clarify and correct them less ... as a result, most girls learn to mind themselves ... to defer to boys and talk only when spoken to' (Sadker and Sadker, 2009 in Seighart, 2021, 91).

As community workers, we need to explore and understand the unconscious biases we have constructed and how we bring them to our work. We can do this through critical reflection and reflexivity (McArdle et al, 2020).

In some of the countries and communities in which we work, the bias will not be unconscious, it will be seen as acceptable, and understood as how the world is and should be. These communities may be openly racist, homophobic or prejudiced towards groups of people with protected characteristics. Sometimes this will be in the form of jokes or name calling and, at other times, it will manifest itself through harmful acts. It is part of our role as community workers to call out discrimination when we see it and work to educate communities about how their views hurt people. This is not an easy task, but it is our role.

I remember hearing recently from David who was chair of the local youth forum of his experiences in primary school. His mum asked his teacher why he never got homework like his peers; to which the response was that she knew he would not do it, so she didn't send any home: David and his family were from the Scottish Traveller community. Unlike other ethnic minorities, overt racism did not just come from other pupils, but also came from teachers. Racism against Gypsy Travellers, it seems, is still an acceptable form of discrimination in the UK in some quarters.

Case study

Janine and Nat are community workers in rural England working with ethnic minorities, who make up less than 2% of the population. The town they work in is one of the most deprived in the UK.

> 'Every time a group does something really lovely with "the refugees", they put it in the local newspaper and I have this really ethical dilemma, because there's hundreds of horrible comments, and the people that we love and care about are compelled to read them, because they say "we want to know what people say about us, so we can protect ourselves and feel safe" … we've really steered away from doing press stuff

around the work we do, because we see first hand the emotional impact that it has on individuals. It hurts them, it makes them feel unwelcome, it makes them feel unsafe, but then we've got this other dilemma – how will we change the systems and hearts and minds if we don't talk positively about the wonderful things these people are achieving?'

'We're one of the poorest towns in the UK. ... So when people read that someone got free driving lessons and you've got young people or younger adults that can't afford that it makes people angry.'

'Our community events are member led, but they're open to our community ... they enable the White residents and minority communities to break down any fear or bigotry that they may have held about a particular group because it really puts it in perspective that they share the same visions and hopes and dreams that we all do. When they see each other in different contexts, rather than a faceless group that they hear about in the mainstream media, they become individual people they can talk to.'

'There's a lot of really brilliant, community groups but sometimes Janine and I get frustrated, because often we see well-meaning, middle-class, older White women who are trying to be helpful, but actually they are really disabling or disempowering. There's a really strong difference between being empowering and enabling and being, disabling and fostering co-dependencies. And so, I think, for me, that's [a] really important aspect. Our work is about enabling, it's about empowering, it's about connecting.' (Janine Adams and Nat Wealleans-Turner, 2021, Focus Group)

Our work as community workers should be about breaking down barriers, helping people to make connections across difference and challenging systems of injustice. The role of the community worker, therefore, goes beyond the work to support and amplify the voices of the group with whom they are working. It is also to influence and inform other groups, organisations and service providers to understand how to promote inclusion in the work that they do. If we see the work we do in isolation and not in the round, then our work will invariably bring harms against others, unless we are able to think critically and reflexively (McArdle et al, 2020).

Many of the people with whom we work in communities face multiple forms of discrimination and barriers. Intersectionality is an approach that explores how overlapping or intersecting identities affect our experiences of society (Crenshaw, 1989). We cannot explore the inequality experienced by one group, such as disabled people, without recognising that these difficulties are alleviated or exacerbated by the other identities we each have, whether that is the colour of our skin, our gender, our sexual preference or our class. Crenshaw (1991) argues that a failure to do this marginalises the less privileged within the group. As community workers, our analysis of the needs of the communities or individuals with whom we work must acknowledge this and our responses must be holistic.

Crenshaw (1991) argues that 'the failure of feminism to interrogate race means that the resistance strategies of feminism will often replicate and reinforce the subordination of people of colour and the failure of antiracism to interrogate patriarchy means that antiracism will frequently reproduce the subordination of women' (Crenshaw, 1991 cited in Bhopal, 2018, 48). We do not agree, and we consider that feminist theory and discourse can offer a helpful lens to the community worker who seeks to promote inclusion and challenge inequalities.

Feminism

Feminist theory is not a unified body of ideas and it is impossible to begin to represent the full range of ideas here. Consciousness-raising approaches in the past drew attention to the binary personal/political dimensions of society and sought to subvert this (Ryan, 2001). Feminist poststructuralism more recently sees the categories of male and female as socially constructed and rejects the idea that human beings have essential gendered natures. Feminist poststructuralism analyses the workings of a patriarchal society in all its manifestations: ideological, institutional, organisational and subjective (Ryan, 2001). Poststructuralism sees women as oppressed by virtue of their sex, but also along other axes, such as age, race, ethnicity, sexual practice, religion, ability and so on (Ryan, 2001). This is described as intersectionality and requires that the community worker does not focus on one dimension of inequality but on multiple dimensions that are usually present.

Emejulu (2011) describes community development as a social and political construction bounded by power relations, identities and social practices and contested by people seeking to preserve, oppose or transform their identities or the rules of behaviour. Emejulu suggests that destabilising and problematising the categories of 'woman', 'practitioner' and 'community development' is crucial because this creates space for articulating broader constructions of political identity, recognising difference and supporting intersectional social justice claims.

Abandoning essentialism or the binary concept of womanhood within feminist community development is, however, a difficult prospect. Having 'women' as a stable and fixed identity can help to bring individuals together to fight for social justice. Recognising difference can, it is argued, undermine women's collective power to advocate for issues that disproportionately affect women, such as, for example, access to affordable and high-quality social welfare services.

The first step in this feminist community development process argued by Emejulu (2011) is to consider whose voices and interests are dominant and whose experiences are missing or marginalised in community development debates. The next step is about creating democratic spaces for dialogue and debate about these issues. If different kinds of women's voices can be articulated and acted upon to shift dominant ideas about what constitutes women's interests, then this might support the creation of a more inclusive form of feminist politics and community development.

In many of the dominant discourses of community development, the practitioner is usually constructed as an active subject, while local people are constructed as passive objects requiring intervention. The result is that agency is understood and conceptualised as a possession that can be given to or taken away from people (Emejulu, 2011). Local people are positioned as requiring community development, to transform from passive objects into active subjects. As a result, community development is defined by some as the process whereby professionals mediate, regulate and control other people's development of agency. Defining local people as deficient creates a hierarchical and unequal relationship between local people and professionals. The result is that local people can never truly have power, be in control or determine their fate, unless they first surrender themselves to outside intervention.

Feminist community development has often avoided successfully constructing local people as passive, since a key concern of feminism is valuing and reclaiming women's voices, concerns and actions. For feminist community development, Emejulu (2011) considers it is helpful to think about political agency as a three-pronged process of:

(i) constructing a political identity based on radical democratic citizenship;
(ii) creating democratic spaces for articulating intersectional claim making and seeking consensus for coalition-building;
(iii) drawing on reclaimed knowledge and experiences of marginalised groups in order to orientate political activities. (Emejulu, 2011, 387)

Research found that female-only spaces for mutual reflection and learning were crucial to influencing the changes that needed to happen to further gender equality locally (Robson and Spence, 2011). Using informal education methods of conversation, small-group work and mobilising the potential of women-only organisations, feminist community development practice has demonstrable success in building skills, knowledge and confidence and enabling a collective voice to challenge oppressive systems and behaviours.

> If community development is to survive as a practice relevant to people encountering structural injustice and oppression, it is important that the central tenets of emancipatory approaches, as exemplified by feminist practice, are revisited and reaffirmed. At its best,

community development protects and develops spaces within which marginality can be mobilised as a source of strength and creativity. (Robson and Spence, 2011, 301)

Promoting inclusion

We like how inclusion was described by the community workers, with whom we spoke in our focus group, as a practice of remembering people.

> 'You'll always find me being the one that goes "don't forget this person, don't forget that person, don't forget this group, don't forget that group, don't forget the kids that aren't at school – those that are in alternative provision or not in education at all, or are marginalised in some way. Let's not forget those". For me, inclusion is about constantly reminding and remembering that there are lots of people that don't fit inside those, perfectly formed boxes that we have in society.' (Janine Adams, 2021, Focus Group)

Often there is a misunderstanding about who is responsible for inclusion. People with privilege may assert that it is the responsibility of people with protected characteristics to integrate or mitigate barriers themselves. Inclusion can only happen if people with privilege and power take responsibility. Even if only a tiny proportion of the overall population have protected characteristics, promoting equality reduces barriers for everyone in the community. Providing transport for all, to enable a wheelchair user to attend an event, also enables the family who can't afford a bus ticket to attend, or it can help someone who, for whatever reason, does not feel safe travelling on public transport alone.

A colleague from a third sector organisation told Kirsty that she often provides bus tickets to women with wealthy spouses. Some relationships are abusive, and not allowing access to money to travel independently is a form of control. As people working in communities, we know that the disadvantage experienced by individuals cannot always easily be captured on a managerial form, and issues around trust or pride or fear of retribution can mean that claiming the cost of a bus ticket through official channels is impossible.

The lack of a budget to promote equal access is sometimes presented as an excuse not to do something which we may be required to do by law. It is of utmost importance that, whoever we work with, we ask them what they need and how they need it and we ensure that they have multiple ways to feed that back to us.

> 'I know that, long term, if we want to change this idea that we can't afford translators or we can't afford whatever, we've got to tackle the system. And that's really difficult, isn't it? 'Cause it's massive. How do we do that without getting really frustrated, 'cause change occurs really slow here, which it's frustrating sometimes, you know.' (Nat Wealleans-Turner, 2021, Focus Group)

We should not forget that most state-funded intervention is a response to a social position or ideology or, it may be argued, to what is in the public's awareness at the time of an election. So, the policy is unlikely to be radical. In appealing to such mass interest, community work has a difficult job in implementing policy.

> Radical and socialist theories locate community work within the struggle for transformative social change, and develop practice based on a wide, critical analysis of political, social and economic factors which interact at local, national and even international levels. The chief proponent of such an approach is without doubt Paulo Freire, whose radical socialist analysis defines a distinct style of practice. (Ledwith, 1997, 7)

We should see the responsibility to ensure equality not as a burden 'but [as] a strategic tool to help [us] achieve [our] goals and to improve equality, eliminate discrimination and foster good relations among those [we] serve' (Equality and Human Rights Commission, 2021).

It is impossible retrospectively to make a project more inclusive, and we should be inclusive from the very beginning. Conducting an Equality Impact Assessment (EIA) is a good way to ensure that fairness is at the heart of our working practices, helping us to avoid unintended consequences for people with protected characteristics. It helps to assess whether your work could discriminate against or unfairly disadvantage people; to assess if there is any potential for a positive or negative impact against people with protected characteristics; and to identify possible action to address negative impacts.

Challenges for the community worker

If we are serious about inclusion, then we need to recognise that, for the people with whom we work, intermediary steps may be required to ensure equal access and full participation. So, it may involve setting up a steering group as a middle ground to build confidence and understanding of what the role entails, to prepare people to be able to come and take their seat at the decision-making table. To be able to do this, we need to invest time in people and communities; something that may not be understood by decision makers, funders and those making policy at government level. There may often be a lack of understanding about the time it takes to do community work well, to engage communities and build trusting relationships. Often, funding criteria reveal a lack of knowledge about the demographics and capacity of communities to engage in a constructive way. We need to identify ways to use our power and influence, within our local communities and within the sectors in which we are working, to help develop understanding and contribute towards long-term systemic change.

Short-term funding and policy will lead to short-lived impact. It takes time to engage with, and build the trust and understanding, of under-represented, disenfranchised or minority groups before any programmes of intervention, be they individual or collaborative projects, can be undertaken and make a difference.

Understanding needs

It is especially important when working with special interest groups to spend time trying to understand the barriers they face. We agree with Tawney (1931) that equality starts with equal care.

Equality of provision is not identity of provision. It is to be achieved, not by treating different needs in the same way, but by developing equal care to ensuring that they are met in the different ways most appropriate to them, as is done by a doctor who prescribes different regimes for different constitutions, or a teacher who develops different types of intelligences by different curricula. (Tawney, 1931, 50)

We believe that it is important to work collaboratively with communities to alter or create new service provision, which increases their engagement and inclusion, and we urge you to bear in mind the Central European political slogan that has influenced and informed disability activism since the 1990s: 'Nothing about us, without us!'

Often, we will not be from the community with whom we are working; and we need to be wary of rhetoric that says you need to be from a particular community to work within that community. While we know this is sometimes partly true, we also know that some young people from ethnic minority communities will better engage with a youth worker from a different community, because they do not have to worry about the worker knowing their parents or seeing them at a community event. Equally, a community worker with a disability may wish to work as a locality-based community development worker rather than in a disability rights context. Sometimes it is our ability to connect across differences that makes us the right person for the task and, at other times, it is our lived experiences around a certain issue or community that makes us effective. Frequently, we may not be from the community with whom we are working, and we need, therefore, to be aware of our privilege and to be aware of whose voice or needs we choose to prioritise.

Understanding privilege

Bhopal (2018) explores the impact of neoliberal ideas around meritocracy (see Chapter 2), which suggest that those who have risen 'to the top have done so because they have worked hard and deserve to be there, in comparison to those who have not – who are lazy' (Bhopal, 2018, 5). Through the steady dismantling of public institutions and a policy-making environment which fails to champion inclusion and social justice, neoliberalism has continued to disadvantage those with protected characteristics by protecting the rights and privileges of those with power. For example, in the UK, neoliberal policies which allow parents to choose the school to which they wish to send their child, informed by published league tables, favour white, middle-class, able-bodied families who have access to transport to get their child to school and the influence and resources to ensure they secure a place.

As people working with communities, as well as understanding how a protected characteristic systematically disadvantages people, it is essential to understand how our privilege advantages us.

> I think whites are carefully taught not to recognise white privilege, as males are taught not to recognise male privilege ... I have come to see white privilege as an invisible package of unearned assets that I can count on cashing in each day, but about which I was 'meant' to remain oblivious. (McIntosh, 1989, 1)

Many people feel defensive about their privilege: 'Many white students feel that affirmative action is a positive initiative, as long as it does not disadvantage them' (Bhopal, 2018, 23). As a community worker developing programmes of learning and achievement with disengaged or excluded young people, Kirsty has seen anger from other young people, families and teachers who perceived that disadvantaged participants were somehow being rewarded for bad behaviour or poor attendance at school, for example. One only has to open some newspapers in some countries to see rhetoric about migrants stealing our jobs, homes and benefits. As community workers, we know that certain groups require additional support to work their way out of poverty and inequality, and it is important that we don't flinch when we start to explore the 'unearned assets' to which we have access. McIntosh (1989) says this process is not about 'blame, shame, guilt, or whether one is a nice person. It's about observing, realizing, thinking systemically and personally. It is about seeing privilege, the "up-side" of oppression and discrimination' (McIntosh, 1989, 5).

Equality and inclusion

Our role as community workers is to amplify the voices of others and, as community workers, we are able to sit around tables to which the communities with whom we are working are not invited. Why do we have more access than anyone else? As a community worker you are well positioned to challenge other organisations and your own to be more inclusive and to ensure that everyone has equal access. We urge you to use your influence and privilege to benefit the communities with whom you are working.

Case study – continued

'We arranged a meeting between local councillors and community members. There were around 13 different nationalities and it gave our local council an insight into how people are feeling: what was affecting them locally, what they'd like to see … and they sat and they listened. There was no jumping in, there was no trying to tell them that it was wrong or minimise their experiences.

'It was a very long meeting, about three and a half hours. I said to them at the end "you're lucky it wasn't longer! If you don't ask people often enough then you will sit for three and a half hours".

'And have they done much with it? Maybe not, but, actually, it was a great opportunity.'

'The feedback from those community members was very positive. They were very angry, but they felt like they had an opportunity to say what was important to them and, even if very little comes from that, they felt that they were heard. And although they've not done much with it, the reality is the follow-up will be the great opportunity for those community members to hold them to account for that.

'There's a cynical part of me that knows that, actually, for people with power and influence, having those conversations is a bit of lip-service and they go away feeling warm and fuzzy, and that they can tick a box about "this brilliant equality and diversity discussion".

And they don't do anything with it. And then they get really shocked when members of the community are really angry. It's like cognitive dissonance – they can't quite manage to understand why people in the community that face additional barriers would be angry with them.' (Janine Adams and Nat Wealleans-Turner, 2021, Focus Group)

Stigmatisation

We need to be wary of ways of working that stigmatise the individuals with whom we work. We need to allow people to be themselves, whether that is the right to be known by your name rather than as a refugee, or to be defined by your contribution rather than your sexuality.

> 'It's so important to have a group where it's not about those overwhelming big issues that they are dealing with – they are always linked to the trauma that they've suffered; but to give them a space just to be themselves, to find their feet again and make new connections; it is a beautiful piece of work if you can do it. A lot of our community events are just that, a place to connect and socialise, nothing else. There isn't any of that heavy load to talk about.' (Janine Adams, 2021, Focus Group)

We also need to recognise that many of the individuals with whom we work want space to not be the disabled person, or the LGBT+ person, and are often looking to us to provide a space for them to just be themselves.

Principles in practice

1. Understand the cultural history and values which have had an influence on the way you communicate, work, lead. Understanding oneself is the first step towards understanding others.
2. When setting up new projects, conduct an EIA; communicate with and make sure that promotional materials represent everyone, including people with protected characteristics.

3. Spend time trying to understand fully the barriers that people face and work collaboratively with these communities to alter or create new service provision that increases these people's engagement and inclusion.
4. Ensure that you identify the costs around reducing barriers for everyone and build this into your budget – do not look to cut corners here.
5. Routinely build critical reflection into your practice to identify unconscious bias and assess your privilege.
6. Ensure that, whatever you do, people can learn about their human rights and how to ensure that their rights are respected.
7. Use your privilege to benefit the communities with whom you are working and find ways to raise their voices.
8. Remember that those with protected characteristics do not all want to be activists; create space for people to be themselves.
9. Ensure that participants are involved in deciding how your work will be reported and promoted and ensure that this is not the point at which the people with whom you work are likely to experience discrimination.

Challenge questions

1. Have there been times and situations where you did not understand what was going on or you felt uncomfortable to speak in public? For example, in a large meeting. Was that to do with your gender, race, class, education, abilities?
2. Are there times when you have been advantaged over a colleague or friend because of your gender, race, class, education, abilities? How did that manifest itself?
3. How can these experiences and understandings inform your work?

References

Bhopal, K. (2018) *White Privilege: The myth of a post-racial society*. Policy Press, Bristol.

Crenshaw, K. (1989) De-marginalising the intersection of race and sex, *University of Chicago Legal Forum* 139: 139–67, cited in K. Bhopal (2018) *White Privilege: The myth of a post-racial society*. Policy Press, Bristol.

Crenshaw, K. (1991) Mapping the margins: intersectionality, identity politics and violence against women of colour, *Stanford Law Review* 43(6): 1241–99, cited in K. Bhopal (2018) *White Privilege: The myth of a post-racial society*. Policy Press, Bristol.

Ditch the Label (2020) *The Annual Bullying Survey 2020*. Ditch the Label, London.

Emejulu, A. (2011) Re-theorizing feminist community development: towards a radical democratic citizenship, *Community Development Journal* 46(3): 378–90.

Equality and Human Rights Commission (2019) *Is Britain Fairer? The state of equality and human rights 2018*. London: EHRC.

Equality and Human Rights Commission (2021) *Letter to the Minister for Equalities on government departments and the Public Sector Equality Duty*. Available at: www.equalityhumanrights.com/en/our-work/news/our-letter-minister-equalities-government-departments-and-public-sector-equality-duty (Accessed: 3 January 2022).

Ledwith, M. (1997) *Participating in Transformation: Towards a working model of community empowerment*. Venture Press, London.

McArdle, K., Briggs, S., Forrester, K., Garret, E., and McKay, C. (2020) *The Impact of Community Work: How to gather evidence*. Policy Press, Bristol, UK.

McIntosh, P. (1989) *White Privilege: Unpacking the Invisible Knapsack*. Wellesley College, Wellesley. Available at: https://nationalseedproject.org/images/documents/Knapsack_plus_Notes-Peggy_McIntosh.pdf. (Accessed: 10 January 2022)

The Papworth Trust (2019) *Facts and Figures 2018: Disability in the United Kingdom*. The Papworth Trust: Cambridge. Available at: https://www.papworthtrust.org.uk/about-us/publications/papworth-trust-disability-facts-and-figures-2018.pdf (Accessed: 3 January 2022).

Robson, S. and Spence, J. (2011) The erosion of feminist self and identity in community development theory and practice, *Community Development Journal* 46(3): 288–301.

Ryan, A. (2001) *Feminist Ways of Knowing: Towards theorising the person for radical adult education*. National Institute of Adult Continuing Education, Leicester.

Sadker, D., Sadker, M. and Zittleman, K.R. (2009) Still failing at fairness: how gender bias cheats girls and boys in school and what we can do about it. In M. Seighart (2021) *The Authority Gap: Why women are still taken less seriously than men, and what we can do about it.* Transworld Publishers, London.

Scottish Human Rights Commission (2020) *Housing Rights in Practice: Lessons learned from Leith.* Edinburgh, Scottish Human Rights Commission. Available at www.scottishhumanrights.com/media/2029/housin-project-report-vfinal-may-2020.pdf (Accessed: 10 January 2022).

Seighart, M. (2021) *The Authority Gap: Why Women are still taken less seriously than men, and what we can do about it.* Transworld Publishers, London.

Tawney, R.H. (1931) *Equality.* George Allen and Unwin Ltd., London.

The United Nations (2022): https://www.un.org/ruleoflaw/thematic-areas/human-rights/equality-and-non-discrimination/ (Accessed: 4 January 2022).

4

Impact, change and making a difference

Karen McArdle

'We find it very difficult to measure the impact of what we do in communities. My colleagues, we all feed into a database system, and your success is generally measured on your learners gaining certification, but the majority of our learners don't gain certification, but their family and community life improves tremendously. And how do we capture that to feed up to the funders? To say, yes, keep the funding coming, we're doing good work here. That's something we've been trying to develop over many years now and COVID, I suppose, slowed down things a bit, but it is very difficult to try and devise a mechanism that we can measure the quality and the impact of the work we do.' (Aine Whelan, 2022, Focus Group)

Introduction

The quotation that opens this chapter illustrates some of the challenge associated with showing impact. Community work can be used for a range of purposes, but we find that the most common overarching goal for community work is to strive for the well-being of individuals and groups in the community and well-being of the community itself. The 'well-being' of communities is of course a contested concept, but here we use it to define, for the individual, a sense of living in hope; and for the community, a shared spirit of hope. Hope is an optimistic way of thinking about the world and implies an expectation of positive outcomes (McArdle et al, 2020). A community focus is common in many different work contexts but, when we are looking for evidence of impact, it is usually change we are seeking to achieve. We should not, however, rule out stasis or continuity as objectives.

Case study

In the following case study, Alan discusses setting up a community larder to meet the needs of people living in poverty in one suburb of the city of Dundee in Scotland. He is focusing on gathering evidence.

> 'Maybe it is about trust in your own observations more. So, food insecurity: over the summer we did engagement with loads of people through community events about setting up a food larder. We got eight volunteers, some of whom have got really quite difficult circumstances themselves, some of whom are further on in terms of their capacity. We got them together and done [sic] loads of work with them around what was needed in terms of infrastructure, around having a committee and in terms of their roles and responsibilities. And the larder's now set up and running really well and they're [the volunteers] really positive about it.
>
> But what is there to capture their learning? We observe their learning, but do we need to get better at helping them reflect on their learning and recording that? I think that's probably something that we don't do well, yet. I think we have those impacts across the board. The focus with the larders can often be the output in terms of the impact it's having on the wider community that are coming for food. You know, the conversations that you're having with people coming into the larder that aren't actually volunteers, but they're really benefiting from the service; from

the connections and the conversations, from the signposting. But we might not be as good at stepping back and looking at the learning and reflections of the people that we're supporting to deliver that.' (Alan Gunn, 2022, Interview)

Gathering evidence for funders of projects is not always straightforward, as described in the following quotation.

'The money comes with so many strings attached and it requires so much compromise, and that becomes a bit of a key question for the health of community work more generally. The fact to what extent we're feeling pushed to the margins or can come towards the centre is almost like a litmus test of how much health is in the system. You know how much we're being tolerated or can be embraced. And you feel that push and pull and this sort of bean-counting of the last ten years has certainly been, you know, pushing anything that isn't obviously quantifiable and onto the back foot to make like three or four cases for something it perhaps should only be making one case.' (Mark Richardson, 2022, Focus Group)

Iain Shaw describes impact over time that is rarely measured.

'You are developing life skills and for years. Afterwards I was constantly bumping into them (people I had worked with as young people). And they had become much less frightened of what the world might offer them. They became more socially mobile, had more ambition, and all those kinds of things. But how did you measure that? You can't measure that on a short-term basis, it has to be something that's happening long term. And if something's just starting and, you know, you've got six months, a year [of funding] even, then you're really in a start-up. You know, you want to get to the point where you are developing something that is embedding and has tradition. And so, in my youth theatre, three people are on the Board who came to me at the age of eight to ten.' (Iain Shaw, 2022, Focus Group)

The two quotations from the focus group illustrate the practical complexity of gathering evidence of impact. Thin (2002, 11) discusses four core themes of social progress:

- Social justice (equal opportunity and progress towards achieving all human rights);
- Solidarity (empathy, cooperation, understanding and associational life);
- Participation (opportunities for everyone to play a meaningful part in development);
- Security (livelihood security and safety from physical threats).

Each of these broad categories can be thought of as the goals for social transformation or processes that may be instrumental in achieving other outcomes. They are expressed positively, but can also be thought of as injustice, fragmentation, exclusion and insecurity or violence. These categories overlap and are generally mutually supportive. These provide benchmarks for thinking about your own practice linked to impact and change. We consider impact to be about change, and this is discussed in the next section.

Change and transformation

Transformation is moving from one state to another, a process transacted through personal or community experience. We have adopted the model of learning of Peter Jarvis, as this is the model of learning that, we propose, is most relevant to the lives of adults. Jarvis (2006) proposes that learning always begins with an experience, an event in unknown circumstances, for which people are unprepared or do not know exactly what to do. The essence of learning is that the initial feeling of confusion or absence transforms into knowledge, competence, attitude, values and emotions. In the course of learning, the individual integrates the transformed contents of the initial disorientating situation into his/her own life history and a new person is 'formed'; one who possesses more experience. The word transformation has a quality to it of significant change and difference. We propose that it applies to communities in the same way that it applies to individuals, embracing the notion of change in form to a new and positive identity (Jarvis, 2006).

Social change, as opposed to change for the individual, refers to significant changes in the ways in which groups interact with each other and the culture within which those interactions take place. Not all change is planned, but it inevitably influences how we practise (Beck and Purcell, 2020). Beck and Purcell discuss the oppressor/oppressed dialectic that Freire (1976) frames as a set of relationships that is played out in the world rather than fixed positions of certain individuals and groups (see Chapter 11). Foucault is discussed in Chapter 2, and his thinking about how power is distributed in complex ways. Beck and Purcell (2020) suggest that Foucault opens up a space for us to think about how every site where power is exercised contains potential for resistance. The following quotation questions our power as community workers.

> 'And why are we assuming that when they enter their programme, there's a need for improvement? And I think having these nuanced conversations internally, but also with our bosses and then, of course, with those people who fund us, whether they be donors or whether they be elected officials or governmental grants or foundations, it really is about re-educating people about "What is the purpose of evaluation? What does evaluation do?" And then as teachers, of course it's part of how we know where the students are. I mean we evaluate or we assess all the time and so you know really taking this idea of the summative evaluation and the endpoint, the number if you will, and backing into this idea of assessment as a tool that's going to enable us to really understand the student and the student's needs and also where the student is ... I think that's where we are right now in our programme, is sort of like, "OK, how can we assume that this is better than this and that it's along a continuum, or

that there's a hierarchy in there?" And I think that's a conversation that's going to take a long time, but I think it's an important conversation to have.' (Lynn Clark, 2022, Focus Group)

Case study

An evaluation was done of a project that sought to be inclusive of migrant populations through the medium of arts in the community. It was a project that offered circus skills to young people, art and design for older adults and many cultural events which focused on the importance of sharing food in social relationships. The impact of the project was assessed in terms of scale, quality and significance. Scale was assessed by the hundreds of people the project had touched but also in terms of the big effect it had had on people's lives through the development of social relationships, as they expressed in interview and focus groups.

Quality was assessed by feedback on each activity from participants, who spoke about the effectiveness of tutors and the quality of the artefacts they had been enabled to create. Significance was shown in the impact on integration of communities where people came together and developed greater understanding of others. The impact had been large scale, high quality and socially important and this could be fed back to the funders of the project.

The case study illustrates effectiveness viewed as scale, quality and significance. We view the concept of evidence as forming a continuum, where on the one extreme evidence may be anecdotal and relatively informal. On the other extreme, evidence may be strong, robust and be formal research data. Both extremes are valuable, as anecdotal/informal evidence, often dismissed as invalid or useless, can be used cumulatively and to bolster other forms of evidence. Strong and robust data is clearly useful but can have its negative side, as it takes a long time to generate and is not always accessible in its presentation to the potential audience of the evidence. Most evidence, we suggest, is located somewhere between the two extremes.

Figure 4.1 shows how these two extremes come together in self-evaluation

There are many approaches to establishing impact, here we have selected approaches as a starting point for work on gathering evidence of impact.

Social impact assessment

There is a field of study known as social impact assessment (SIA). It is conceived as being the process of managing the social issues of development projects. There is consensus on what 'good' SIA practice is: it is participatory; it supports affected peoples; it increases understanding of change and capacities to respond to change; it seeks to avoid and mitigate negative impacts and to enhance positive benefits across the life cycle of developments; and it emphasises enhancing the lives of vulnerable and disadvantaged people (Esteves et al, 2012). SIA is complex, an interdisciplinary and/or transdisciplinary social science that incorporates many fields including sociology, anthropology, demography, development studies, gender studies, social and cultural geography, economics, political science and human rights, community and environmental psychology, social research methods and environmental law (Esteves et al, 2012).

SIA researchers and practitioners are interested in the processes of analysing, monitoring and managing the social consequences of planned interventions. SIA requires an understanding of its core concepts such as culture, community, power, human rights, gender, justice, place, resilience, sustainable livelihoods and the capitals, as well as of the theoretical bases for participatory approaches (Esteves et al, 2012; see Chapter 5). It is crucial to understand how these concepts influence the way social relationships are created, change and respond to change, and hence how such concepts should frame analysis in an SIA (Howitt, 2011).

There are many frameworks for managing SIA, all of which seek to manage the complexity of community projects. Frameworks can give a sense of security and be evidential, but need to take

Figure 4.1: The evidence continuum

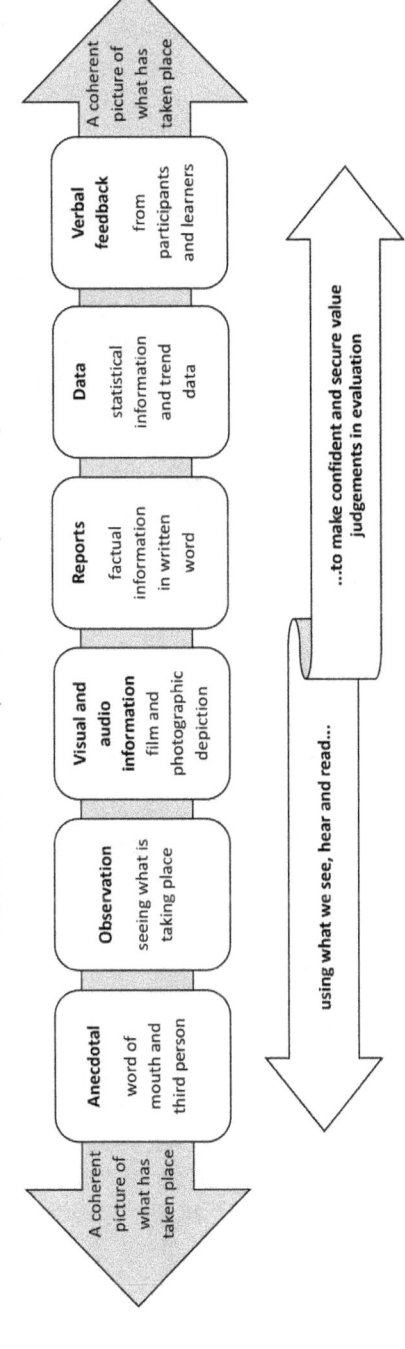

account of this complexity. Simple frameworks can provide a structure and provide guidance, but none of these should be viewed as being definitive, because social impact is notoriously difficult to measure and is often, we suggest, better being described rather than measured.

Social return on investment (SROI) and social accounting

The approaches, just described, to showing social impact, and SROI and social accounting, have much in common. They share common principles and similar stages in their approach. They aim for a rigour and comprehensiveness that may be seen to be missing from other more descriptive approaches. Because of these aims, they require resources in terms of time and skills that other approaches do not necessarily involve.

All the approaches follow a broadly similar structure:

- Planning stage, in which the organisation is explored – its stakeholders, its beneficiaries, the changes it aims to bring about and how it does this. An impact map can be the result of this stage;
- Evidence gathering and analysis stage, in which evidence is collected to report on impact;
- Reporting and verification stage, in which a report is drawn up and verified.

SROI most distinctively attaches a financial value to the understanding and measuring of change. This attaching of financial value allows for the capturing of impact from a range of stakeholders while at the same time calculating an overall value.

This translating of value into financial terms allows for a ratio of benefits to costs to be calculated. For example, if £5 of social value is created for every £1 invested, then we have a ratio, or an SROI, of 5:1. Of course some changes are hard to value in monetary terms. However, it is important to value them, or they can get lost when an assessment of overall impact is made. This valuing of all stakeholders' perspectives is important, as it gives a particular emphasis to the value from the perspective of participants or beneficiaries, a perspective which, unfortunately, can often be ignored in this process. SROI is also much more than these financial valuations or the final ratio; the testing of the theory of change, an analysis of how change occurs for a given organisation and its work, is just as significant.

Social accounting is a longer-established process than SROI. It is based on the understanding that social value should be reported on and audited, just as we report on financial performance. It shares the same basic stages as SROI, as already outlined, but doesn't necessarily involve giving a financial value to social value. Qualitative evidence of social value can stand as it is, without also being given a financial value. An SROI analysis can, however, be part of the social accounts.

Key to social accounting is that it is regular, so that the concept and the practice become embedded in the culture of the organisation. This regularity provides a means whereby the organisation can compare its own performance year on year and against appropriate external norms or benchmarks; and provides for comparisons to be made between organisations doing similar work and reporting in similar fashion. Finally, the accounts need to be verified, just as financial accounts are verified, by a suitably qualified panel.

The scope of an SROI report or a set of social accounts can be more or less limited, from covering a particular project to the work of a whole organisation. Regardless, these are approaches which take some time, both in the planning and in the execution. They need commitment from all parts of the organisation and particular skills for those leading on the process. Another of the challenges of impact, where impact was too strong, is outlined in the following section.

Showing impact

> 'And I ran a programme for a year at a home, where we were working with people with dementia. And, at one of them, it was a two-year programme; there were World War II vets [veterans]. We actually left the programme, because it got so successful that the staff complained it was too much work for them to bring everybody, because so many people wanted to

> do it. The families were saying we want our loved ones involved.' (Joan Harrison, 2022, Focus Group)

This quotation from the focus group also shows how, although success was apparent, it put pressure on other parts of a service. It shows that we can, arguably, understand dimensions of our success through popularity.

There are many models of evidencing impact, but here we choose to explore the scale, quality and significance of impact. Scale refers to the size of the impact. Did our work affect one person or a whole community of 30,000 people, for example? The quality of impact refers to the nature and also the strength of the impact. Did our work affect people in a particular way, such as enhanced community spirit, and was this widespread? Finally, significance is important. This is more difficult to pin down and refers to why it matters. Our impact on community spirit matters for reasons linked to society caring that people have a sense of well-being in their communities; it matters because it costs less in terms of services for unhappy people; it matters because community spirit may lead to additional volunteering; and there are sure to be other significances. You may have spotted the link to values and judgements that are inherent in scale, quality and significance. Scale is not always a numerical judgement. The term 'widespread' can mean, for example, 100 or 1,000 people. Scale can mean having a 'large' impact, where the term 'large' needs to be defined further. Similarly, quality and significance are qualitative terms and are linked to the value placed on ideas and the services described (McArdle et al, 2020). The following quotation questions the assumptions behind evaluation as a form of gathering evidence of effectiveness.

> What is the purpose of evaluation? What does evaluation do? How can we assume that this is better than this and that it's along a continuum, or that there's a hierarchy in there?
>
> Why are we assuming that when [adult learners] enter their programme, there's a need for improvement? We need to have these nuanced conversations internally, but also with our bosses and with the people who

fund us, whether they be donors or elected officials or governmental grants or foundations. Really, it is about re-educating people about the purpose of evaluation and I think that's a conversation that's going to take a long time, but I think it's an important conversation to have.' (Lynn Clark, 2022, Focus Group)

Principles in practice

1. Assessing the social impact of what is done in community work is important. This requires planning at the start of a project as to exactly how you will measure impact.
2. Outcome impact considers whether targets have been met, and process impact looks at what is going on in an activity. Both are about what has changed.
3. Change and transformation are fundamental to our work, so we should always be aware of the change we are seeking for both the individual(s) and community.
4. Frameworks and models of social impact can be reassuring, but they have both pros and cons and should be considered carefully.
5. Human rights are fundamental to community work and we should be aware of our own stance on human rights and our own prejudices and how these have an impact on what we do.
6. All projects can be analysed in terms of scale, quality and significance. These can be built into planning, monitoring and evaluation.

Challenge questions

1. How do you go about measuring the impact of what you do in your work and why do you do this?
2. What is the scale, quality and significance of your current mainstream work, as described in the second case study? How do you know?
3. What is the change that you currently seek with individuals and communities?
4. Do you have a preferred framework for working with the community? If so, what are its pros and cons?
5. Which dimensions of human rights give you niggling doubts? Does this or could this have an impact on your work?

References

Beck, D. and Purcell, R. (2020) *Community Development for Social Change*. Routledge, London.

Esteves A.M., Franks, D. and Vanclay, F. (2012) Social impact assessment: the state of the art, *Impact Assessment and Project Appraisal* 30(1): 34–42, DOI: 10.1080/14615517.2012.660356

Freire, P. (1976) *Education, the Practice of Freedom*. Writers and Readers Publishing Cooperative, London.

Howitt, R. (2011) Theoretical foundations. In F. Vanclay and A.M. Esteves (eds) *New Directions in Social Impact Assessment. Conceptual and methodological advances*. Edward Elgar, Cheltenham, pp 78–95.

Jarvis, P. (2006) *Towards a Comprehensive Theory of Human Learning: Theory and practice*. Routledge Falmer, London.

McArdle, K., Briggs, S., Forrester, K., Garret, E. and McKay, C. (2020) *The Impact of Community Work: How to gather evidence*. Policy Press, Bristol.

Thin, N. (2002) *Social Progress and Sustainable Development*. Kumarian Press, Inc. Broomfield CT.

5

Participation

Karen McArdle

Introduction

Thinking about working with participants usually includes working with community activists or residents, volunteers or people with whom you have an empowerment agenda, as well as people in organisations who wish to engage with these participants. An empowered person is one who can take initiative, exert leadership, display confidence, solve new problems, mobilise resources and undertake new action (Saxena, 2011). In this chapter we focus on the empowerment agenda; we look at working with community activists and volunteers in the chapter on community engagement (Chapter 7).

Power and empowerment

Empowerment practice enables people to gain influence and control over their lives, particularly with social institutions. When thinking about participation it is crucial to think about empowerment, and hence power (see Chapter 2), including how and where it impacts on people and how it impacts on some people more than others. Empowerment may be thought of as a product of participation in decision making (see Chapter 17)

Popular participation as an idea entered into our community understandings in the 1960s and 1970s, linked to many different ideologies (Stiefel and Wolfe, 2011), but was often about democracy, critical reflection and problem solving. It has changed over time to become linked to means of overcoming the limitations of governmental arrangements to meet changing needs; it is supposed to allow governments and their structures to act in a more flexible and local way. Empowerment participation usually implies action from the grassroots but, in our experience, participation is increasingly a 'top down' approach, which seeks to embed people in existing systems rather than thinking of changing systems to meet people's ability to participate readily.

Power may be understood as something that circulates, rather than as something some people have and others do not. So, a Foucauldian (1976) understanding is that there is a power dynamic in every human transaction. Empowering people to take part in systems is, in a Foucauldian sense, a form of manipulation of them for a purpose. It is crucial in thinking about empowerment to think about empowerment for what purpose and for whose purpose (Cooke and Kothari, 2004).

Cooke and Kothari state:

> There are acts and processes of participation that we cannot oppose. Some of these such as sharing knowledge and negotiating power relations may be part of everyday life; others such as political activism or engagement in social movements are about challenges to day-to-day and structural (for want of a better word) oppression and injustice within societies. But it is also the case that acts and processes of participation described in the same way – sharing knowledge, negotiating power relationships, political activism and so on – can both conceal and reinforce oppression and injustices in their various manifestations. (Cooke and Kothari, 2004, 13)

The very notion of 'community', it may be argued, conceals power relations, masks biases in interests and needs. Local knowledge reflects local power, authority and gender, for example (Cooke and Kothari, 2004). The people we choose to include in participation are often perhaps those who are most accessible to us, rather than being those most in need or most relevant to the purpose. Cleaver (2004) states that development projects are 'commonly cloaked in the rhetoric of empowerment' (Cleaver, 2004, 37) but often take place within the efficiency- and project-dictated imperatives of public bodies, for example. Empowerment has become a buzzword in development but its radical, challenging and transformatory edge has been lost over time. In effect, empowerment has become depoliticised in many participatory activities (Cleaver, 2004).

Case study

> Participatory budgeting is very popular in Scotland in local government, as a means of including people in deciding on what money should be spent. One local government in Scotland set up a system of asking people in a relatively disadvantaged community to put forward ideas for a small pot of funding. People in the community could vote for the project they preferred, which would then receive the funding. Groups in the community decided they would like this money and set out the necessary plans for using the funds, if awarded them. The community worker, Ramesh, noticed that groups who had previously worked together now did not partner each other, as the funding was too limited to share and competition for the funding divided the community. Rather than being a celebration and rewarding of community activity, it set up rivalry.
>
> The projects were voted on by all members of the community and voting was observed to be limited to those who were engaged with community groups, so those who knew about the opportunity voted. People who were friends of the citizens proposing projects lobbied hard and were successful in securing funding. Other groups who had put in a lot of work writing a bid and presenting it were very disappointed and saw it as a popularity contest that they had lost!
>
> The community worker recognised that the approach to participatory budgeting had been very

well intentioned, but the limitations had contributed to fracturing a community that was already divided in many ways. She thought that the process had been too rushed and too competitive; and the community could have been consulted about the use of the funds in a more sophisticated manner, so that choices were not a popularity contest or competitive. Community needs were not taken into account in the process, either. The community worker sought additional funding to assist unsuccessful community groups to work together to create as shared partnership project.

The political context

It is impossible to talk about participation or work to include people, without thinking about politics at local, national and international levels. The work we do in communities must always be in the self-identified interests of the communities with whom we are working. Sometimes community workers, in our experience, are seeking to further their own political ends, rather than those of the people with whom they are working, often assuming they are one and the same. At other times, community workers consider they have to be apolitical, especially when working in the public sector. It is our firm viewpoint that it is impossible to be apolitical. The context in which people live and develop, or not, is characterised by politics. This book is intended to be relevant in all countries, but certain trends in politics cannot be overlooked, across the world.

Tett (2018) cites Pickett and Wilkinson (2009): 'Inequality in income and wealth has been rising dramatically across the world during recent decades and these inequalities are associated with negative social outcomes in a range of areas: from public health and well-being, to social trust, political engagement, social mobility and crime.'

The authors feel that this inequality is a result of neoliberalism, the impact of which has been felt all over the world. Imogen Tyler (2021) describes the movement known as neoliberalism with reference to the British experience –neoliberalism being a form of governance, which concentrates, in particular, on the 'mechanisms through which public consent is procured for policies and practices that effect inequalities and fundamentally corrode democracy' (Tyler, 2021, 5). It is about governing for the marketplace, Tyler explains, and has resulted in Britain in the erosion of workers' rights, civil liberties and human rights. Neoliberalism (see Chapter 2) is characterised by generation of fear and anxiety linked to labour precariousness, which in turn links to material deprivation, family hardship, uncertainty and personal anxiety, as well as increased stigmatisation of 'others'. People become scapegoats, and Tyler cites the media's being involved in this process of scapegoating populations such as refugees, 'economic migrants', the 'work shy', those on benefits, which is common across Europe (Tyler, 2021). Many community workers are practising in societies where opposition and dissent are not tolerated or where corruption erodes the belief that meaningful participation is even possible. This is why politics is so important to participation. As people are 'othered', their point of view is not heard, and if heard, it is not valued. People who are afraid and anxious and just coping with fear or chaotic lives are unlikely to wish to participate in a system or structure that feels un-inclusive. Working 'with' the media, including social media, is most important to avoid 'othering' people.

Case study

> Councillor Rajan was newly elected to local government and was very keen to be seen as democratic. The proposed new flyover in his constituency on a dangerous stretch of dual carriageway was controversial, but there had been deaths at the junction on occasions over the last few years. It was a commuter route for many working people, who lived in the vicinity and travelled from the relatively rural area to the city to work. A group of three farm-worker cottages lay in the path of the proposed flyover. Councillor Rajan decided to invite residents to a planning meeting to hear their views.
>
> A display of plans was sited at the front of the village hall and a panel of speakers were seated at the front

of a theatre-style seating arrangement. Councillor Rajan was delighted with the turnout; people had to stand at the back of the large hall, as all the seats were full. The speakers included the Director of Planning and the Environment, who described the proposed flyover plans and was met with a round of applause and questions about the disruption to traffic during construction. Councillor Rajan spoke about the importance of the flyover and how pleased he was to see so many people interested and how he was confident the funding would be there. A representative of the Community Council spoke about what they had achieved in lobbying for the flyover and how it was good to be heard, as, indeed, it had been a long time coming.

The speakers were followed by an open discussion, which focused on how to minimise commuter disruption. One of the farm workers, Colin Robertson, put up his hand and was invited to speak and asked what would be the implications for his home. Another resident called out, "You will get a good load of money from compulsory purchase". This was followed by grunts and nods of agreement from other residents. Colin sat down. Councillor Rajan closed the meeting and was very pleased with the way the meeting had gone. The community worker, Jean, went to speak to Colin after the meeting. They sat down beside each other and Jean noticed Colin had tears in his eyes. He explained he loved his home and his family had lived there for three generations. He felt unable to do anything because opinion was so against him. He also said the other families were too worried to come to the meeting and expected him to report back. Jean said she would organise a meeting with Councillor Rajan and the Director of Planning. She offered to go too, which Colin said would be great. She also suggested he contact the local Advice Centre and ask about the legal side of what might happen and what his rights would be. She agreed to knock on doors and assist with communicating with neighbours.

On reflection, Jean wondered about the purpose of the public meeting. Everyone had agreed with each other, except Colin Robertson. So, one of the outcomes was mutual hand shaking and agreement and another outcome was a disempowered citizen and probably a cluster of other disempowered citizens from the three cottages.

It can be hard to participate and share our opinions, especially if it is not the view shared by others. In the following example, Ross, an adult education worker in Scotland, describes how he facilitates the participation of the adults with whom he works.

'We have a students' forum, where we invite students to come along and it's that kind of, you know, your voice does matter. And if you're worried about just putting your voice yourself forward, let's do it as a collective. ... So, for example, if somebody comes in and they've had their benefits cut or whatever, we will then as a group look into that and then we will petition whoever; we'll go to the door with a person or we'll send an e-mail ... but yeah, we can say what we want to see and it's a lot more powerful in that group saying it, it comes across a lot better, if that makes sense.' (Ross Weatherby, 2022, Focus Group)

Governance

Participation is frequently thought of currently in terms of governance. Gaventa (2011), in discussing rights of citizenship and democratic governance, poses six propositions, which provide us with critical challenges for how participatory local governance may be done (Gaventa, 2011: 253–62):

a) A key challenge for the 21st century is the construction of new relationships between ordinary people and the institutions which affect their lives.

He refers to the growing gap between the poor and institutions which affect their lives, especially government.

b) Rebuilding relationships between citizens and their local governments means working both sides of the equation – that is, going beyond 'civil society' or 'state based' approaches, to focus on their intersection, through new forms of participation, responsiveness and accountability.

He states there is growing consensus that the way forward is to focus on both a more active and engaged citizenry and a more responsive and effective state, which can deliver needed public services.

c) The call for new forms of engagement between citizens and the state involves a fundamental rethinking of the ways in which citizens' voices are articulated and represented in the political process. Also a reconceptualisation of the meanings of participation and citizenship in relationship to local governance is required.

Traditionally, preferences have been expressed through electoral politics in many countries, but increasingly forms of engagement known as 'empowered participatory governance' link 'bottom up' and 'top down' forms of governance to create a new middle path between the polar opposites of devolution and centralised democracy (Fung, 2002). This can be thought of as a new way of meeting in the middle for citizens and governments.

d) A fourth challenge is that the enabling conditions for the better-known successful experiments in participation are limited to a few countries. Effective intervention strategies in most cases therefore must begin with how to create the prerequisite conditions necessary for participatory governance to succeed.

Gaventa (2011) cites Fung and Wright (2001), who point to one background enabling condition for participation, which is that 'there is a rough equality of power for the purposes of deliberative decision between participants' (Gaventa, 2011, 25). To gain this condition means work on local democracy building, which is linked to work on empowerment, especially of oppressed and marginalised groups.

e) While the 'local' and related themes of participation and empowerment are increasingly part of the development discourse, the 'local' has many conflicting political meanings and is itself a problematical concept, especially in an era of increased globalisation.

Gaventa (2011) points out that the idea of locality is often used by non-local actors and can be used to support different agendas. Also, the local discourse may screen out the importance of extra-local factors that equally shape the possibilities for democratic participation locally.

Encouraging participation

Participation should include the notions of contribution, influencing, sharing or redistribution of power and of control, resources, benefits, knowledge and skills to be gained though beneficiary involvement in decision making (Saxena, 2011). Saxena states that the essence of participation is 'exercising voice and choice and developing the human, organizational and management capacity to solve problems as they arise in order to sustain the improvements' (Saxena, 2011, 31).

The literature on participation is often rather vague on incentives that will encourage participation (Cleaver, 2004). It is often assumed that people will see actual benefits of projects or will participate out of social responsibility, for the community as a whole. In explaining motivations, Cleaver states that social norms are seen to occupy a secondary place to economic rationality; social relations and participation are seen to serve the ends of economic development. Such perceptions do not allow for personal, psychological motivations, for the need for respect, recognition and purpose and possibly other individual motivations. Age, gender and class, for example, among other characteristics, will impact on an individual's willingness and ability to participate. The structure and systems for participation will enable and constrain the choices people have about whether to participate. Often the systems and structures require people to fit in, rather than being adapted to facilitate participation.

Alan, a community worker whom we talked to, discussed how he used the arts to enable people's participation in an engagement activity without taking up too much of their time. He felt that it allowed people to participate at different levels.

> 'I think need to be careful about how we term lived experience, but I think using media was a really kind of powerful way of sharing people's stories without going down the road of unintentionally exploiting people … it was a way of capturing people's voices, but without taking up too much of their time and, you know, leading to them being exposed and vulnerable in ways that they maybe weren't quite ready for. So, I do think that [arts and media] are a tool that we don't probably utilise enough, and I think it can be really effective.' (Alan Gunn, 2022, Interview)

Cleaver (2004) states that participation had been translated into a management 'toolbox' of procedures and techniques rather than being used as a means of critical engagement and empowerment of people. The authors agree that tools and techniques for community participation are abundant but there is a need to focus on the linkages between participation and the furthering of social and economic goals for the community, rather than on the latest trendy method, which has commodified community development. One model is not relevant everywhere.

Hung et al (2011) originally developed the Motivation, Opportunity, Ability (MOA) model as a way of explaining and determining the level of local participation in tourism development in their study. The MOA model aims to provide a more holistic view of how local people are either empowered or inhibited to participate and become active, in the example of a tourism planning process. Motivation can be taken as the driving force behind a person's decision-making process, as it can affect the intensity and direction of behaviour for participation (Jepson et al, 2014). Opportunity is the open (or closed) gate for participation, which we suggest may occur through relevant systems, inclusion and provision of participation chances. The final aspect of the MOA model is ability, which is seen as complex, including a combination of factors such as awareness, experience, knowledge, skills, accessibility of information and financial resources.

We would argue that there are factors which are even more complex. Processes are very important too; relationships; and the need to manage values of dignity; mutual respect; and reciprocity. This is linked in a neoliberal context to a reintegration of self into community for both participants and community workers so that procreating knowledge together can occur (Ledwith, 2021). We need to build trust. Trust may be defined, by us, as the promise of a continuing positive relationship in the best of all worlds. This is of course time consuming and expensive, and needs to be recognised to be so in planning and costing, so that participation is authentic. Trust is also needed by those who may be in more powerful situations but feel vulnerable and exposed by the participation of those with whom they are unfamiliar. One of the characteristics of participation is that you cannot turn it on or off like a tap; it's an evolutionary process that gathers momentum and defies breaking down into neat compartments (Saxena, 2011).

Learning is an important dimension of participation. The aim of learning is to enable learners to develop abilities for critical analysis, and the skills and ability they need to put their values and beliefs into practice. Facilitators of change processes need to learn how to use their potential influence on institutions that determine power structures and relations (Taylor, 2008). Individual learning, when based in a process of critical reflection on experience, is vital to both individual and community change. There is a need to exploit opportunities also for changing institutions that seem resistant to change. Institutional change is not a linear or necessarily a cumulative process; often the most powerful influences for change are not even intellectual, but emotional. Taylor (2008) suggests, for example, using the arts for change brought about through artistic or creative expression – by poetry or music.

Taylor (2008) addresses the importance in community development of ethics, of reflective practice and of an awareness of the need for a morality which helps us to be conscious not only of what we ought to do or should do, but also what we can do. Morality in this light may be seen as equivalent to the respect that we afford our relationships with others and with the world which we inhabit. The knowledge we need to develop our moral awareness is often not constructed through an intellectual process. Indeed, it may be thought of as wisdom – to do what we can, and then to manage the risk (Taylor, 2008).

Having what might be construed almost as a 'sixth sense', or even 'wisdom', is necessary because those engaged in participation processes cannot escape from the need to address issues of power and politics that arise inevitably within change processes. Facilitators working with communities of all kinds need to learn about power, both conceptually and also by letting new theory emerge collectively with others as knowledge is co-created in real contexts, action is taken and consciousness is promoted (Taylor, 2008).

Taylor (2008) goes on to discuss the role of educators as facilitators. Educators do need to be realistic about how much participation is good participation. Resources, including time, are expensive and context dependent. Change requires both will and action from above and below, and an awareness that 'invited participation' may be driving out popular mobilisation through co-option of agendas for change by powerful actors and institutions that then control it. A challenge for educators is to explore ways in which individuals may learn through a self-awareness, or consciousness, of their own power and knowledge in relation to that of others and to use this consciousness as a means of informing their practice.

Voice

Voice is often considered to be important, across the full range of services offered by the public and third sectors. For example, lay knowledge is now considered to be a key component of the development of health policy at local, regional and national levels in the UK (Williamson et al, 2009). The effective use of lay knowledge can often result in improved representation and a sense of ownership at local level, with increased levels of involvement of all members of the community. The inclusion of the voices of children and young people in health service provision and development has become increasingly important (Williamson et al, 2009).

Having a voice is both a presence and supplies the agency to affect one's own well-being (McArdle et al, 2020). Voice is important, as it embraces how people choose to frame their 'lived experience'. There is a perennial difficulty, however, in deciding who speaks for a community of any kind, be it geographical, social or a community of interest. Often, the more empowered will come forward to speak for a community. Building trust is key to securing the participation of those who are at the margins of society and are seldom heard. Trust is arguably more difficult to generate for those in the public sector than for those in the third sector. There is an implicit contract in the relationship in the public sector. They have a service to provide and are backed by an edifice of bureaucracy that can be disempowering for the participant (McArdle et al, 2020). Another view is that clients trust and respond to anything from their local public sector, because it is a trusted system, but ignore the third sector organisations.

Doherty et al (2004) (cited in Williamson et al, 2009, unreferenced) suggest that the following broad terms might be useful when discussing 'hard to reach' groups, which are increasingly referred to as 'seldom heard':

- Minorities – traditionally under-represented, marginalised, disadvantaged and socially excluded;
- Service resistant – those who are overlooked, the invisible and those unable to articulate their needs;
- Slipping through the net – the over-targeted and disaffected, 'known' families and those who are wary, suspicious or distrustful.

Bifulco (2012) discusses the capability of voice as the capacity to express one's opinions and thoughts and to make them count in the course of public discussion (Bonvin and Thelen, 2003). Voice is equivalent to having powers of choice and, at the same time, is a premise for, and result of, public democratic debating. The conditions for voice are complementary to the conditions necessary for good health and well-being. By means of voice, which is precisely the capacity to debate, contest, inquire and participate critically, there is a link between capacity to aspire and voice (Bifulco, 2012). This brings us back to the first point in this chapter and the link between aspiration and empowerment. Voice, we suggest, underpins empowerment.

Principles in practice

1. Be clear about the values that underpin what you are trying to do. Values, we propose, must include equality, diversity and inclusion.
2. Make those in more powerful positions, and those who are relatively disempowered, experience trust, honesty and respect. Be sure that you know what you mean by trust.
3. Recognise and plan for a long process – participation is time consuming and therefore expensive.
4. Learn to work 'with' arts and media to avoid contributing to, or reinforcing, 'othering' the participants.
5. Seek to balance power dynamics by stimulating mutual trust.
6. Seek to promote critical reflection, problem solving and active citizenship so that the participants may benefit from the purpose of the activity. Help participants to understand and question problems – how did this happen? Co-investigate.
7. Seek to find out what will genuinely motivate participation. Is an activity in the participants' interests?
8. Check that all doors to participation are open, that there are no social, physical or structural barriers.
9. Facilitate learning of the knowledge, skills and attributes required for participation.
10. Be aware of intersectionality. Disadvantage characteristics are inter-related. Different oppressions can interlink.

Challenge questions

1. What are your deeply held beliefs or values about participation?
2. How do these values affect what you do in practice?
3. What are three key principles or characteristics of your political views?
4. How do these political views affect what you do?

5. Have you ever found yourself in the situation of Jean in the case study? If so, what did you do?
6. What do you do to influence MOA in participation?

References

Bifulco, L. (2012) Citizen participation, agency and voice, *European Journal of Social Theory*. Available at: https://doi.org/10.1177/1368431012459695 (Accessed: 12 December 2021).

Bonvin, J-M. and Thelen, L. (2003) Deliberative democracy and capabilities. Paper presented at 3rd Conference on the Capability Approach, 7–9 November, Pavia.

Cleaver, F. (2004) Institutions, agency and the limitations of participatory approaches to development. In B. Cooke and U. Kothari (eds) *Participation: The new tyranny?* 2nd edn. Zed Books, London.

Cooke, B. and Kothari, U. (2004) *Participation: The new tyranny?* Zed Books, London. UK

Foucault M. (1976) *The Will to Knowledge: The history of sexuality: 1.* Trans R. Hurley (1998) Penguin Books, London.

Fung, A. (2002) Creating deliberative publics: governance after devolution and democratic centralism, *The Good Society* 11(1): 66–71

Fung, A. and Wright, E. (2001) Deepening democracy: innovations in empowered participatory governance, *Politics and Society* 29(1): 5–41.

Gaventa, J. (2011) Towards participatory governance: six propositions for discussion. In A. Cornwall (ed) *The Participation Reader*. Zed Books Ltd, London.

Hung, K., Sirakaya-Turk, E. and Ingram, L.J. (2011) Testing the efficacy of an integrative model for community participation, *Journal of Travel Research* 50(3): 276–88.

IACD (2023) Recalling our core values www.iacdglobal.org/2019/01/01/recalling-our-core-values/ (Accessed: 13 March 2023).

Jepson, A., Clarke, A. and Ragsdell, G. (2014) Integrating 'self-efficacy' theory to the motivation-opportunity-ability (MOA) model to reveal factors that influence inclusive engagement within local community festival, *International Journal of Event and Festival Management* 5(3): 219–34.

Ledwith, M. (2021) Personal communication in focus group (12 November 2021).

McArdle, K., Briggs, S., Forrester, K., Garret, E. and McKay, C. (2020) *The Impact of Community Work: How to gather evidence.* Policy Press, Bristol.

Saxena, N. (2011) What is meant by people's participation? In A. Cornwall (ed) *The Participation Reader.* Zed Books, London.

Stiefel, M. and Wolfe, M. (2011) The many faces of participation. In A. Cornwall (ed) *The Participation Reader.* Zed Books, London.

Pickett, K. and Wilkinson, R. (2009) *The Spirit Level: Why equality is better for everyone.* Penguin, London UK.

Taylor, P. (2008) Where crocodiles find their power: learning and teaching participation for community development, *Community Development Journal* 43(3): 358–70.

Tett, L. (2018) Participation in adult literacy programmes and social injustices. In M. Milana, S. Webb, J. Holford, R. Waller and P. Jarvis (2018) *The Palgrave International Handbook on Adult and Lifelong Education and Learning.* Palgrave Macmillan, London.

Tyler, I. (2021) *Revolting Subjects: Social abjection and resistance in neoliberal Britain.* Zed Books, London.

Williamson, T., Ryan, J., Hogg, C. and Fallon, D. (2009) *Younique Voices. A study of health and well-being: experiences, views and expectations of seldom heard and marginalised groups in Rochdale Borough,* final report. Manchester: University of Salford.

6

Working with communities

Karen McArdle

Introduction

Community matters because:

- It makes people feel connected;
- It helps people avoid loneliness or social isolation;
- It provides people with recognition and identity;
- It contributes to a sense of place and belonging;
- It provides a frame within which to understand individuals;
- The whole is greater than the sum of its parts.

This list is only a beginning, derived from our focus group for this chapter, and you may be able to think of many more reasons why community matters. There is, however, a new mantra in town (Tam, 2021). Global pandemics and economic crises, and Brexit in the UK, have resulted in a siren call for communities to be more resilient. Given that the causes of shock and strain are global, this is a big expectation to place on geographical communities, which are often small and local. There has been much talk during and post the COVID-19 pandemic about the return to normal, but also a feeling that we cannot go on like this with a galloping climate crisis, widening inequality, worldwide threat to human rights (Chanan, 2021) and, we would add, global insecurity between nations. The ability of communities to respond is unlikely to be achieved through occasional short-term projects, we suggest; rather, there is a need for strategic public investment in community development and this is something for which we should be advocating. There is a requirement for a national strategy on community involvement to revive and improve community development (Chanan, 2021). In summary, community development, often thought of as a local activity, has a new strategic dimension which may be implemented at local, national and international levels, and community workers can and should operate at these levels. Wyler (2021), in discussing the report *A Better Way* (2019), indicates the ways in which both top-down and bottom-up work and support communities so that:

- Everyone is heard and believed in, given a fair opportunity to thrive and has the ability to influence the things that matter to them;
- Every community comes together, looks out for each other, respects difference and enables everyone to belong;
- Society as a whole values and invests in everyone and in every community. (Wyler, 2021, 103)

Given that 'wicked' problems affect people, communities and society,

> the transformative impact of community development on people's lives must be recognised in terms of both integrating it into public policy making and investing in its quality and expansion. It is not enough to aspire to reach out and engage community in shaping public policies and services; the confidence and capacity of communities to play an influential role must be effectively cultivated. ... Community development is a key discipline in providing outreach workers/advocates who can connect with diverse members of communities and help them explore how to deal with certain differences and also to reach consensus, and find ways to put forward their common concerns and agreed proposals. (Tam, 2021, 242)

Values and community work

Community work in the context of community development is underpinned by values and principles. Without this, it is simply a set of practices; a set that has as much potential to manipulate and exploit communities as it has to support empowerment (Beck and Purcell, 2020). Values are our moral compass. Values determine what we do and how we do it. Unfortunately, values can become tired terms through overuse and tokenistic use of the concepts. It is important to use processes of critical reflection and reflexivity (see Chapter 1) to ensure that, for example, equality becomes more than simply opening an invitation to everyone to participate and becomes embedded in the goals of social justice.

When we discuss community, we often implicitly are referring to disadvantaged and vulnerable communities. It is important, however, to be aware that all communities will have some degree of disadvantage associated with them and to not overlook the sometimes hidden needs of more affluent communities. Disadvantage and vulnerability are relative terms, and every community has strengths, limitations and needs. It is helpful once again to be reflective and reflexive about who we think is disadvantaged or vulnerable and why; and to think about who we consider deserves our effort.

> 'Are we actually working with the most vulnerable? Because we'll often find the same faces. That's kind of what you get when you work with the people who want to be actively involved, but, actually, are they in need of support? It's such a tough one to really do in terms of community empowerment. You know, our role is very much looking at building capacity and supporting people to find solutions and do things within their own community but sometimes it's like you need to take it back a step just to get those initial relationships.
>
> We need to know what to do with people. We need to know what they actually want and need, and what

would actually help and if we don't know that, then what are we offering?' (Alan Gunn, 2022, Interview)

The choices we make about many things, including with whom to work, are closely linked to our values. Values are our deeply held beliefs and are far from immutable. They affect what we do; how we do it; and with whom. There may be things we consider non-negotiable, and these are linked to values. What is intrinsically valuable is the subject of philosophical discourse, but it may, arguably, be seeking others' or society's well-being – but what this entails depends where you stand in politics (McArdle, et al, 2020). Being aware of your own values and how you interpret the professional values already stated into practice is important, and we suggest this is done through reflection and reflexivity (see Chapter 1).

The core values defined in the Scottish National Occupational Standards for Community Development are defined as:

- Social justice and equality;
- Anti-discrimination;
- Community empowerment;
- Collective action;
- Working and Learning together. (CLD Standards Council, https://cldstandardscouncil.org.uk/wp-content/uploads/SummaryCDNOStandards2015.pdf [Accessed: 1 June 2022])

The Standards theoretically applied to practice will ensure that community development impacts on poverty, racism and social exclusion in a way that empowers, enables and encourages participation.

Core principles for community development have been described by the International Association for Community Development (IACD). They provide a helpful and all-inclusive definition of community development and a statement of core values. 'Community development is a practice-based profession and an academic discipline that promotes participative democracy, sustainable development, rights, economic opportunity, equality and social justice, through the organisation, education and empowerment of people within their communities, whether these be of locality, identity or interest, in urban and rural settings' (IACD, 2020).

The core values are:

1. *Participative democracy*: Working to ensure the active participation of people and communities in planning and decision making on all matters that affect their lives.
2. *Sustainable development*: Working to secure fair, just and equitable social, economic and environmental development based on climate justice, respect for biodiversity, the protection of the natural environment and all life on earth.
3. *Equality and human rights*: Promoting and respecting the equal worth, dignity and diversity of all people and working to ensure their equitable access to resources, services and opportunities. Ensuring that fundamental and internationally recognised human rights are respected, promoted and protected.
4. *Social and economic justice*: Promoting a just society through collective action that challenges injustice, poverty, inequality, discrimination and social exclusion through policies and procedures that lead to the fair and equitable distribution of resources, sustainable production and democratically controlled decision making.
5. *Empowerment*: Working collectively with people in ways that value lived experience, build on existing strengths and support the development of awareness, understanding, knowledge and skills, contributing to greater participation, collective action and community resilience in planning and decision-making processes on all matters that affect their lives. (IACD, 2020)

Social change

In working with communities, change is what we are usually striving for. Change is usually planned in the face of, or as a response to, community social change. Social change may be thought of as change in the ways in which individuals and groups interact with each other and the culture within which these interactions take place. It also encompasses changes in the values and beliefs that may be held by different groups (Beck and Purcell, 2020). Change may be thought of as making a difference, contributing to innovation or modification of the existing state. Change may be thought of as change for individuals; change for groups in society; or change in society itself. We propose that community workers should be acting at all these levels simultaneously (as described by Janine a community worker, working in the north-west of England).

> 'Yeah, I think for me personally in the work that I do, it's about having that voice and giving a voice to the community members that I work with and whether that's that I sit around tables which they're not sometimes privy to. I make sure that their voices are heard across the board, and you know, we do have big discussions with our local council, Cumbria Council, and we do have discussion about what they're doing to make their service better and more inclusive.' (Janine Adams, 2021, Focus Group)

Community resilience

Many people experience chaotic lives, with multiple challenges from interlinked sources of difficulties, such as, for example, economic downturn or absence of employment, inadequate housing or failing schools. These people often know a lot about being resilient. They may have the ability to rebound from stress, to regain equilibrium and to return to a state of health and wellbeing. They may have social capital that contributes to the ability to rebound.

As a response to stressful events, resilience focuses on recovery. It includes the ability to rebound from stress. It also often implies a sustainability of the recovery and growth and enhancement of the individual or community (derived from Reich et al, 2010).

Resilient community structures provide a means of 'circling the wagons' to provide defensible space and build on people's hopes (Hall and Zautra, 2010). Hall and Zautra cite Boothroyd and Eberle (1990), who define a healthy community as one in which all organisations, large and small, formal and informal, work together successfully to enhance the quality of life of all its members. Health of individuals and communities not only refers to levels of pain but also takes account of opportunities for enrichment in family and civic life and qualities that sustain well-being for individuals and build vibrant communities for generations. The value of the arts and culture in building quality of life is important here (see Chapter 14).

A search of the literature on community resilience found many models of community resilience and what to do to promote this. Adoption of a model can give a feeling of certainty, but when we sought to tease out the common elements, we found that we were developing another model, and we propose that, as all communities are different and the layers of individual, family, group and community are multiple, interlinked and complex, we should hold onto our professional values and manage each community differently (see Chapter 7). A resilience portfolio can help to inoculate communities against potential threat and crises and this means, in practice, identifying, conserving and investing in human, social, intellectual and physical capital (Hall and Zautra, 2010) and, we would add, emotional capital. Hall and Zautra (2010) advise against expending this effort in short-term, narrow programmes.

Physical capital, already mentioned, is largely self-explanatory and usually refers to community physical assets, such as halls, housing and amenities, but it is important to think of physical assets in terms of the cultural dimension of place and belonging. Social capital is often thought of in terms of networks of people who trust and assist each other (Putnam, 2000), but Putnam claimed this was in decline. Human capital refers to the growth and development of people over their life span and embraces education through lifelong learning, leisure and the arts. Intellectual capital refers to creativity and ideas in the community, associated with a sense of agency or being able to do things. Emotional capital refers to the *Zeitgeist* of the community or its mood. We have often heard communities described as depressed, and this goes beyond the physical infrastructure.

Sometimes community resilience is criticised as being the source of blame for communities from authority for not coping with challenge. We suggest that resilience is crucial to coping, and the methods should not be lost because the term is becoming tired and is sometimes abused.

Asset-based community development

Asset-based community development (ABCD) builds on the assets that are found in the community and mobilises individuals, associations and institutions to come together to realise and develop their strengths. This makes it different to a deficit-based approach that focuses on identifying and servicing needs. ABCD was forged as a working approach to community development in the 1960s and its roots can be traced back to the work of Saul Alinsky (Reich et al, 2010). There has, however, been a resurgence of interest in this approach.

The ABCD model suggests that there are seven types of assets in a community. It adds to the capitals listed in the previous section: economic, institutional and cultural, which refer to jobs/ businesses, civic abilities and a belief in positive change. Reich et al (2010) describe asset mapping:

1. Organise and brief people to tackle each of the headings;
2. Pool what people know already;
3. Walk around the neighbourhood;
4. Tabulate the assets;
5. Have a further collective discussion to uncover overlaps.
 (Derived from Reich et al, 2010, 109)

In the health professions, ABCD has been described as a move from a 'disease' prevention model to a more positive approach that aims to empower communities to tackle the social 'determinants' of health by targeting general health and well- being. The ABCD approach aims to move away from top-down delivery with measurable targets for health that are put in place without consideration of the context in which they sit, to a model that explores the links between individual health and social determinants and looks for ownership and accountability at an individual and community level. It is an approach that values capacity, skills, knowledge, connections and supportive potential in the community (Harrison et al, 2019). ABCD sees populations as co-producers of health rather than consumers (Blickem et al, 2018).

Appreciative inquiry (AI) is a similar significant theory within organisational research and developed from social constructionist theory. It chimes with the values of community work by focusing on the positives of individuals and communities. AI is a strengths-based, positive approach to organisational change. It helps people to move toward a shared vision for the future by engaging others in strategic innovation. It is seen as an alternative to deficiency models, which focus on problems and solutions. AI looks at the social potential of a social system and begins with appreciation, followed by collaboration, and this process should be proactive and applicable (Blickem et al, 2018). These techniques are seen as alternatives to diagnosing problems and instead focus on positive conversations with people, who are empowered to set the agenda for change and improvement.

Since ABCD relies on existing community assets to create change, it has been criticised for suggesting that disadvantaged communities may have all the resources they need to solve community problems. This may be countered by the recognition that communities can seek support and resources from outside. It is also criticised for sometimes being a bit too positive where positives do not exist. There is a need for a balanced viewpoint on the part of the community worker.

In the next section we present key asset-based principles

Asset-based principles

1. *Place-based approach*: A focus on local communities. Asset-based community development is a place-based approach focusing on the assets of an identified geographic area, a place residents describe as 'home'.
2. *Local leadership*: The community leads its own development by identifying its interest, and community leaders are themselves capable of opening doors to the wider citizenry. Local leaders are therefore defined by the relationships they have within the community, by their social, rather than political or financial capital – people as citizens rather than clients in development.
3. *Focus on community assets*: Community development starts from existing community capacity and assets, building on what we have, as opposed to what is absent or problematic in the

community. It is focused on indigenous assets as opposed to perceived needs. These assets are resources that the ABCD approach mobilises to achieve sustainable change.
4. *Relationship driven*: Increases the social capacity of community members and focuses on the maintenance of productive relationships between community members. It includes a focus on the power of relationships and informal linkages within the community, and the relationships built over time between community groups and external institutions. In association people join their gifts and strengths together and these become amplified, magnified, productive and celebrated.
5. *Equality and social inclusion*: All community members, regardless of gender, age, ability (or disability), race, culture, language, sexual orientation or social and economic status have equal opportunity to become engaged in the community development process and are able to access its social and economic benefits. ABCD is about change for the better as defined by the community itself.
6. *Balance*: Community development builds on a balanced approach that addresses and integrates economic, social, environmental and cultural considerations.
7. *Transparency and accountability*: This framework encourages and requires government, non-governmental organisation and any other outside involvement in community development to be transparent, accountable and participatory. In turn, communities hold each other to the same values of transparency and accountability, expecting no less of each other than of external agencies.

Community interventions and action

Community action is often issue-based, and it aims to assist those excluded from influence and power to achieve social change, collectively (Payne, 2020). Issues that the community feels strongly about can be identified, individuals and organisations mobilised and community activists engaged (see Chapter 8). Community work often is and should become involved in public policy and may become involved in social conflict. Inevitably one is included in struggles between people in powerless positions and the powerful (Payne, 2020). Look for support from the profession and be ready with careful justification of your choices or decisions.

Principles in practice

There are many, many models of community development practice and we cannot reproduce them here. We suggest only principles to follow.

1. Check that you are operating at more than one level. Are you operating locally or more strategically to facilitate change?
2. What are the values that underpin your community development work? Are they related to the standards presented in this chapter? If so, why? If not, why not?
3. Community practice is about social change. Be clear what the change(s) is that you wish to achieve. Ask yourself who desires this change and for what purpose.
4. If you adopt a model of community development, ask yourself why this model, and be critical of its relevance and usefulness to your context.
5. Consider the value of asset-based approaches in contrast to deficit models. What are the strengths and limitations of each of these for your context, and can a balance be formed?
6. What are the vagaries of your situation in community development? Consider where the power lies and develop professional and personal networks of support.

Challenge questions

1. What, for you, is non-negotiable in community work? What does this say about your values?
2. Do you think that values are bland or tired? If no, how do you incorporate them in practice? If yes, how can you refresh your values practice?
3. What are the key assets of your community? What are the key deficits? What does this mean for community development practice?

4. What change have you made to a community in the last year? What social change do you look for in the future? How will you contribute to this social change?

References

Beck, D. and Purcell, R. (2020) *Community Development for Social Change*. Routledge, London.

Blickem, C., Dawson, S., Kirk, S., Vassilev, I., Mathieson, A., Harrison, R., Bower, P. and Lamb, J. (2018) What is asset-based community development and how might it improve the health of people with long-term conditions? A realist synthesis. *Sage Open*, July–September: 1–13. Available at: https://journals.sagepub.com/doi/pdf/10.1177/2158244018787223 (Accessed: 1 June 2020).

Boothroyd, P. and Eberle, M. (1990) *Healthy Communities: What they are, how they are made*. UBC Centre for Human Settlements, Vancouver, BC.

Chanan, G. (2021) Regeneration in partnership with communities. In H. Tam (ed) *Tomorrow's Communities: Reasons for community-based transformation in the age of global crises*. Policy Press, Bristol.

Civil Exchange and Carnegie Trust (2019) *A Better Way: A call to action for a better way*. Civil Exchange and Carnegie Trust, London.

CLD Standards Council (2015) *Community Development National Occupational Standards*. Available at: https://cldstandardscouncil.org.uk/wp-content/uploads/CDNOStandards2015.pdf (Accessed: 12 January 2023).

Hall, S. and Zautra, A. (2010) *Indicators of Community Resilience: What are they, why bother?* In J.A. Reich, A. Zautra, and J. Stuart Hall (eds) *Handbook of Adult Resilience*. Guilford Press, New York.

Harrison, R., Blickem, C. Lamb, J., Kirk, S. and Vassilev, I. (eds) (2019) Asset-based community development: narratives, practice, and conditions of possibility – a qualitative study with community practitioners. *Sage Open*, 1–11. Available at: https://journals.sagepub.com/doi/pdf/10.1177/2158244018823081 (Accessed: 1 June 2022).

International Association of Community Development (IACD) (2020) *IACD Strategic Plan 2020–2024*. Available at: www.iacdglobal.org/wp-content/uploads/2020/07/IACD-Strategic-Plan-2020-2024-English.pdf (Accessed: 1 June 2022).

McArdle, K., Briggs, S., Forrester, K., Garrett, E., McKay, C. (2020) *The Impact of Community Work: How to gather evidence*. Policy Press, Bristol.

Payne, M. (2020) *How to Use Social Work Theory in Practice: An essential guide*. Policy Press, Bristol.

Putnam, R. (2000) *Bowling Alone: The collapse and revival of American communities*. Simon & Schuster, New York.

Reich, J.A. Zautra, A., Stuart Hall, J. (eds) (2010) *Handbook of Adult Resilience*. Guilford Press, New York.

Tam, H. (ed) (2021) *Tomorrow's Communities: Reasons for community-based transformation in the age of global crises*. Policy Press, Bristol.

Wyler, S. (2021) Four factors for better community collaboration. In H. Tam (ed) *Tomorrow's Communities: Reasons for community-based transformation in the age of global crises*. Policy Press, Bristol.

7

Community engagement

Ed Garrett and Karen McArdle

'Thinking back to when I first came up to Grampian [a region of Scotland] in the mid-80s, it was about understanding what was going on within the different villages in the Mearns [local area of Grampian]. It was about speaking to people, so a lot of it was just soaking it up, you know? And I guess reacting to some of the interests that were beginning to emerge from those discussions and that began to create the agenda. So, the stuff that I was involved in was just picked up through the village hall committee. So, it was just getting to know the community and meeting people that were interested in their community. I wasn't going in with any particular agenda, but it was about trying to understand what people were interested or concerned about.

'You were engaged with people in communities, because you wanted to help and that created a relationship that created trust. So that when somebody else needed help there was some somebody to go back to. So, you went in with a few tools, whether it was your grants for the youth club or the capital grant scheme for the village hall or whatever, but it gave you a starting point for an ongoing conversation, but

I think it was just around helping them.' (Ken Milroy, 2022, Focus Group)

Introduction

The quotation that opens this chapter describes an approach to community engagement as a starting point for other activities. Community engagement is important to any community work. It is only by knowing what the community wants and needs that we can work to achieve this engagement. Engagement can create ways and spaces which address inequalities in decision making and which tackle social injustice. By recognising the value of everyone's contribution it builds on community assets. It can also generate social capital which can drive further change, which is more likely to be sustainable. Describing a process, this chapter is more practical in its focus than previous chapters but is also built on theory and ideas about the way the world is.

The value of community engagement is increasingly recognised, which seems on the face of it to be positive. Lots of people and lots of organisations in Scotland, and perhaps your country too, are undertaking community engagement. For example, in Scotland, we have the National Standards for Community Engagement to support good engagement practice (Scottish Community Development Centre, 2022a).

There are many definitions of community engagement, but we like one often used in Canada, cited by Tinglin and Joyette (2020), as it captures some of the potential energy that goes with community engagement: 'People working collaboratively through inspired action and learning, to create and realize bold vision for their common future' (Tinglin and Joyette, (2020, 20). It is a process that, typically, makes connections with people to get to know their views and how they feel about a particular matter, with some kind of behavioural response anticipated (Tinglin and Joyette, 2020). We suggest that it is usually about action on the part of the community.

However, community engagement is not always valued well. People in some sectors may be asked to undertake community engagement without the skills or experience to do it well. The resulting engagement may be tokenistic and, in fact, at its worst can be disempowering and damaging to communities. It also means that those doing the engagement work may be left exposed and unsupported. Doing community engagement work can often be quite challenging, having to deal with difficult issues in communities, with strong views expressed. It is important for community workers to support those involved in community engagement by providing the knowledge and experience that will assist others to do it well.

This chapter connects closely with a number of other chapters in this book, most particularly those on participation (Chapter 5), social justice (Chapter 2) and equality (Chapter 3), so there is a crossover in terms of relevant theory. Of particular importance for this chapter is the concept of voice and power.

Voice and power

As community workers we are frequently interested in social justice (Chapter 2). In working with communities, we need to not only know what is important to people but also understand how power operates to constrain any process of genuine engagement. We need to make sure that communities, and particularly the most marginalised, matter in any process of engagement. In Chapter 2 we discussed Foucault and how power pervades every transaction of life, and this is particularly complex with community engagement where the transactions will be multiple. Voice (see Chapter 4) is an important idea; it is about people being able to talk about their experience in a way that makes sense to themselves, as well as to others. Voice is about empowerment. McArdle and Mansfield (2007) describe it as the sense of self which provides the lens through which we view the world. Some voices are valued more highly than others. For example, the voice of a middle-aged male may often be valued more highly than that of a young, single mother. Voice is also about making sure that voices from all parts of the community are heard. It is only with this voice that power and the traditional systems of representation that often support this power can be challenged.

Valuing our knowledge

When we undertake community engagement, we are collecting lots of bits of knowledge about a community. This knowledge will be sourced in a variety of ways and these different ways may give these pieces of knowledge different status. Understanding this differentiation of status is important when we present a picture of our engagement. We will want to triangulate between different kinds of knowledge. Data from a survey is given depth by being overlaid with a case study from a focus group, for example. It is important to be confident about the value of our knowledge. As community workers we value and thrive on the local and the anecdotal; these are rightly as important as figures collected in a survey. Some other professionals may value these less. When we come to making sure that our engagement findings matter in terms of decision making, we may need to convince these people. This convincing will work best if we are confident in and understand the knowledge base of our engagement.

This chapter takes a practical approach to exploring the process of community engagement in four main stages:

- Beginning the engagement
- Planning the engagement
- Doing the engagement
- Making the engagement matter and bringing about change.

As already mentioned, community engagement is in part a matter of information gathering with communities; what their priorities are, what they want, what they need. However, it is also about much more than this gathering of information. As discussed regarding voice, it is also about bringing about change, about social justice and power. Good engagement is about involving communities in bringing about the change that is important to them. For the authors, community engagement is underpinned by community development and its values of empowerment, equality and inclusion.

Another way of understanding community engagement is to think about why we do it. Brunton et al (2017) distinguish between two ways of thinking about it. There are instrumental or utilitarian reasons for why we might engage; these reasons concern improved outcomes. Then there are reasons to do with social justice and empowerment. So, engagement is the right thing to do, regardless of whether it leads to improved outcomes.

Of course, the two positions may well often align; improved outcomes are often produced when we take social justice and empowerment into account. It is important to recognise this difference in positions, particularly when dealing with and understanding people and organisations, who may have a more instrumental understanding of the value of engagement.

In the following case study engagement does not take proper account of social justice, power and voice, causing problems in the long term.

Case study

> Tara works for the sports and leisure team in a large city. She has been asked by her manager to engage with local communities on the siting of new outdoor gyms in parks throughout the city. She decides to do a survey using an online engagement portal. She also has stalls at libraries in the area where she can talk to people directly and run through the survey with them.
>
> Response is quite good, although monitoring feedback indicates that most people taking part are middle aged and middle class. Findings from the engagement are fed into the local government committee, who act on these findings and decide to go ahead with new projects. Over the following years, there continue to be disputes with some parts of the community, particularly those in more deprived areas, who feel they were not properly asked for their views.

Beginning the engagement

Many engagements, or certainly larger ones, begin with organisations such as public sector services, businesses or charities. The organisation may want or need to know about some proposed change, the siting of a new school or the development of a new strategy, for example. The organisation then proceeds to engage with the community about this change. Although this way of proceeding may seem understandable, it is also clear that there is an imbalance of power. It is the organisation, or in the case of the new school, the local council, which holds the power; they are the ones who have defined the engagement.

Accordingly, if we, as people engaging with the community, are serious about challenging power, we also need to look at how we begin engagements. Managers need to understand that engagement should not be a series of one-off events. Only if engagement is embedded into all our work as an ongoing process will organisations and communities be working together properly to create engagements. For those actually doing the engagement, we need to think carefully about how the engagement can be constructed, involving the community as co-creators. Engagement is essentially a matter of building relationships.

The next case study is a good example of how communities can define the focus of the engagement and then work together with organisations to do the engagement.

Case study

> Tim manages a team of youth workers. According to feedback from his team as well as professional partners, he gets the impression that there is some interest among parents of teenagers in reopening the youth centres that been closed over the past few years. To find out more about this interest and what young people think themselves, he meets with some interested parents and the local youth forum to look at a possible engagement. They work together on planning and organising the engagement, including what questions should be asked and the method of gathering data. In the event, they run an online engagement using social media, which has an extremely good response. Tim and his team continue to work with the parents and youth forum as the project develops, supporting their ongoing involvement.

Key to the outcome here is the importance of sustained social capital; those networks, relationships and support that exist within communities which Tim could engage, including interested parents, a youth forum and professional networks. It was also important to build the capacity of communities to take the lead on engaging with organisations concerning their priorities. Without this social capital, ongoing community engagement would have been much more difficult to sustain. For example, a focus group participant said that South Africa has seen an increasing loss of the community structures and institutions that allowed for effective community engagement over a 20-year period. To reinvigorate effective community engagement, social capital needs rebuilding.

Planning the engagement

Like all community work, community engagement needs good planning. Planning does mean that we have to make links between theory and practice. In the planning process, thinking about theory, such as voice and inclusion discussed earlier, and how you will address this in practice, is important. It is a reminder that community engagement is a skilled process that needs reflection in and on action (see Chapter 1).

In Scotland, there is an engagement planning tool called Visioning Outcomes in Community Engagement (VOiCE) (Scottish Community Development Centre: 2022b) linked to the National Standards for Community Engagement. This tool is a useful way of making sure that you have thought about the main stages of an engagement. The tool asks questions about community engagement:

- Why you are doing it? What difference do you want to make?
- How will you do it? What methods or approaches will you use?
- How will you know if you have been successful?
- Who do you want to speak to? How you can be inclusive?
- What resources do you need? Who else should be involved?

The last point is often particularly important, we propose. Work with other organisations is needed to make sure that communities do not feel overly consulted by a barrage of people asking them similar sorts of questions. Identifying and involving other organisations in planning is one way to avoid the consultation fatigue which communities can experience from organisations not working together.

Doing the engagement

There are lots of ways to implement community engagement. What methods you use will depend on the aims of the engagement as well as the time and resources you have to support it. Here a number of ways are explored, thinking particularly about them in terms of voice, power and knowledge. Chapter 16 discusses community research approaches in more detail.

Surveys

Surveys are perhaps the most obvious way to ask people for their views. They can capture views from a large number of people, are fairly easy to collate and need not be too time consuming for the community and for the community worker. While time can be an important consideration, we suggest that surveys should not be used as the only, or even the main tool, in most engagements. For example, for some people literacy or language may be a barrier to taking part in a survey. With many surveys being online now, digital skills or access can also be significant barriers.

It is important to look at other ways of engaging than just surveys, either paper or electronic. Door-knocking or outreach are ways of ensuring that you can speak to people who may not answer a survey. Snowballing, or using contacts of people you have already spoken to, is another way of speaking with more people, though you need to be careful here that you are not limiting yourself to one social grouping or demographic. If we are thinking about voice, we need to make sure that we are speaking to those who are most often excluded from speaking, through power. We also need to make sure that this speaking can be done in a way that makes sense to the community.

Focus groups

Focus groups are a good way to collect rich feedback. This is not only because they are structured to allow precisely for more extended discussion, but also because they allow for this discussion to be led in part by what the participants themselves think is important. A good focus group will have a set of questions to be explored. The parameters are set in advance, but the skill of good facilitation is to explore these in ways that make most sense to the participants, also taking into account additional themes they may want to raise. This creation of discussion by participants is important when we are thinking about voice.

In the following case study a creative approach allows wider participation as well as a different voice.

Case study

> Lesley is a deputy manager in a care home. She wants to know more about what people in the care home think about living there and, particularly, how it has been living there during COVID-19 lockdown. She works with a community worker to run a focus group, which is well attended, but she is conscious that it was only the most able residents who were able to take part. She decides to work with an existing residents' creative writing group to write a poem about their experiences of the home. She finds that several people take part who would not get involved in a more structured process. She also finds that the openness of the approach means that people feel free to express ideas which did not come up in the focus group.

Community forums

Forums are an example of managing community engagement which are often more community-led. Forums bring together people around a particular issue or demographic. For example, youth forums and older people's forums are popular ways of engaging with these groups. The groups are organised and led by their members, though support is sometimes provided by community workers. Not only are forums a good way to ensure real community-led engagement, they are also ongoing groups which can be involved in the sustainable co-creation of engagements in the longer term.

The next case study provides an example of a forum providing the structure for ongoing co-creation of engagements between communities and organisations.

Case study

> Leanne is a community activist who has long been involved in trying to improve public and other forms of transport in her area. There is a local bus forum, but this is run by the local council and many people see it as capable of bringing about only limited change. Leanne brings together a community-led transport forum consisting entirely of community members, who are able to respond to consultations as well as take forward emerging issues in their communities. Also, as a group meeting regularly they contribute to wider discussions about what, in the longer term, should be the focus of engagement.

Engagement having a grip: working with power and bringing about change

At the end of the engagement process, it is of course important that we feed back the results of the engagement to all those involved. It is also important, we suggest, to make sure, as far as possible, that change occurs and that communities are involved in bringing about this change. One hears too often, when talking with communities, that nothing ever happens as a result of them being asked their views. Accordingly, right from the start of any engagement, you need to make sure that the engagement can be part of any decision-making process.

Kurt Lewin (1947) sees change as a three-step process. He suggests that change starts when driving forces question the status quo and challenge norms, creating an opening for something different. This is the unfreezing stage. The second stage is the moving stage, where new behaviour becomes the norm. The third stage is refreezing, where systems are established to support and reinforce the new system.

Clearly, in very practical terms, knowing how the system works and how and where to influence it best is critical. Community workers need to have an understanding of the political context in which they are operating. Engagement also means thinking about ways in which you can best work in your context to influence change. Mini publics (like citizens' juries) (What Works Scotland, 2022) are a good example of how community members can be involved in decision making. Typically, they bring together a body of randomly selected community members to discuss and make decisions/recommendations on issues of public concern. They are widely used to ensure inclusive community voice in shaping decisions on often complex or controversial issues. They use a process called dialogue and deliberation in order to discuss issues and reach conclusions in ways that are non-conflictual and which openly recognise the value of different viewpoints (Escobar, 2011).

All engagements produce knowledge. Some people, and some professions in particular, value some kinds of knowledge more than others (McArdle et al, 2020). When you are using the knowledge produced by an engagement, it can be helpful to understand some of theory behind this valuing, giving you confidence in the value of your engagement knowledge.

The following case study takes up this bringing together of different kinds of knowledge. It is also an example of how a mini public can be used as a structure to bring about change.

Case study

Jane works in public health. She has been asked to support a community engagement process around tobacco-related harm, with the aim of having significant community input into the development of a local action plan. Towards the end of the process, she is hoping to organise a mini public for community members, to make recommendations for this action plan. She is struggling to convince some partners. They are worried that community members do not have the expert knowledge to make these kinds of decisions. Jane argues that their knowledge, although more localised and less rigorous than other database based knowledge, is nonetheless just as important. The mini public goes ahead, with community members and professional partners working together, as equals, to decide on priorities for the action plan. There is a genuine exchange of views and increased understanding of different perspectives from all those involved. In this way, community views genuinely contributed to the action plan.

Community organising

Community organising is an approach which is focused on building connections between and across communities. Developed significantly in the US by Saul Alinsky in the 1940s through his Industrial Areas Foundation (IAF), it has more recently gained popularity elsewhere. Alinsky outlined his model in his book *Rules for Radicals* (1971). The model sees community organisers training local leaders to use one-to-one interviews with local people to identify issues within communities. It prioritises finding connections and building trust between local people to enable them to take action together. The ideas of Saul Alinsky are often compared to those of Paulo Freire. Edward T. Chambers, Alinsky's mentee, is credited with creating a systematic scheme of training for organisers. He describes the development of the practice: 'Under Alinsky, organizing meant "pick a target, mobilize, and hit it" In the modern IAF, it's "connect and relate to others". Issues follow relationships. You don't pick targets and mobilize first; you connect people in and around their interests' (Chambers, 2003, 46). Like community development, community organising also focuses on supporting local people to identify their own solutions, but while community development focuses on building capacity within communities at a local level, community organising is more focused on making change occur around community issues at a more structural level.

Underpinning community development practice is an understanding of the power within relationships and interactions in the community with individuals, networks and organisations. Community organising takes this a step further, focusing in more detail on a critique and analysis of the distribution of power 'in order to build alliances for political leverage' (Gilchrist, 2019, 67), targeting those in positions of influence through '"mass mobilisations to exert disciplined and organised pressure' (Gilchrist, 2019, 67) to hold them to account.

Community organisers maintain independence through fundraising, which often takes the form of membership fees or 'dues' (Hothi, 2013), so they are able to negotiate for real change in the community without being beholden to funders and the public purse.

Relational meetings

As initial engagements with communities are focused on building connections and identifying leaders, underpinning the community organiser's approach are relational meetings, short meetings of no more than 30 minutes, focused on learning about one another's motivations and skills. By asking someone to meet with us to tell us about themselves and their community, we are telling them that '"their perspective is of value' and, as conversation is 'a two-way street', we also share our own perspective and 'must be prepared to be vulnerable about his or her own social passions, values, frustrations, and concerns' (Chambers, 2003, 49).

> Mixing human spirits has a certain form and requires certain skills to practice. Those of us who become practiced in the art of the relational meeting have learned to use our whole selves – body and spirit, charms and personality, compassion and wit, humor and anger – in short, intense, focused human encounters. When a good one-to-one occurs, two people connect in a way that transcends ordinary, everyday conversation. Both people have the opportunity to pause and reflect on their personal experience regarding the tension between the world-as-it-is and the world-as-it-should-be. At that moment, a new public relationship can be born, two human spirits can mix, and both people can gain power to be truer to their best selves, to live more effectively

and creatively, to take action together for the common good. (Chambers, 2009, 32)

The quotation from Chambers describes some of the attributes needed for good engagement. Our final point in making sure that the engagement matters returns to the danger of tokenism. Tokenism leads to engagements that merely act as processes, through which those who already have power can consolidate this power. In this sense, community engagement can be part of what Gramsci (1971) referred to as the hegemonic process through which we continue to consent to our relative powerlessness because we do not recognise the ways in which we are being dominated. As community workers, we have a role to critically interrogate how this process works, valuing voice, inclusion and multiple forms of knowledge.

Principles in practice

1. Community engagement is underpinned by a commitment to social justice and empowerment. Think about how you contribute to this.
2. Thinking about the different kinds of knowledge that are collected in engagement and how they can be valued differently is an important dimension of practice in community engagement.
3. The development and harnessing of social capital is key to an ongoing equality between services and communities in engagement.
4. Thinking about voice in the methods that you use will raise issues of power differentials. Think about how you will manage these.
5. Be clear about change and how to bring this about through the engagement.

Challenge questions

1. Think about engagements you have been involved in. Have they had an instrumental or social justice understanding of the value of engagement?
2. What kind of knowledge do you value in your work? How confident are you in explaining why this knowledge is important?

3. How is social capital important to community engagement in your work?
4. Do you feel valued in your community engagement work?
5. Thinking about the case studies in this chapter, do these match your experience of community engagement?
6. How can you ensure that engagements move beyond tokenism and can be genuinely transformative?

References

Alinsky, S. (1971) *Rules for Radicals: A pragmatic primer for realistic radicals.* Vintage Press, New York.

Brunton, G., Thomas, J., O'Mara-Eves, A., Jamal, F., Oliver, S. and Kavanagh, J. (2017) Narratives of community engagement: a systematic review-derived conceptual framework for public health interventions, *BMC Public Health* 17: art 944.

Chambers, E.T. (2003) *Roots for Radicals: organising for power, action and justice.* Continuum, New York.

Chambers, E.T. (2009) *The Power of Relational Action.* ACTA Publications, Skokie.

Escobar, O. (2011) *Public dialogue and deliberation: a communication perspective for public engagement practitioners.* Available at: www.ed.ac.uk/files/imports/fileManager/eResearch_Oliver%20Escobar.pdf (Accessed: 23 December 2022).

Gilchrist, A. (2019) Developing the well-connected community. In *The Well-Connected Community: A networking approach to community development*, 2nd edn. Policy Press, Bristol, pp 195–210.

Gramsci, A. (1971) *Selections from Prison Notebooks.* International Publishers, New York.

Hothi, M. (2013) Growing Community Organising London: The Young Foundation. Available at: https://youngfoundation.org/wp-content/uploads/2013/05/Growing-Community-Organising-FINAL-V3.pdf (Accessed: 7 August 2022).

Lewin, K. (1947) Frontiers in group dynamics: concept, method and reality in social science, social equilibra and social change. *Human Relations* 1(1): 5–41.

McArdle, K. and Mansfield, S. (2007) Voice, discourse and transformation: enabling learning for the achieving of social change, *Discourse: Studies in the Cultural Politics of Education* 28(4): 485–98.

McArdle, K., Briggs, S., Forrester, K., Garrett, E. and McKay, C. (2020) *The Impact of Community Work: How to gather evidence.* Policy Press, Bristol.

Scottish Community Development Centre (2022a) *National Standards for Community Engagement.* Available at www.scdc.org.uk/what/national-standards (Accessed: 23 December 2022).

Scottish Community Development Centre (2022b) *VOiCE.* Available at www.scdc.org.uk/what/voice (Accessed: 23 December 2022).

Tinglin, W. and Joyette, D. (2020) *Community Engagement in a Changing Social Landscape.* Friesen Press, Tamarak Institute, Victoria, Canada.

What Works Scotland (2022) *Mini Publics.* Available at http://whatworksscotland.ac.uk/topics/mini-publics/ (Accessed: 23 December 2022).

8

Networking and partnership

Kirsty Forrester

Introduction

A good community worker has, as a matter of course, a broad network and a range of connections, an understanding about the different layers of organisation and power within communities and how to connect them together, as described by Gilchrist: 'The organisational and demographic environment in which community workers and activists operate is becoming increasingly dynamic, complex and diverse. Practitioners need to be ever more agile in working across boundaries' (Gilchrist, 2019, vii). In this chapter we will explore how we can better use our networks to develop strong partnerships for and with communities.

Networking

Networking is about good relationships. It can save time and gives us access to resources. By picking up the phone to call someone in our network, we can more quickly get the answer we need to a problem. Ideas around networking are fundamental to ideas of community; by making connections with others, we can build community and find collective strength. The following quotation describes how relationships make up a sense of community: 'In modern parlance, community comprises the informal interactions and connections that we use to coordinate everyday life. These links enable us to exchange resources and ideas for mutual benefit and to share experiences in ways that are usually supportive' (Gilchrist, 2019, 3).

Most of us have social ties across many different communities and we might consider someone tied to only one community as socially isolated. To feel a connection to only one community 'is both illogical and dangerous' (Sen, 2006, 106). For example, we may have met migrant women who are victims of domestic violence but feel unable to leave their abusive relationship because, with low English-language skills, little knowledge of UK systems and a lack of friendships beyond their own cultural group, it feels easier to stay, rather than face being ostracised by their community. Sadly, 'networks also include relationships based on fear, jealousy, animosity and suspicion' (Gilchrist, 2019, 84). Therefore supporting individuals and communities to build and expand their networks underpins good community development, allowing 'a form of intelligence gathering, enabling people to gain access to advice, services and resources that they might not otherwise know about or be able to influence' (Gilchrist, 2019, 94).

Gilchrist (2019), who has written extensively on the subject, says networks are based upon shared values and interests and identified by interpersonal relationships, where power is a decentralised web of connections. To use Gilchrist's term, 'a well-connected community' is one which pulls in additional resources and supports the most vulnerable residents during challenging times. She says that a community with strong networks will be more resilient and better able to respond to catastrophe and, while we agree, our personal experiences of living in communities affected by severe floods or storms tells us that communities can, through the solidarity of the shared experience, become networked overnight. We saw numerous examples of this during the worldwide COVID-19 pandemic in community settings with which the authors are familiar.

The 'Voices for Indi' campaign, described here, is an excellent example of how a group of activists used a networking approach to build connections to make real change for their community. In 2012, dissatisfied with their sitting political representative, a group of 12 citizens in Indigo Valley, Australia, started to meet informally to discuss what they could do to improve the quality of their political representation. Using a community conversation model, they asked their community what mattered to them. What they heard led the group to decide to field their own, independent candidate, taking their report as a manifesto (Voices for Indi, 2013). Across Indigo Valley's large geographical area, they set up localised hubs and encouraged people to connect with their communities, using digital tools to network. Their government candidate, Cathy McGowan, won, beating the incumbent and positioning herself as a partner to the electorate (Tattersall, 2022). She invited local volunteers to come in to her office to work with her, giving them the opportunity to build their own networks and access the power normally privileged by elected officials. What happened in Indi led to independent candidates winning seats in the 2022 election and the beginning of a new kind of Australian politics, with local communities and local issues very much at the centre. This example shows how effective networking can be in facilitating change.

Glasby and Dickson (2014) say that we must be aware of the multiple hats we wear as community workers, organisational or team representatives and advocates for the communities with whom we are working. It has been argued that community development workers '"fostered dependency and "learned helplessness" among those whom [they] purported to empower' (Gilchrist, 2019, 68). Understanding our role in the creation of independent networks may be a helpful way to look at things. The asset-based community development approach to community development acknowledges the benefits of a community with strong social networks and may be a helpful tool, focusing on the positives of communities, not the deficits.

Communicating well

Gilchrist (2019) defines the qualities required to network well: affability, integrity, audacity, adaptability and tenacity – qualities that we feel are synonymous with being a good community worker. To that list, we would add the ability to tune in to other people – what they're saying and what is their meaning. Developing an awareness of our own language and behaviours to help relationships and communication to develop is key.

Each of us has a responsibility as a human being to communicate as effectively as we can with each other. To communicate effectively, we must transmit our messages in a way that strangers can understand what we mean, and we need to interpret strangers' messages in the way they meant them to be interpreted. (Gudykunst, 1994, 6)

Every single one of us changes our language throughout the interactions we have, in the course of a day, shifting from the formal, to informal; from parent, to child, to colleague, to friend to neighbour. As complex beings, we all have a range of different identities and selves that we move in and out of. Code-switching, a term introduced in 1954 by sociolinguist Einar Haugen, is the act of changing or adjusting your language, accent, style of speech or behaviour to assimilate to the environment and people present. It can also describe the mixing or alternating of different languages and dialects within a conversation. Sometimes we choose to or are forced to code-switch our authentic selves so as to gain trust or position, and it is how power and our sense of self are experienced in these interactions that becomes positive or negative. The ability to code-switch is of benefit to the community worker who wishes to network effectively, and our ability to speak in the vernacular with local people and in a more professional English with senior managers and elected officials is a benefit.

Partnership

Taylor (2003) suggests that, across the world, ideas about government have changed, acknowledging that complex social issues cannot be solved by government alone. Governance, with partnership and cooperation very much at the core, allows knowledge, expertise and, ultimately, responsibility to be shared; in the words of Jones and Little (2000, 171), 'partnership is seen exclusively as positive currency'. Since the 1960s, partnership has underpinned most economic development and local regeneration initiatives in the UK, where the authors work, and it is one of the five universal building blocks of all United Nations (UN) Global Goals, with the UN suggesting that sustainable development can be realised only with strong global partnerships and cooperation (United Nations, 2022).

Partnerships exist at the micro, meso and macro levels of community work, whether that is in a youth-work setting, delivering a programme with a local school or sports club, team managers coming together to respond to the adult learning needs across an area, or at a more strategic level with public and voluntary sector leaders, working with government and industry to develop innovative programmes of learning and training to promote employment and reduce poverty. Glasby et al (2011) describe these as the individual, organisational and structural levels of partnership.

Edwards et al (1998) suggest that motivations for forming partnerships are:

- As a forum for strategic discussion, representation or consensual planning;
- To pool resources for efficient delivery of services;
- In response to the requirements of regeneration programs in order to bid for funding for identified objectives;
- At a local level to create a proactive network around a specific project or social group. (Edwards et al, 1998, cited in McArdle, 2012)

Partnerships can be contrived, and Jones and Little describe these as 'false partnerships' (Jones and Little, 2000, 181). Such relationships can develop into genuine partnerships over time, or they may simply disappear. Organic partnerships which develop in response to a well-articulated local need are perhaps more likely to succeed, especially when those involved in their inception have power to identify who should be involved, rather than governance structures and membership being forced upon them. A community worker with whom we spoke discussed how shared challenges helped people to work together to share resources, promote each other's opportunities and signpost people to other agencies and services.

'We've got a vested interest in terms of things that happen in the community, but I just try to take a holistic view of that and have the same kind of input with some of the groups that work locally as well, because they're really well placed to be supporting the community as well. And a lot of the cost-of-living stuff, we just don't have the capacity to do it alone, we don't have the workers to do it and we're reliant on the third sector to do that with our support and coordination, and we're doing really positive work together.' (Alan Gunn, 2022, Interview)

Partnership is often a condition for funding, and this can be challenging in areas of deprivation, whether urban or rural, and where partners to work with are thin on the ground. Areas where resources are needed most are, therefore, often excluded from the initiatives that should benefit them most, or one of the partners may find themselves involved in purely tokenistic fashion, without access to any real power. As community workers, we must consider power within partnerships. If they are created and viewed as the property of public sector organisations, then this places the voluntary sector and local communities themselves immediately on the back foot. The community worker quoted earlier explained how unhelpful it is when agencies are pitted one against the other.

> 'I think [the challenges of partnership are] competition and territorialism. And you know, funding is finite and it's going to become more so, so, there's a natural concern, I think, specifically in terms of the third sector, who are completely reliant on grant funding, so there is a real challenge there.
>
> 'I think the third sector and statutory organisations complement each other and that should be the focus. It is not an either/or. I think if you take the competitiveness for funding out the way people will naturally work together.' (Alan Gunn, 2022, Interview)

It is understandable that local communities and organisations are willing to engage in partnerships, especially when resources are available, but to do so often requires them to formalise structures that work precisely because of their informality or to expand their reach more quickly and beyond the geographical boundaries with which they are comfortable. McArdle (2012) described the pressure that one successful rural partnership faced to expand its geographical coverage to include more urban settlements with very different concerns and aims.

Success also depends on accountability among all members. We have a responsibility to the communities with whom we work, but also to the people and organisations with whom we are working. Gilchrist (2019) suggests that accountability must involve:

- giving an account of what was done and why;
- taking into account the interests of different stakeholders; and
- accounting for the use of resources, especially finances. (Gilchrist, 2019, 99)

Working in partnership is not easy: it takes time, skill and energy, as 'partners bring very different expectations, goals, cultures, worldviews, skills, powers and resources to the process' (Taylor, 2003, 116). Often, we can feel that it would be easier to get on and do the job ourselves, but the benefits of good partnership working far exceed the challenges. As one of the community workers with whom we spoke said, 'One of the reasons why partnerships don't last is about resources, but it is also because it takes time and it is also about valuing it as well' (Gunn, 2022, Interview).

Challenges arise from 'conflicting objectives' (Jones and Little, 2000, 177), and for partnership working to be effective all partners around the table need to be clear about their organisation or group's mission and what their own unique contribution is to the collaborative work. If we are all trying to do the same thing, we will find ourselves in competition with the partners who could be our closest allies. For example, when Kirsty started working as a local authority adult learning worker there was a lot of duplication. Through a process of review, partners were able to each identify their unique contributions in responding to adult learning needs across the city and how they could better work together to support people to progress in different areas of their lives. Kirsty's public sector adult learning team identified that their unique role was in supporting the lowest-level and most vulnerable learners in the city, both men and women, to gain language and other skills to progress in life, learning and work, while the local women's centre offered a safe, women-only environment and college partners offered progression into further study. By clarifying our unique contributions, the strategic partnership was able to increase capacity and respond to a high demand for community-based learning. For our voluntary sector colleagues, who must compete for funding, being clear about their core purpose and unique role within a locality was even more important. Indeed, clarifying roles, identifying new partners and working together can lead to much better outcomes for communities, as described here by a colleague working within a multidisciplinary partnership:

> 'The only way we can improve outcomes is through deepening connections to well-being and learning. … But we know that there are lots of people who don't feel connected to what they're learning about. … One of the things that we're looking to do is mix stronger and more accessible pathways that are offered to young people. … So, we are absolutely looking at the partners that can help to offer those wider pathways for our learners across the area.' (Kathleen Johnston, 2022, Focus Group)

In the same way that it is important that we are clear about our organisation's unique contribution to a partnership, we need to also be clear about the purpose of the partnership and how working together can add value to existing work. In previous employment, I have heard colleagues express frustration about a local strategic forum that would, for its strategic plan, just write down all the work that was being done in the area and in isolation by the partners who attended their meetings. The existence of partnership did not bring anything new into the area and, for workers, it was just another meeting to attend in an already busy week. Unfortunately, those directing the work and leading the forum had failed to understand the nature of collaborative partnership working.

While partnership working should never be an end in itself, it is easy to see how this happens when an already busy manager is tasked with setting up a new partnership. However well intentioned, it is all too easy to lose sight of why the partnership was so important in the first place and the outcomes it was meant to deliver. (Glasby et al, 2011, 4)

Theory of change approaches have become very popular in the UK, particularly for health and social care partnerships (Glasby et al, 2011), as a way to establish shared goals, address any conflicting ideas and pre-empt any future challenges. The following questions may be helpful:

- Where do we want to be/what do we want to achieve? (outcomes)
- Where are we now? (context)
- What do we need to do to achieve our desired outcomes? (process). (Glasby et al, 2011, 4)

Research by McArdle (2012) found that an ethos that emphasised collaboration was felt, by those involved in a successful rural regeneration partnership, to be key to its success. 'People respected each other's roles and did not push their own agenda; rather they looked for mutual achievement. The key quality that contributed to this ethos was considered by one respondent to be respect' (McArdle, 2012, 341).

The successful partnerships in which we, as practitioners, have worked have been characterised by a variety of staff and leadership groupings, encouraging ideas from staff at all levels and across organisational boundaries, so that they feel they have a stake in how work is designed and delivered. While such collaborations achieve a variety of outcomes for service users, they also lead to the growth of independent, confident, agile staff, wider professional networks and understandings, streamlined efficient services and professional satisfaction for those involved. Collaboration within a multi-agency partnership with different professional and organisational backgrounds and ways of working, and coming together based on mutual trust and respect while remaining independent, breeds a different kind of loyalty and commitment based on shared values and mission and purpose. It is important that these shared goals are defined early into the relationship. Indeed, the independence of organisations within partnerships is a strength allowing them to 'remain flexible and responsive to changing circumstances' (Gilchrist, 2019, 12).

Collaboration

While networking, cooperation or partnership may be defined as collaboration, they are not necessarily so. When we cooperate with other organisations, we may achieve a shared goal, without increasing our capacity. True collaboration comes from two or more parties working together to produce something which is far greater than that which they could have produced alone. Collaboration involves sharing the risks, the responsibilities, resources and the rewards. It is also about allowing the ownership for decision making and planning to be shared from the beginning. Collaboration is about recognising and valuing the other party and their unique contribution. Collaborative relationships are synergistic, they break down silos and afford us a wider pool of colleagues with whom to work. Collaboration cannot be forced; it develops organically. Good communication is key to good collaboration. As practitioners, we need to demonstrate a commitment and an openness to collaborative ways of working for it to become the norm, and we need to start by ensuring that collaboration is the way we work within our teams. Collaboration, we argue, underpins good leadership; we explore it in more detail in Chapter 17.

Partnering with communities

Taylor (2003) argues that, as community workers, it is essential that we ensure that the community is at the heart of policy making and decisions that affect them, through involvement in strategic decisions, partnerships and groupings, because we simply cannot address all the things that community development seeks to achieve alone, as the following quotation illustrates.

'Some of [the challenges] are structural. Like we rely heavily on the community and voluntary sector, on there being volunteer-led groups who can work with the funding that we can give or volunteer management committees. And if the community and voluntary sector isn't strong, then our work is not strong because [my colleague] covers a whole county and you just can't be in the whole county.' (Fran Kennedy, 2022, Focus Group)

In the following case study, Lynn describes an experience, as a practitioner in a strategic role, of partnering with a community of young people in a way that enabled them to hold real power and decision makers to account, creating learning programmes that made a real impact.

Case study

'When I was doing reproductive justice work in Louisiana, and we had a very high STI [sexually transmitted infections] rate. We were given funding to get sex ed [sex education] in the schools, but we weren't quite sure. You know it never happened in Louisiana, we were what they call the buckle of the Bible Belt. We wanted middle school and high school youth to be able to hear the information they needed to stay healthy. This was really important for us. And there was a lot of push-back. And so, this organisation, Advocates for Youth, worked with us and a number of organisations throughout Mississippi and Louisiana to be able to help us to work productively with youth to give us the skills to allow them to lead. It was hard because, you know, we had all these different barriers, with age being a huge one, but there were all sorts of other cultural barriers. It was one of the most useful training series that I have been part of because the youth basically said to us, you know, "You've got a vision, but you really need to sit down and shut up and listen because we know what we need!" You can come up with this lovely programme, but if it's not valued by them, all your work will be for nothing. I thought it was interesting because it was really led by the youth; the people who trained us were young people who've been through this programme, and it's a national movement and they bring the youth together, so once they get into this programme, then they're sort of cross-pollinating all over the place.' (Lynn Clark, 2022, Focus Group)

Involving the community makes interventions more sustainable, pulls in local knowledge to inform solutions, allows for better monitoring of outcomes and 'develops the skills and social capital in communities that are needed to tackle exclusion' (Taylor 2003, 115). To involve the community, we must ensure that the community is an active partner with real power and access to resources and that partnerships do not serve to exclude them further (Taylor 2003). While it is important that communities are able to make decisions about investment in their area, we must also consider what we are asking of local people if they are to be involved as equal partners; they need to have considerable knowledge, not only of their own community, but also political knowledge, and strong local networks, and they must also be willing to give a considerable amount of their time and sometimes personal resources, usually unpaid. We must challenge situations where the people with whom we are working feel they are not valued. For example, as a community development worker supporting community alcohol and drug forums, Kirsty worked hard to challenge professionals to moderate their language and stop wearing their badges and using their titles, as this made community members feel inadequate and uncomfortable. The team worked hard to value all contributions to the work and to ensure that everyone could participate. We argue that if we are serious about local involvement, then we should recognise and reward local expertise. We know that strategic partnership meetings can be formal and complex in both language and structure, what Jones and Little describe as the 'private/public sector mould' (Jones and Little, 2000, 177), and we must consider how we can address this and be aware of the time it may require to get up to speed if the community is to be involved as an equal partner.

The community workers with whom we spoke told us that partnership working underpinned all the work they did in the community. As community workers, we know the incredible rewards that come personally and professionally for strong collaborative relationships and partnerships, and we know that these surpass those experienced when we work in isolation. The authors would argue that community work is fundamentally a collaborative endeavour, but it would be naive to think this is always straightforward. Working in partnership with communities and other organisations is complex and often challenging, and to be successful we must define roles and expectations from the beginning, but we consider that community workers are well placed to do this important work and ensure that communities are at the centre.

Principles in practice

1. Take a networking approach to your practice, seeking new connections and supporting those with whom you work to build theirs.
2. Make sure that your work supports the creation of new or stronger networks and independent communities, rather than a dependency culture.
3. In the partnerships in which you participate, be clear about your role, and the role of others, to ensure there is accountability and a shared vision.
4. Analyse your existing networks and partnerships, describing the role of each partner and assessing the purposes, mission and value to your work. What is the outcome of partnership for your participants?

Challenge questions

1. Spend time thinking about the multiple hats you wear in your role as a community worker. How do you use these to support work outcomes?
2. Think about your professional relationships and projects. Which of these are truly collaborative? How do these differ from other

relationships and projects? What was different about how these relationships and projects were formed?
3. How do the partnerships in which you are involved help to create stronger and more inclusive pathways for the communities with which you are working?
4. Think about who holds power within the partnerships and networks in which you participate. Is power shared? Are some less able to influence and make change? Does everyone have their voice heard? How can you ensure there is parity of esteem and influence moving forward?
5. Have you ever been in the same situation as Lynn Clark described in her focus group? What did you feel and do?

References

Edwards, B., Goodwin, M., Pemberton, S. and Woods, H. (1998) *Findings: Partnership working in rural regeneration. Research in progress.* Joseph Rowntree Foundation, York.

Gilchrist, A. (2019) *The Well-Connected Community: A networking approach to community development*, 2nd edn. Policy Press, Bristol.

Glasby, J. and Dickinson, H. (2014) *A–Z of Interagency Working.* Palgrave Macmillan, Basingstoke.

Glasby, J., Dickinson, H. and Miller, R. (2011) Partnership working in England – where we are now and where we've come from. *International Journal of Integrated Care*, 11 (Special issue) e002. 10.5334/ijic.545.

Gudykunst, W.B. (1994) *Bridging Differences: Effective intergroup communication.* SAGE Publications, Inc., Thousand Oaks, CA.

Gudykunst, W.B. (2004) *Bridging Differences: Effective intergroup communication*, 2nd edn. SAGE Publications, Inc., Thousand Oaks, CA.

Jones, O. and Little, J. (2000) Rural challenge(s): partnership and new rural governance, *Journal of Rural Studies* 16: 17–183. Available at: www.academia.edu/362175/Rural_Challenge_s_partnership_and_new_rural_governance (Accessed: 28 August 2022).

McArdle, K. (2012) What makes a successful rural regeneration partnership? The views of successful partners and the importance of ethos for the community development professional, *Community Development* 43(3): 333–45.

Sen A. (2006) *Identity and Violence: The illusion of destiny*. W.W. Norton, New York.

Tattersall, A. (2022) Changemaker Charts: Independents and Elections, 16 May 2022. Available at: https://changemakerspodcast.org/nick-haines-changemaker-chats-independents-and-elections/ (Accessed: 8 August 2022).

Taylor, M. (2003) *Public Policy in the Community*. Palgrave Macmillan, London.

United Nations (2022) Web page: www.un.org/sustainabledevelopment/globalpartnerships/ (Accessed: 11 September 2022).

Voices for Indi (2013) *Voices 4 Indi Report*. Think Print, Wangaratta. Available at: https://voicesforindi.com/wp-content/uploads/2020/04/V4I-Report.pdf (Accessed: 4 September 2022).

9

Health and well-being

Ed Garrett and Karen McArdle

Introduction

Some community workers may have a specific focus on health and well-being, but for anyone doing community work, the health and well-being of the individuals and communities they are involved with will no doubt be important to them. It really is, we suggest, the role of all community workers.

Jane Mitchell, who manages a community-led health charity, emphasised the importance of the role the community plays in community in health and well-being in an interview for this chapter:

> 'COVID-19 really showed the need for a community-based response to addressing health. Local communities know and understand their issues and have the networks to drive forward support. They have local knowledge and people buy into local things. We had so many people get in touch during COVID wanting to volunteer. They didn't know about, or didn't want, to go through area-wide organisations. They wanted to go through a local group.' (Jane Mitchell, 2022, Interview)

There has of course been a long tradition of community involvement in health. For example, in the UK, where the authors live and work, public participation through the charitable movements and the burgeoning Labour movement was responsible for driving health improvement in the 19th century. The advent of a National Health Service (NHS) in 1948 in the UK led to an understanding that health was more the preserve of the NHS and the experts within it than of the community or patients. Since the 1970s there has been increasing recognition at both international level and more locally of the importance of understanding health from this broader, community perspective (Taylor, 2003).

This recognition is driven by a clear imperative to focus on prevention. Increasing pressures on health services, because of ageing populations and changing professional and patient expectations, have confirmed the need to look for more upstream and preventative interventions in the social determinants of health – these determinants being the economic, social, environmental and cultural conditions that influence our health.

> The social determinants of health are the non-medical factors that influence health outcomes. They are the conditions in which people are born, grow, work, live, and age, and the wider set of forces and systems shaping the conditions of daily life. These forces and systems include economic policies and systems, development agendas, social norms, social policies and political systems. (World Health Organization, 2023)

There is a need to address health inequalities linked to these conditions. The report on the Marmot Review of health equity in England (2020) made clear how inequalities in these conditions are leading to inequalities in health outcomes in the UK.

> The last decade has been marked by deteriorating health and widening health inequalities. People living in more deprived areas outside London have seen their life expectancy stalling, even declining for some, while it has increased in more advantaged areas. ... This damage to health has been largely unnecessary. There is no biological reason for stalling life expectancy and

widening health inequalities. Other countries are doing better, even those with longer life expectancy than England. The increase in health inequalities in England points to social and economic conditions, many of which have shown increased inequalities, or deterioration since 2010. (Marmot, 2020, 4)

Different models of health

Research by the Joseph Rowntree Foundation tells us about the COVID-19 pandemic in the UK. This may apply to your country too.

> The pandemic has really put a spotlight on our health, both physical and mental. Many people have struggled with the emotional and psychological toll this period has taken on us. Those of us with disabilities or health conditions that prevent us from working have been held back further because of the reduced number of face-to-face doctors' appointments, referrals, treatments and assessments.
>
> The problem will not go away by itself – it's time to step in and do what we can to weaken the links between poverty and ill-health. None of us should be pulled into poverty because we are unwell, and none of us should be put under such pressure and strain by poverty that we become sick. (Joseph Rowntree Foundation, 2023, 4–5)

As community workers interested in social justice, it is social determinants of health, and how they produce health inequalities, that will likely be the focus of our work. As we have said earlier in this chapter, health and well-being really are part of the role of all community workers and there is much work that we do; from early years, through attainment in education, to work around employability and literacies that have an impact on health and well-being. These focuses of the community worker are key in contributing to positive health and well-being outcomes. Health literacy, for example, can be important in mediating inequalities, and supporting health literacy may well be a key role for community workers.

Nutbeam and Lloyd (2021) describe three levels of health literacy: functional, interactive and critical. Functional describes the basic literacy and numeracy skills required to gain basic health information and carry out prescribed tasks such as taking medication. Interactive literacy describe the more advanced skills required to find and extract information from a range of sources and apply new information in changing circumstances. Critical literacy describes the ability to analyse information from a range of sources and apply this information in a wide range of circumstances for people to gain access and advocate for themselves, their families and their communities. This may involve people developing an understanding of the impacts of social determinants of health and taking action to reduce them.

Health is a big and complex area of work, where we will be working alongside many different partners. Given this, it is important to be aware people may have two distinct understandings of health. Firstly, we have the medical model, where health is seen as the absence of disease. This model has a long history, with its roots in the dualism of Descartes in the 17th century and the subsequent rise of modern science. Here the separation of the body and mind means that the body is seen simply as a machine which can be treated (Bowling, 2001).

Then we have the social model of health, which focuses on the conditions in which people live, including their communities, as much as on their bodies (Bowling, 2001). It also emphasises that health is not always some objective state but also, vitally, includes how the person experiences their life. The World Health Organization (WHO) defines health as a state of complete physical, mental and social well-being and not merely the absence of disease or infirmity (WHO, 2022).

This social definition links health and well-being, with well-being seen as a constituent of health. It contains a strong element of self-definition; it is simply our own sense of life going well (Ruggeri, 2020). In terms of valuing individual autonomy, subjectivity and the uniqueness of individual experience are important. Nevertheless, there are problems, most obviously with the measurement of these understandings of health and well-being.

If well-being is simply what the individual says it is, how do we know that we are promoting it as community workers? There are certainly difficulties in providing some measures here (Ruggeri, 2020). We prefer a tighter definition of well-being, as living a life of value, for self and for others. More fundamentally, and linked to broader discussion around health in the next section, we need to consider the way in which well-being has, in part, become both a discourse and an industry that can promote certain ways of life. This discourse is often challenged, of course, but by choosing our own well-being we may be sometimes internalising a particular discourse, which may often be a discourse of capitalism and consumption.

Dawn Tuckwood, a public health worker involved in discussions for this chapter, noted the multiple and complex discourses that exist around health, with an emphasis increasingly on self-care and the value of community support and capacity building – arguably part of a shift towards a community/place-based paradigm. There is much here to be positive about for the community worker. Yet these discourses need to be set against other understandings of health, more closely linked to the medical model, which we will come across in our work.

It is a response to the need for critical engagement with these discourses and associated health practices that the theory in this chapter takes as its focus. We first explore the links between health and control, before considering the importance of community voice in addressing health inequalities. We conclude with a discussion of social capital and its contribution to health, in particular looking at what has been called 'the modern epidemic' (New Scientist, 2014), loneliness. The philosopher Hannah Arendt, writing in the 1950s, suggested that solutions to these problems lie in the political as well as the personal and social domains.

Health and control

Case study

>Jimmy was a volunteer for a community food larder, helping people out with food and other essentials that they might struggle to afford. It was clear to

him and to other volunteers that some larder users were struggling to know what to cook with some of the food available, so they organised with colleagues some healthy cooking courses. These courses were well attended, but not necessarily by the people that Jimmy thought might most benefit from them. He talked to some of these people to find out why they had decided not to come. One person said that they thought that healthy cooking was all about being put on a diet. Another said that they struggled with their weight and had experienced stigma around this right through their life. They associated health with this stigma and being told what to do.

As this case study shows, some people can experience health and its institutions and discourses as disempowering. This shows that a link can exist between health and control of the individual and communities. The medical model has its roots in the birth of modern science. The scientific paradigm is positivistic (Bowling, 2001). Positivism essentially asserts that there is some objective reality which can be tested and discovered through scientific method. The scientific project is about discovering this reality. In contrast, much of the work done with communities, we argue, stresses the multiple nature of reality; that reality is not some abstract realm beyond the social world, but is in fact constituted by the social world (Bowling, 2001; Graney, 2002). In consequence, lay knowledge about health may be seen as a completely different kind of knowledge to that of medical knowledge (Taylor, 2003).

It should be noted that the choice between the scientific and other alternative paradigms need not be stark. With science itself conceived as a social activity, the gap closes considerably (Israel et al, 1998). Accepting this distinction, however, the challenge of alternative paradigms to the scientific – particularly those driven by community empowerment –is, in part, an epistemological challenge; a challenge about different ways of knowing. This epistemological challenge is significant when considering who owns the knowledge or the 'guarding' of professional knowledge. Naidoo et al (2002) argue that central to professional knowledge and practice is the acquisition of a monopoly in valued areas of

Health and well-being

expertise. To challenge the value of this professional expertise is to challenge a whole social and political system built on distinctions of what is valuable and who is allowed to know and practise this knowledge.

People working with communities, and particularly those in the third sector, may well have experienced a negative valuing of what they do. In Scotland, there are Health and Social Care partnerships, which recognise the importance of all services and organisations involved in delivering health support working together. Third sector organisations delivering support at a local level, often through volunteers, may be integrated into these partnerships. This practice can result in inward leverage of significant funding to support locally based action in health and well-being contexts.

There are of course understandable challenges for these partnerships in knowing how to work with communities, but the fact that this integration of services is happening very slowly reflects at least in part the undervaluing of this community-level support from some health professionals, as described here by a community worker.

> 'From our point of view, as an organisation, integration between the third sector and health and social care services isn't happening as it should. There isn't that close working with the statutory sector. There doesn't appear to be a wide understanding of the benefit and added value third sector organisations can offer in terms of community-based support, nor the respect and trust that we are all working in a professional manner.' (Jane Mitchell, 2022, Interview)

Of course, there are lots of positive examples where a problem of undervaluing community work is not the case. A participant in our youth work focus group said:

> 'We've been partnering with a consultant clinical psychologist for a couple of years and she'll come and visit us and observe the youth work in full swing, even if it's kicking off and chaos, and she'll say "You know

> you are doing therapy by stealth, even if it is therapy with a small 't' you're offering the kind of consistency that these young people need".' (Charis Robertson, 2022, Focus Group)

There is, however, a further and more important implication of this epistemological difference when we are thinking about health. Theodor Adorno (1991), for example, claims that the scientific project is theoretically committed to domination. He argues that the rationality of science objectifies the particular objects of nature, under its dominant value system. Taylor (2003) suggests that the traditional scientific approach involves an objectification of the patient as the object to be 'done to'. To objectify something, we suggest, is to empty it of its inherent value. She continues that the scientific model is about the isolation of the health problem to specific and achievable interventions, within the sphere of specific medical expertise, thus retaining power and status in the encounter (Taylor, 2003). So, the patient is characterised as simply part of the medical system and loses any control as part of this system. Furthermore, medical intervention is arguably committed to retaining this control, not just as an accident of a particular intervention or system, but in its status as part of the scientific project. As patients, we may internalise this control. For example, in a recent community health needs assessment, Dawn Tuckwood noted in an interview how some people, particularly older participants, understood health to be the realm of health professionals. We suggest that a challenge to the epistemology of science is not just an epistemological challenge, but is also a challenge to the structures of control of health practice. Community research generates, we propose, a different kind of knowledge and is an interesting example of such a challenge, as the following case study shows.

Case study

> Two community choirs in North-East Scotland applied for and received some funding to do some research on the value of community singing. The research was led by the choir leader and music director with support

from other choir members. The research looked at and explored the accepted benefits of community singing, such as increased well-being and confidence. By allowing the groups to explore and understand, on their own terms, these benefits, the research achieved a wonderful depth of understanding that makes sense of what matters to those involved. This understanding also gave the groups a confident picture of the value of what they do. This value may be picked up by health professionals and form part of the emerging practice around social prescribing, where wider contributions to addressing health issues are given value.

As well as the medical model, health more generally (both medical and social models, including well-being) can be used as a form of control. Foucault (1991) outlines how power as discipline has reached into every part of our lives. There has been a shift in power and yet, he argues, this shift has not resulted in empowerment, rather it has resulted in power as what he calls discipline, exercising a much more pernicious and wide-reaching effect on our lives. To put it another way, the shift in power is not a shift from one source of power to another source of power within the same understanding of power. Power itself has been transformed in this shift. Power as discipline becomes 'A certain way in which political power touches and affects bodies, in all their actions and reactions, even down to the "soft fibres of the brain"' (Elden, 2006, 46).

Power as discipline becomes inescapable. How this power works varies in different contexts. For our purposes here, what Foucault (1991) says in regard to psychiatry is interesting. Psychiatry moves from something which seeks to control and correct what Foucault would call madness, to something which defines what it is to be abnormal and to control and correct on this basis (Elden, 2006). Medicalisation may be practised as a form of control. This medicalising not only tells us that we are medical subjects who need treatment from medical experts. This discourse is also internalised so that we understand ourselves in this way. We become our own forms of control (Hancock, 2018). All of us become caught up in this process. The process of control becomes part of the fabric of who we are. Health becomes a way of exerting power through the creation of notions of what it means to be healthy and the consequent marginalisation of those who are deemed to be unhealthy. It is in this way that public health as part of the disciplinary society, it is argued, becomes a control on individual liberty (Elden, 2006).

Foucault does, however, offer forms of resistance to this disciplinary society. Just as we are constituted by power relations, we are also empowered by these relations to move beyond them. In terms of modern health, we have capacity to understand and advocate for our own health and to work with health professionals as equals in this process (Hancock, 2018). As community workers we need a reflexive awareness of how power both controls and liberates us.

Health inequalities: community voice and social capital

Case study

> A community-based participatory research programme started in a disadvantaged area of a city in Sweden in 2016. A partnership between the local community, academia, the private and public sectors as well as non-governmental organisations was initiated for innovative solutions for health equity. According to the needs of the community, a women's health group was established as one of many initiatives within the programme. Mainly women migrants from various countries of the Middle East participated in the group, which was managed by a lay health promoter with the same cultural background as the group. The group met for health circle meetings in a common municipality space that became a familiar environment for the women. Guests, such as health professionals from the primary healthcare service or personnel with more strategic positions, were invited to the meetings for dialogue about health issues or the healthcare system. The advantages of such meetings were that the group helped each other to understand the information and that one could ask questions in a calm environment.

> The group is also helpful in putting words to a situation and story. Hearing others with same experiences describing their situation helps others in the group to find the words. The story dialogue method, described by Labonte, Feather and Hills (1999), promoted this process. The women's health group also met for physical activity, modified according to the needs of the group. The bilingual lay health promoter adapted the session according to who showed up. A social coherence was created by the activities. (Lindsjö et al, 2021)

This case study shows the significance of community interventions and their role for a particular population. A key role for community workers in supporting health and well-being will often be to focus on health inequalities and the conditions which create these inequalities. Workers from different professional backgrounds may have different approaches, however, and it is worth being aware of these possible differences. Some community workers with a background in health may be interested in supporting communities to achieve particular health outcomes; for example, helping people to achieve a healthy weight. Other community workers may be more interested in developing capacity in individuals and communities so that they can make decisions about what is healthy for them, which may be achieving a healthy weight.

The value of community voice in addressing inequalities is particularly important from a community work perspective. The participation of communities in ways that make sense to them, and including the most disadvantaged, means that services and activities are a better fit with what people want and need. It is also a challenge to the inequalities in power which underpin other inequalities. In Scotland, there is a training programme called Health Issues in Communities which aims to build capacity in communities to identify and address health issues that they think are important. As Jones (2021) says, this popular education model has its roots in the work of Freire, starting with people's own experience of health and then building a critical consciousness around this. This course may improve health outcomes, but it also does much more than this. As Jones (2000) notes, it involves a challenge to existing social and political relationships, which see the professional role as ameliorating individual dysfunction.

In practice, we can see changes in how people view themselves and others. For example, Jones (2000) describes involvement in the management of a community health project: people who had seen themselves as merely 'users' of services began to provide services and support for others. This idea is often visible in practice through recovery forums and peer-education mental health programmes in schools and self-organising walking groups at grassroots level.

What we see here is a shift in power from being a recipient of services provided, to being in control of services; a shift that can challenge existing power structures as well as having important health benefits in terms of experience and confidence gained (Jones, 2000). It increases social capital, which can improve health more widely. Social capital building is a form of upstream intervention to improve health. There is certainly much evidence for a link between improved health and increased social capital (Rocco et al, 2012). Exploring this link critically through the particular issue of loneliness is useful.

Case study

> Sheila is the chair of the board of a community-led health project working with older people in a rural part of Scotland. She has been involved in the project from its beginning and knows that a lot of the need for its services and activities boils down to the numbers of older people experiencing loneliness. These numbers increased with the COVID-19 pandemic and the lack of opportunity people had to see each other. She could see people she knew declining in their physical and mental health. Within the social restrictions linked to the pandemic, she worked closely with staff and older people to ensure the return of activities, such as lunch clubs and exercise groups, giving people more chances to get together. She was also keen for the local older people's forum to start meeting again as a way of building people's knowledge of what was

happening in their local communities and to provide a voice and influence for older people in what happens in these communities.

What we see here is how social capital building in the form of social connections and capacity is used to address loneliness. Putnam (2000) identified some of the conditions of loneliness in the US in *Bowling Alone*. There is a decline and change apparent in social capital. This decline will be replicated in countries where there are cuts to public services and to spaces which allow people to come together.

Loneliness is a subjective experience. Loneliness is, we suggest, the difference between your actual social connections and those you would like to have (Perlman et al, 1981). The effects of loneliness on mental and physical health (as Sheila sees in the case study) can be very significant, and attention and resources need to be put towards addressing these effects. Much of the work done to address loneliness has been focused on increasing social capital. For example, in Scotland, building on the case study of older people presented here, Age Scotland, a third sector organisation, emphasises the need for community connections in its work to tackle loneliness. A problem is that this rebuilding of social capital does little to address the causes of this decline in the first place. As community workers we need to be politically engaged. In the case study, Sheila recognises this, seeing the value of the older people's forum as a way of addressing loneliness. The political theorist and philosopher Hannah Arendt offers us a useful way in here.

In *The Origins of Totalitarianism* (Arendt, 2017), she gives a political analysis of loneliness, linking it to the rise of totalitarianism. She argues that in loneliness she found the essence of totalitarian government, and the common ground of terror (Rose Hill, 2020). Essentially, not only does loneliness cut people off from each other, but a totalitarian regime also may then replace social connections with an ideology of mistrust and cynicism. Collective action to bring about change becomes impossible. Loneliness needs to be distinguished from isolation and solitude, which often are the conditions for some kind of agency in the world.

Clearly, we live in a world with different political concerns than those of the 1950s, when Arendt was writing. However, just as totalitarianism uses loneliness to confirm its power, so should loneliness be seen as part of the conditions allowing for the flourishing of neoliberalism (see Chapter 2). Separated from each other, we feel powerless and incapable of change. So as important as social capital building can be in addressing loneliness, we also need critical engagement which understands loneliness as a political as well as personal and social issue. To overcome loneliness, we suggest, we need political engagement and action.

This chapter has emphasised how health and well-being are based in discourses and practices that can be problematic for the community worker, who may be interested in social justice and power. Having a critical awareness of these discourses and practices is crucial to effective working together with other services and communities to support sustainable community-led change. We have also recognised the valuable role of community participants in identifying issues and levering in funding to address these in a capacity-building approach, where the support and interventions of community-based practitioners are important.

Principles in practice

1. Think about the different models of health and how these models can impact on your practice in different ways.
2. Health is a contested concept which needs to be understood critically. What is your understanding of health?
3. As community workers we need to work with health inequalities and the social conditions which produce these inequalities.
4. Community voice in health can be seen as challenging to professional status. Has this been your experience?
5. Discourses of health can be used as forms of control. But the power that controls can also liberate. How does this impact on your practice?
6. Building social capital is an important way of improving health, but this needs to be understood critically. Loneliness, for example, is a problem of citizenship as much as a social or personal issue.

7. Networks of professionals and interested parties across disciplines are vital to a coherent approach in tackling health and well-being issues. Reflect on collaborative approaches in this context.

Challenge questions

1. What does health mean to you in your work? How does well-being relate to health?
2. What are the dominant discourses of health that you come across in your practice? How do different discourses affect what you can do?
3. In your work are you looking to achieve particular health outcomes? Or are you looking to support people to make their own choices about health?
4. How can you move beyond power that constitutes us as medicalised subjects?
5. How do we know that we are making a difference in terms of health and well-being? What shows us that this is the case?
6. Thinking about Jimmy in the case study, what would you do in the same situation?

References

Adorno, T. (1991) *The Culture Industry*. Routledge, London.
Arendt, H. (2017) *The Origins of Totalitarianism*. Penguin Books, London.
Bowling, A. (2001) *Research Methods in Health*. Open University Press, Maidenhead.
Elden, S. (2006) Discipline, health and madness, *History of the Human Sciences* 19(1): 39–66.
Foucault, M. (1991) *Discipline and Punish*. Trans A. Sheridan. Penguin Books, Harmondsworth.
Graney, A. (2002) Effectiveness and community empowerment. In S. Cowley (ed) *Public Health in Policy and Practice*. Bailliere Tindall, Edinburgh, pp 164–88.
Hancock, B. (2018) Michel Foucault and the problematics of power: theorizing DTCA and medicalized subjectivity, *The Journal of Medicine and Philosophy: A Forum for Bioethics and Philosophy of Medicine*, 43(4): 439–68.

Israel, B., Schulz, A., Parker, E. and Becker, A. (1998) Assessing partnership approaches to improve public health, *Annual Review of Public Health* 19: 173–202.

Jones, J. (2000) Private troubles and public issues: a community development approach to health. In *Community Learning Scotland*, pp 71–81.

Jones, J. (2021) Popular education, health inequalities and resistance to stigma, *Concept* 12(2): 1–12.

Joseph Rowntree Foundation (2023) The essential guide to understanding poverty in the UK. Available at: UK Poverty 2023: The essential guide to understanding poverty in the UK | JRF (Accessed: 19 February 2023).

Labonte, R., Feather, J. and Hills, M. (1999) A story/dialogue method for health promotion knowledge development and evaluation, *Health Education Research* 14(1), pp 39–50.

Lindsjö, C., Sjögren Forss, K. and Rämgård, M. (2021) Health promotion focusing on migrant women through a community based participatory approach, *BMC Women's Health* 21(1): 365. Available at: https://europepmc.org/article/med/34656089 (Accessed: 4 July 2023).

Marmot, M. (2020) *Health Equity in England: The Marmot Review 10 years on*. Available at: www.health.org.uk/publications/reports/the-marmot-review-10-years-on?gclid=Cj0KCQiAwJWdBhCYARIsAJc4idCJvzICYIT4-PrOrhhNkw8x70dhGYFmnP2QOye9eCwfvNR42ULq6QQaAn0DEALw_wcB (Accessed: 23 December 2022).

Naidoo, J. and Wills, J. (2000) *Health Promotion: Foundations for practice*. Bailliere Tindall, Edinburgh.

New Scientist (2014) Loneliness is a modern epidemic in need of treatment. Available at www.newscientist.com/article/dn26739-loneliness-is-a-modern-epidemic-in-need-of-treatment/ (Accessed: 23 December 2022).

Nutbeam, D. and Lloyd, J.E. (2021) Understanding and responding to health literacy as a social determinant of health, *Annual Review Public Health* 42(1): 159–73. Available at: https://doi.org/10.1146/annurev-publhealth-090419-102529 (Accessed: 14 January 2023).

Perlman, D. and Peplau, L.A. (1981) Toward a social psychology of loneliness. In R. Gilmour and S. Duck (eds) *Personal Relationships: 3. Relationships in disorder.* Academic Press, London, pp 31–56.

Putnam, R. (2000) *Bowling Alone: The collapse and revival of American communities.* Simon & Schuster, New York.

Rocco, M. and Suhrcke L. (2012) *Is social capital good for health? A European perspective.* Available at: www.euro.who.int/__data/assets/pdf_file/0005/170078/Is-Social-Capital-good-for-your-health.pdf (Accessed: 23 December 2022).

Rose Hill, S. (2020) *Where loneliness can lead.* Available at: https://aeon.co/essays/for-hannah-arendt-totalitarianism-is-rooted-in-loneliness (Accessed: 23 December 2022).

Ruggeri, K., Garcia-Garzon, E., Maguire, A., Matz, S. and Huppert, F. (2020) Well-being is more than happiness and life satisfaction: a multidimensional analysis of 21 countries, *Health and Quality of Life Outcomes* 18: art 192.

Taylor, P. (2003) The lay contribution to public health. In M. Grey, T. Harrison, J. Orme, J. Powell and P. Taylor (eds) *Public Health for the 21st Century.* Open University Press, Maidenhead, pp 128–44.

World Health Organization (2022) *Constitution.* Available at: www.who.int/about/governance/constitution (Accessed: 23 December 2022).

World Health Organization (2023) *Social determinants of health.* Web page. Available at: www.who.int/health-topics/social-determinants-of-health#tab=tab_1 (Accessed: 14 January 2023).

10

Youth work

Kirsty Forrester and Karen McArdle

Introduction

'Youth' is often presented as a problem (Carpenter, Freda and Speeden, 2007; Giroux, 1997; Hunter, 2022), but alongside any discourses of 'problem' youth in the media or in policy is the lived experience of young people themselves. Youth work, it is suggested, is a highly skilled practice which seeks to raise the voices of young people and journey alongside them, while we learn and develop together (Robertson, 2022):

> 'Often our field is not as valued as it could be because folks look at us and think "Well, you're just having a game of pool with a young person". Actually, that collaborative approach, whether it's in an informal universal setting or within the delivery of a course, that takes an incredible amount of skill: of reflection-in-practice and reflection-on-practice; and that, I would argue, has much more of an impact and value for the young person's learning as well. I mean, delivering a standard curriculum is relatively straightforward, but it's being able to adapt and weave with the young person. I think that's the key.' (Charis Robertson, 2022, Focus Group)

We return to this focus on education as the foundation of youth work later in this chapter.

Young people are viewed differently in different cultures. So, we need to begin by asking two questions:

- What value does your country place on youth work?
- How does it show up in your work?

You can answer these questions by thinking about the discourses of youth present in different media and by the assumptions behind youth services and systems in your country. The following quotation from Jarman applies, we suggest, to young people as well as children: 'The measure of a society's civilization can be judged by the way in which it treats its children' (Jarman, 1996, cited in Roberts and Sacheder, 1996, ix).

Brierley (2021) discusses how it takes a village to raise a child, in a context of thinking about young people. He also emphasises the influence of the family on young people. For example, the children of doctors are 24 times more likely than their peers to become doctors; and for others it is just as difficult to *not* follow in their parents' footsteps as a result of the social marginalisation and exclusion that goes with, for example, violence, unemployment or familial substance misuse. 'Life is full of choices for children; however the family we are born into or the "village" we develop in is never a choice' (Brierley, 2021, 20).

Arguably, common to young people in many cultures is the discourse of being othered, excluded or despised. Giroux (1996) expresses the experience of youth, looking back on this denigration as an adult. He focuses on culture and class, which are important in the context in which youth work frequently takes place, being seen as a solution to youth 'problems'.

> For the youth of my neighbourhood, schools and other mainstream public spaces both positioned and excluded us. As an outlaw culture, we were labelled as alien, other, and deviant because we were from the wrong culture and class. Class marked us as poor, inferior, linguistically inadequate and dangerous. We were feared and denigrated more than we were affirmed. (Giroux, 1996, 8)

Defining youth

An ongoing challenge for youth workers is that 'youth' as a definition is not fixed. The age at which we are considered adult varies depending on whether we are seeking to vote, to drive, to travel on public transport, to have sexual experiences, to buy alcohol, to make medical decisions about our own bodies or be represented within the law. Depending on which work definition is used, young people can be denied or given access to services; can be advantaged or disadvantaged; and can be included or excluded. Like adults, young people mature and make friends at and with different ages and these arbitrary numbers are not necessarily helpful to the youth worker.

> The notion that 'youth' is a problem, an uncertain transition, not least in a rapidly changing 'knowledge' economy, rather than young people sometimes have problems, lies at the heart of discriminatory processes, with varying class, race and gender and religious subthemes. ... Our analysis therefore challenges government policy discourses, which view youth as a uniquely 'transitional' social status. Instead, we see it as a set of socially variable experiences, rather than defined in terms of socially prescribed 'adult' destination. As the boundaries between various stages of life become blurred, factors such as extended family dependence, growth of higher education and postponing childbearing further call into question the viability of describing youth as a brief transition. Rather than extending the boundaries of youth, we need to revise standard ideas of what it means to be 'adult'. (Carpenter and Freda, 2007, cited in Carpenter et al, 2007, 88)

Case studies

The following case studies show how youth workers in Scotland think about defining youth and the challenges that arise from different definitions within a youth work context.

Susan is the manager of a youth work organisation:

> 'We expect a lot from young people in really short spaces of time, which are exceptionally stressful and formative years for young people. So, I think, we could do well to think about young adulthoods not necessarily cutting off at 18, but seeing youth work over that longer term. Because I think that's actually where you build in habits of volunteering and community activists and place-making and change – making over that longer term. You can see it really effectively in things like student associations that are largely self-organised or if you look at an organisation like the young farmers; they don't have Youth Workers, they are a self-organised young people's movement. There's something exceptionally powerful about how that operates.
>
> Some agencies talk about young people, but I don't think they mean young people, like we mean young people and Youth Work. I think they mean people under 40 because they're talking about people that are going to buy houses or relocate into the area, that they're going to bring up children, or start businesses. They're not necessarily the 14, 15, 16-year-olds that we have in youth projects at the moment.
>
> We had a study visit from Hong Kong and they had a youth policy, rather than a youth work policy, and it was up to about 30 or 35 years old. Their youth policy covered housing, health, employment and it was a relatively short document, but it was really integrated, as it looked at all aspects of the transition from childhood to adulthood, which is, really, what youth is.' (Susan Hunter, 2022, Focus Group)

Connor leads a youth work team for a public sector organisation. He says:

> 'At the moment, we aren't using age to define our groups, we are using the appropriateness of the

young people, their needs and established behaviours. From working with the young people, we are able to identify which groups would be suitable for them to hopefully get the most benefit. The thinking is that young people could be 11 or 16 but may have similar issues and need an appropriate environment where the conversations are suitable for their needs, rather than having the 'junior or senior' approach. This is currently working and is something we will review to ensure we are doing our best to support our young people.' (Connor Maxwell, 2022, Focus Group)

The following quotation summarises the challenge faced in grappling with age complexity:

'In youth work, everything depends on if you're willing to grapple with that complexity and not just slot people into easy conventional approaches, like the school system; the factory model; and all that kind of thing. We need to grow our confidence in saying "actually we are going at that age appropriateness thing or just appropriateness generally". We often come across that, because a 12-year-old versus a 21-year-old, that's a huge age range and there's so much risk within that, that we're having to manage on a day-to-day basis.' (Charis Robertson, 2022, Focus Group)

The three quotations from the focus groups begin the process of defining youth or what age young people are for different purposes, and show the complexity of this process, its difference in different cultures and its arbitrariness.

Educational imperatives

Youth work is often described in terms of non-formal learning (Stuart and Maynard, 2015). Non-formal learning is learning outside the formal school, vocational training or university system which takes place through planned activities. Because of the planning and intention, Stuart and Maynard suggest, non-formal learning involves some form of facilitation. This does not equate to 'teaching' because learning is viewed as an active rather than a passive process. It tends to be short term, voluntary and has few, if any, prerequisites (Stuart and Maynard, 2015).

Informal learning is learning that is not organised or structured in terms of goals. There is no teaching or facilitation. Informal learning refers to the skills acquired unintentionally through life experience, and the skills are not acquired in a planned or deliberate manner. Informal learning also occurs in the context of the private and social lives of young people, but also includes the informal learning that occurs around educational activities, rather than as an intended aspect of a planned educational intervention (Stuart and Maynard, 2015).

Many professionals work with young people in a variety of contexts and environments. We would argue that the approach often taken by community workers when working with young people is both educational and relationship focused, as described here by Jeffs and Smith (2005, 20–1):

> Education ... embraces a commitment to: respect for persons, the promotion of well-being, truth, democracy, fairness and equality. It is also an intensely hopeful activity. For us education is founded on the belief that things can be improved, that people can change. We have to have an idea of what is possible and a belief that we can make some difference. This involves us looking for, and building up, the good in others and ourselves.

Furlong et al (1997) conducted research to identify the different models of youth work that existed in Scotland in the 1990s. They identified four distinct models, which, we believe, are still relevant today.

- *Control model* – Assumes that young people are a threat to the prevailing social order and that action by the state or voluntary organisations is required to help control and monitor young people.

- *Socialisation model* – Begins with a similar premise to that underlying the control model; that young people should be acclimatised into the values and norms of society as part of the transition to adulthood.
- *Informal education model* – Argues that informal education can help to empower young people and ultimately help them to take more control of their lives – key functions include the emphasis on programmes which encourage participation and decision making. This model is identified by characteristics.
- *Citizenship model* – Citizenship is a concept related to an individual's access to services or to social integration or social solidarity. The citizenship model of youth work evolves from a concern to help young people become active citizens within their society. (Furlong et al, 1997, 6–9)

The first two models listed here are arguably concerned with containment. Youth workers commonly emphasise young people's active participation and voice in a community work context, which would be embraced by the third and fourth models.

Brierley (2021), in discussing 'young people in trouble' and the youth justice system in the UK, refers to the PACT model, the principles of which, we think, apply to all young people in a youth work context. PACT stands for *presence, attunement, connection* and *trust*. We seek here to present his model for a more general purpose than youth justice.

- *Presence* is about being available and recognising life experience; not patronising or pathologising young people but respecting them, explains Brierley. If young people feel that we respect who they are, they are more likely to allow us to be present in their lives. 'Presence is the power of showing-up for the young person in a way that surprises them' (Brierley, 2021, 175).
- *Attunement* is the step of meeting young people where they are emotionally and ensuring that they sense they are being seen and felt (Brierley, 2021). Attunement requires recognition of disparities in power. We need to redress that power as and when we can. This does not mean colluding but recognising that a bridging relationship is important.

- Brierley suggests getting rid of the term 'engaging with young people and prefers *'connecting'*. Brierley says that engaging places responsibility on the young person for not connecting with a professional or service. If we speak of connection, we acknowledge the reciprocity of all relationships. We should make sure that we feel connected to the young person, and not just the other way around.
- *Trust* may be defined as the promise of a good future relationship. Trust is linked intersectionally to presence, attunement and connection.

Brierley emphasises the importance of reflection on the part of the worker in the PACT process. We need to be very sensitive to and aware of our own attitude, prejudices, thoughts and behaviours in our youth work. Indeed, youth work can be identified by looking at the values that underpin it. The National Youth Work Agency (England) defines these as:

- Young people choosing to take part.
- Utilising young people's view of the world.
- Treating young people with respect.
- Seeking to develop young people's skills and attitudes rather than remedy 'problem behaviours'.
- Helping young people develop stronger relationships and collective identities.
- Respecting and valuing differences.
- Promoting the voice of young people. (National Youth Agency, 2022b)

Challenges for young people and work with young people

Social problems affect young people; for example, poverty, parental substance use, caring responsibility, indeed there are many other problems and the impacts are far-reaching. Particularly in the media, the consequences of social problems are sometimes ascribed to the young people, not society as a whole (Giroux, 1997), further compounding their sense of marginalisation and limiting potential sources of support. The following quotations illustrate the impact of poverty and the resulting social marginalisation, and how young people are able to engage with youth work. A few of the knock-on challenges this provides in our work with young people are included.

> 'Money is tight, parents are working shifts overnight, they're putting their young person out to the youth club and not going to be there when the young person gets home. Young people are staying in the house overnight by themselves and some young people are being picked up by detached youth workers; the young people under the influence of alcohol. But they were just going to go home to an empty house, you know? So, we're really testing what the youth worker's role is. You know, there's obviously the child protection threshold, but beyond that, how do you, how do you support that young person to challenge what their parent thinks is acceptable? What's the boundaries? Where's the trust? What's safe? What's the risk? And if we don't have, you know, strong family support and, you know, family learning and parenting support that is really difficult for young people and youth workers.' (Susan Hunter, 2022, Focus Group)

> 'I've been working in community work for 20 years ... I've worked with lots of young people who could not care less about the political process, you know, and they're not interested because, actually, lots of those young people live in families where they're concerned about surviving ... someone who's not very sure about whether they're gonna be having a dinner next week or dealing with parental substance issues, they're not caring about climate change. And often when I'm involved in lots of, what I would consider, very middle-class endeavours, like helping young people talk about social action programmes, it's the same old young people, isn't it? And a lot of the time I will challenge that like, well, where are the working-class kids? It is important that they be part of the change, but actually, they're dealing with multiple

disadvantages, just to get through a week. They're not interested in some kind of amazing project about climate change, you know.' (Nat Wealleans-Turner, 2021, Focus Group)

Buchroth and Parkin (2010) state that youth work is inherently an educational activity based on dialogue and conversation, working with the issues that young people bring from their everyday lives. We agree with Mackie, who suggests that youth work is 'fundamentally a practice aimed towards combating social injustice' (Mackie, 2019, 95) and, as youth workers, we must consider the impact of such social problems upon the young people with whom we are working. We have argued elsewhere (see Chapter 11) about the importance of seeing our community work participants within their social context. Fyfe and Mackie (2022) suggest that, without this analysis, any educational endeavour is potentially doomed to irrelevance. Given the challenges that some young people face, we must also be clear about the nature and purpose of their practice intervention (Fyfe and Mackie, 2022).

The youth workers we spoke to in writing this book were clear that youth work was a negotiated educational relationship, with the youth worker and young people figuring out the curriculum or programme of activity together and, as such, it would be unique each time. They discussed the risks when attempts are made to replicate successful programmes in other locations; and the challenges of outcomes-driven and targeted youth work, which forces youth workers to define programmes of learning before they have even engaged with any young people to identify what their needs are, or the issues facing them. " 'Let's scale it up and roll it out' without any thoughts to what you're talking about, and the context and things" (Charis Robertson, 2022, Focus Group).

These challenges are very real, and increasingly youth workers are finding themselves forced to design programmes of learning to fit a set of narrow funding criteria rather than respond to the needs of young people within the community. While we may need to define outcomes to secure funding, or to plan a targeted engagement in response to data about youth disorder, we would argue that this should not require the community worker to define a rigid programme of learning without first engaging with young people themselves. Engaging with vulnerable young people to identify their issues and to co-design learning programmes can tick lots of boxes for funders and achieve a range of outcomes for the young people and communities involved. In the following quotation, Connor Maxwell discusses how this can work within framework systems that may be prescribed.

> 'As youth workers, we need to have that skill to make it adaptable, to meet the needs of the individuals we're working with on that 12-week block or however you're going to run those programmes. We facilitate groups that are skills-based programmes for school non-attenders and we've got a sort of skeleton base. But it's never the same stuff, because you don't know who you're going to get in front of you and that's what we recognise really well. I think that we can say that this is what we're presenting the schools; and this is what they are sort of going to be doing, but having that adaptability to understand the needs of the young people, to speak to, have that consultation with them to then meet their individual needs through our programmes.' (Connor Maxwell, 2022, Focus Group)

Our ability to understand and describe the impact of our interventions is important; as a sector, we need to be confident in making the case that outcomes will be achieved, even if we do not yet know what the programme will be, if investment is to be sustained.

> 'We accept that the outcomes of individual youth work relationships can be hard to quantify and the impact of encounters with young people may take time to become clear and be complex. In that context, it is hard to reject the basic tenet expounded by a range of youth service representatives and young people themselves, that "you know good youth work when you see it". However, with a tight spending settlement and an increase in commissioning of youth services at a local level we also believe it is essential that publicly

funded services are able to demonstrate what difference they make to young people.' (Select Committee on Education, 2011, paragraph 39, cited by Stuart and Maynard, 2015, 232)

The youth workers with whom we spoke for this book talked about the need for youth work to be understood and valued by colleagues from other sectors, particularly education. We believe that by better describing the impact of our interventions our work will be better understood by stakeholders. In Scotland, youth work is increasingly linked to schools; we need to think carefully about the future of our sector if young people's participation is timetabled and part of an activity agreement. We reiterate the views of our focus group members who emphasised the importance of the voluntary aspect.

> 'I have advocated and campaigned for such a long time around the incorporation of an internationally recognized convention [UN Convention on the Rights of the Child], which doesn't specifically include the right to youth work, but it does include lots of the elements that we would see manifest in really good youth work, around care and protection, and play and leisure, and access to information ... we need to be really clear how youth work advances children's rights. Youth work is voluntary and it must remain voluntary.' (Susan Hunter, 2022, Focus Group)

Power and young people

> 'Research which looks at young people's views on communication with adults makes it clear that they have little confidence that they will be listened to or that their opinions will be respected. One of the most common findings is that adolescents do not feel that their views are taken seriously by adults. One of the things they most wish for is for adults to show them some respect, to listen to them, and to treat what they have to say as a legitimate contribution to any

discussion or conversation.' (Coleman, 2004, cited in Roche et al, 2004, 22)

This quotation illustrates well the impact of power in relationships between adults and young people. Understanding and seeking to mitigate the nature of power should be fundamental to our practice (Giroux, 1997). If we, as community workers, truly wish to build authentic, trusting relationships in which young people can safely explore and develop their ideas, we must, at times, give control about the direction of travel over to them. Youth work, within the context of informal education, is characterised by both youth and adults recognising 'the other as possessing knowledge skills and feelings and each values the others' experience' (Bill Roseter, 1987, cited in Jeffs and Smith, 1987, 53).

The youth workers with whom we spoke in Scotland, where the authors practise, talked about a culture of risk aversion, in which organisations were often reluctant to give young people any real power, and they felt that this could be seen by young people as lack of trust: "Our default is the risk assessment rather than the trust assessment" (Charis Robertson, 2022, Focus Group).

Many had, both as young people and later as community workers, been on youth exchanges to see practice elsewhere in Europe, and they felt that much could be learnt from some of the practice they had seen in terms of how young people were trusted and were given "genuine freedom" (Susan Hunter, 2022, Focus Group). Often this trust was expressed by governments at local and national level by allowing young people to decide how they wished to spend budgets, and in other cases it was simply allowing young people to experiment, to build and create things even when there was an element of risk or danger in the activity.

Relationships

Building effective and meaningful relationships is central to youth work. In principle, practitioners work alongside young people, with the educational focus firmly placed on issues of interest and concern to them. The interaction and relationship between adult practitioners and young people are mediated by principles of trust, respect, sincerity and, above all, authenticity (Fyfe and Mackie, 2022).

The following quotation from Jeffs and Smith (2005) provides a helpful way to understand authenticity:

> To fully engage in conversation, we have to be in a certain frame of mind. We have to be with that person, rather than seeking to act upon them. This is of great importance. If we enter into conversation with the desire to act upon the other participants, then we are seeing them as objects; things rather than people. (Jeffs and Smith, 2005, 31)

A crucial dimension of multifaceted authenticity for practitioners is to maintain and cultivate an awareness of what matters in the lives of the young people with whom they work. It is vital for authentic practitioners to stay informed about what is important in the lives and life-styles of those young people with whom they work (Fyfe and Mackie, 2022)

Youth voice

One of the key roles of youth work is to support young people's voices to be heard. We agree with Giroux (1997, 32) that 'young people need to become critical agents able to recognize, appropriate and transform how dominant power works on and through them'. Unfortunately, young people are rarely afforded the opportunity to contribute to discourse about themselves (Giroux, 1997, 32). Thus marginalised, it is no wonder that many young people feel powerless to change their situations. Susan Hunter, from our focus group, echoes this marginalisation of young people who are not seen positively but as problems:

> 'We see certain young people as deficits, like they are problems that need [to be] fixed. We must see young people as asset[s] … I speak to organisations and they're saying, "Well, we don't have any young people that are participation ready, because young people's lives are so complex." They're working

with young people quite often at the point of crisis. But I've always believed that every young person is "participation ready" if adults can change what you're doing to make it work.' (Susan Hunter, 2022, Focus Group)

As youth workers we must, therefore, ensure that programmes are co-designed with young people themselves and their needs and desires are at the fore. We agree with Pauline Rettie that young people

> 'have a right to directly influence how they can have their voices heard when services are being designed and evaluated. ... Being an active contributor to the solution means young people are more likely to buy into what they come up with – and let's be honest – their ideas are often far better than ours!' (Pauline Rettie, 2022, Angus Youth Engagement Case Study)

Conclusion

In this chapter we have explored the many challenges that youth workers have to consider and address in the course of their practice. Despite these challenges, youth work continues to be and will always be a transformative practice which seeks to work with young people and communities towards positive outcomes. We have heard stories of youth workers being told by the young people with whom they worked many years later, "you changed my life", "I would never have gone to college if it wasn't for you", "you taught me to stand up for my beliefs" or "you helped me speak".

Across the UK and in Ireland, youth agencies are keen to emphasise that youth work changes lives (YouthLink Scotland, 2016; National Youth Agency, 2022a); Youth Cmyru, 2022); National Youth Council of Ireland, 2022). We agree that youth work is 'life-changing, life-enhancing, even life-saving' (de St Croix and Doherty, 2022, 3), but to flourish, youth work needs continued investment and youth workers who are inspiring, confident and brave.

'We're not resourcing it in a way that gives young people the message that youth work is for everyone ... there's not enough youth work in the world to meet the needs of young people or to shift it from a deficit- to an asset-based model or a genuine participating model or community action model or to social action. You know, we need more of it.' (Susan Hunter, 2022, Focus Group)

Principles in practice

1. Be aware of the purpose of what you do with young people and who controls the context in which you are working. How does this have an impact on your work?
2. What is a common life experience of the young people with whom you work? Obviously, every individual is different, but what challenges will they likely present? How can you accommodate this in your practice?
3. Think about your own approach to youth work. What are your goals, and are these emancipatory or educational, both or different?
4. Think about youth work as relationship building. What are the characteristics of your relationship with young people? Does the PACT model work for you?
5. Ensure that the voice of young people is heard in your practice, working *with* not *on* or *for* young people, wherever possible.

Challenge questions

1. What is it that you do with young people? Why this? What is the theoretical underpinning of what you do? How do you define youth or young people?
2. What is it that you do that has an impact on young people? What is that impact? How do you know?
3. What is your relationship like with young people with whom you work? What is it that you do or think that makes this the case? How could you improve?
4. What are the key challenges to hearing the voice of young people? Why are they referred to sometimes as the 'seldom heard'?

References

Brierly, A. (2021) *Connecting with Young People in Trouble: Risk, relationship and lived experience*. Waterside Press, Hampshire.

Buchroth, I. and Parkin, C. (2010) Theory and youth and community work practice. In I. Buchroth and C. Parkin (eds) *Using Theory in Youth and Community Work Practice*. Learning Matters, Exeter, pp 4–19.

Carpenter, M., Freda, B. and Speeden, S. (eds) (2007) *Beyond the Workfare State: Labour markets, equality and human rights*. Policy Press, Bristol.

de St Croix, T. and Doherty, L. (2022) *Valuing Youth Work: Seven evidence-based messages for decision-makers on youth work and its evaluation*. Policy Briefing on Youth Work and Evaluation. Available at: www.kcl.ac.uk/ecs/assets/rethinking-impact/valuing-youth-work-seven-evidence-based-messages-for-decision-makers.pdf (Accessed: 19 November 2022).

Furlong, A., Cartmel, F., Hall, S. and Powney, J. (1997) *Evaluating Youth Work with Vulnerable Young People*. The Scottish Council for Research in Education, Glasgow. Available at: www.researchgate.net/publication/237341019_Evaluating_Youth_Work_with_vulnerable_young_people (Accessed: 6 November 2022).

Fyfe, I. and Mackie, A. (2022) Are you for real? Investigating authenticity in community-based youth work practice, *Journal of Youth Studies*, 1–16. Available at: https://doi.org/10.1080/13676261.2022.2101353 (Accessed: 6 November 2022).

Giroux, H.A. (1996) *Fugitive Cultures: Race, violence, and youth* (1st edn). Routledge, London.

Giroux, H. (1997) *Channel Surfing: Race talk and the destruction of today's youth*. Palgrave Macmillan, London.

Hunter, S. (2022) *Contribution to Youth Work Focus Group*.

Jarman, 1996, cited in Roberts, H. and Sacheder, D. (eds) (1996) *Young People's Social Attitudes: Having their say, the views of 12–19 year olds*. Dr Barnardo's, Ilford.

Jeffs, T. and Smith, M. (eds) (1987) *Youth Work*. Macmillan Press Ltd., London.

Jeffs, T. and Smith, M. (2005) *Informal Education: Conversation democracy and learning*. Educational Heretics Press, Shrewsbury.

Mackie, A. (2019) *Young People, Youth Work and Social Justice: A Participatory Parity Perspective*. PhD thesis, University of Edinburgh. Available at: https://era.ed.ac.uk/bitstream/handle/1842/36184/Mackie2019.pdf?sequence=1&isAllowed=y (Accessed: 19 November 2022).

National Youth Agency (2022a) *How we can help you create a skilled diverse and inclusive workforce*. Available at: www.nya.org.uk/kevin-jones-head-of-workforce-and-professional-practice-on-how-we-can-help-you-create-a-skilled-diverse-and-inclusive-workforce/ (Accessed: 28 November 2022).

National Youth Agency (2022b) *Youth work values*. Web page. Available at: www.nya.org.uk/career-in-youth-work/what-is-youth-work/ (Accessed: 19 November 2022).

National Youth Council of Ireland (2022) *Youth work changes lives*. Web page. Available at: www.youth.ie/get-involved/campaigns/youth-work-changes-lives/ (Accessed: 28 November 2022).

Rettie, P. (2022*), Angus Youth Engagement Case Study* Angus Council

Roberts, H. and Sacheder, D. (eds) (1996) *Young People's Social Attitudes: Having their say, the views of 12–19 year olds*. Dr Barnardo's, Ilford.

Robertson, C (2022) *Contribution to Youth Work Focus Group*.

Roche, J., Tucker, S., Thomson, R. and Flynn, R. (eds) (2004) *Youth in Society*. 2nd edn. Sage Publications Ltd., London.

Roseter, B. (1987) cited in Jeffs, T. and Smith, M. (eds) (1987) *Youth Work*. Macmillan Press Ltd., London.

Select Committee on Education (2011) *Conclusion and recommendations*. Available at: www.publications.parliament.uk/pa/cm201012/cmselect/cmeduc/744/74412.htm (Accessed: 28 November 2022).

Stuart, K. and Maynard, L. (2015) Non-formal youth development and its impact on young people's lives: case study – Brathay Trust, UK, *Italian Journal of Sociology of Education* 7(1), 231–62. Available at: http://journals.padovauniversitypress.it/ijse/content/non-formal-youth-development-and-its-impact-young-people%E2%80%99s-lives-case-study-%E2%80%93-brathay-trust (Accessed: 28 November 2022).

Youth Cmyru (2022) *Our purpose, vision and values.* Web page. Available at: https://youthcymru.org.uk/our-purpose-vision-values/ (Accessed: 28 November 2022).

YouthLink Scotland (2016) *Youth Work Changes Lives: A prospectus.* YouthLink Scotland, Edinburgh. Available at: www.youthlinkscotland.org/media/1257/prospectus-eversion.pdf (Accessed: 28 November 2022).

11

Adult learning

Kirsty Forrester

Introduction

Adult learning encompasses different types of provision, designed to address various education and training objectives. It takes place in communities, further education colleges, higher education institutions, training centres and the workplace, as described in the following quotation:

> The work that adult educators do is, and should be, essential for the well-being of the societies in which we live. Adult educators train members of our military, provide continuing education for health care providers, and offer EAL to newcomers. They help low-level literacy learners obtain skills to gain better employment and teach grandmothers to read so that they can assist their grandchildren with their schoolwork. In colleges and universities, they provide formal education, and in community groups and organizations they facilitate on-the-ground learning opportunities to advocate for resources and participate in governance. ... Adult educators work in all walks of life. The way in which they approach this work matters significantly, because adults need to engage in learning not just for individual career success or to develop workplace competencies

but also to be critically informed and thoughtfully engaged citizens, capable of creative thought, and able to adapt to change. (Gouthro, 2019, 73)

We acknowledge that the adult education landscape is different in different countries, across different regions and within different localities, informed by different political systems, views of welfare and the role of the state. Adult learning is a wide topic and we have had to make choices about what to cover. In this chapter, we have chosen to explore what is distinct about the community-based adult learning that takes place in community settings, focusing in particular on basic skills education for adults. This includes informal learning and Adult Basic Education (ABE) programmes provided for adults at the elementary level of literacy, with an emphasis on communicative, computational and social skills. We would argue that these social practices are different to other forms of adult education, which focus on fixed programmes of learning that are institutionally determined and are more likely to have a fixed curriculum.

Context

In the US, one in five adults have low literacy skills, reading at or below a third-grade level (Morgan et al, 2017). One in five working-aged Australian adults have low literacy, numeracy and digital skills (OECD, 2019). One in five European adults have not completed their secondary education and a significant number are affected by low levels of literacy and numeracy and are at risk of digital exclusion (European Commission/EACEA/Eurydice, 2021). The picture is much the same across the rest of the developed world with, on average, around 20% of adult populations struggling with low literacy, numeracy and digital skills. In developing countries, the situation is far worse (OECD, 2019). Undoubtedly, migration patterns related to conflict, climate change and poverty will change demographics, thereby having an impact upon the learning needs presented in communities. For example, it is anticipated that by 2030, 15–20% of all American workers will be immigrants (Morgan et al, 2017). The impact of these statistics is significant, with multiple research studies revealing that these populations, often affected by unemployment, poverty, poor health and incarceration consistently demonstrate low literacy and numeracy rates (Bynner and Parsons, 2005; Morgan et al, 2017; Grotlüschen et al, 2019; OECD, 2019).

> 'There's this idea that, if you don't have these basic skills, it's too late for you and you should have had that early on. But we know that in the US, the education system isn't like that for a lot of people and depending on where you're coming from, race, class, gender, really influence the way that people are treated in education, particularly when they're young. So, what stems from that is that they may or may not get those basic education skills that you would assume an elementary school child would receive.' (Kimiko Petsche, 2022, Focus Group)

There is evidence that these issues are entrenched and multi-generational, as parents with low levels of literacy and numeracy and negative experiences of education struggle to support their children to develop their literacy and numeracy (Morgan et al, 2017). Their children are exposed to fewer words and enter kindergarten with a much larger skills gap than their peers, a skills gap that these parents themselves faced and which they have been unable to overcome. Research from Australia reveals that children's 'experiences of and success in school, is significantly impacted by the educational experiences of their parents and grandparents' (Adult Learning Australia, 2014, cited in Adult Learning Australia, 2021, 10). Family-learning work to promote the idea of the parent as a child's first educator is important but must be supported by opportunities for parents to develop their own skills.

'Educational attainment appears to be a strong determinant of participation in adult education and training: across all countries analysed, low-qualified adults participate less in education and training than those with higher educational attainment levels' (European Commission/EACEA/Eurydice, 2021, 15). The attainment gap is just as relevant for adults as for children. According to a 2019 UNESCO report on adult learning and education, the lowest levels of participation in adult learning were among adults with disabilities, older adults and minority groups; provision for vulnerable adults and rural communities is decreasing (UNESCO, 2019). This is concerning, as those who are already advantaged are more able to increase their skills and advantage through education. We place community-based adult learning within the traditions of social justice (see Chapter 2); adult education is therefore concerned with inequalities linked to issues such as class, gender and race oppression. The work we do in communities with adults must be targeted, we believe, to those who need our services most.

> If things continue as they are and – without a significant sea change in political outlook, there is every chance they will – the benefits of adult learning will continue to coalesce around the better off and most advantaged in society, reinforcing and even intensifying existing inequalities, rather than helping the least advantaged individuals and communities. Who takes part, and who does not, has consequences. (UNESCO, 2019, 12)

Barriers to engagement

Many adults face multiple barriers to learning and have to balance complex responsibilities in order to participate in education; for example, caring responsibilities, health issues which limit participation, shift and work patterns and the cost of transport.

Earlier this year a colleague of Kirsty, whose name is Diare, met with a woman who had self-referred to the adult learning service. This woman had arrived in the country a year ago but had no money. She had got a part-time job and had been saving up to pay for English lessons. At the end of the meeting, the woman asked how much they would cost. When she discovered they were free, she burst into tears, telling Diare that now she could buy herself a new pair of shoes. She had been struggling to make ends meet but felt that learning English was essential and so was prioritising it over buying other essential items.

Financial constraints can prevent adults from participating in education and training; in particular, adults with low levels of basic skills and those with low levels of or no qualifications are most likely to experience precarious situations in the labour market and to be affected by low incomes. These individuals may wish to develop their skills and qualifications but are unable to afford the time or cost of participation. When designing our programmes and policies we must bear them in mind. It is also important to remember that adult education as, largely, a voluntary endeavour, is influenced by the adult learner's own perceptions of education and how they conceptualise their involvement. Therefore, previous negative experiences of education, or ideas about the activity as a training course rather than remedial help, matter. The following quotations illustrate these negative experiences and their impact on people.

> 'People are still stigmatised for not being able to read and write. Society doesn't seem to be very forgiving and understanding of the situation. We have a whole generation of people who don't recognise dyslexia as a possibility, "God forbid, not me, I don't have dyslexia", but they can't read and write because of that not being recognised in time in school and support not being given. Stigma is a huge thing.'
>
> 'That's what we are seeing too, particularly in my programme, a lot of people live in shame and secrecy around not being able to read in their 40s or 50s … and I don't think people understand how prevalent that is, not just in New York City, but throughout the United States. And because there's a lot of secrecy, people assume that, well, everyone can read or at least the basics of reading.' (Lada Copic and Kimiko Petsche, 2022, Focus Group)

In our experience, because of this lack of understanding among many authorities about the scale of the problem or what the issues actually are, one of the most tragic barriers that adult learners may face in accessing provision is a lack of programmes which meet their needs.

> 'We notice a lot of [other adult education providers] aren't a good fit for our students. They'll either have

> a cut score for language acquisition or they don't start, kind of, at that (foundation level) phonemic awareness, because the test, that you have to use, starts at the 1st grade level. Students have all these great work-arounds and they've got a really good sight-word vocabulary, but they're not independent readers, because they really haven't been taught the skills that they need to be able to be empowered and set free.' (Lynn Clark, 2022, Focus Group)

This quotation illustrates tests as barriers that inhibit adult learning. The adults we work with in communities have developed, highly sophisticated strategies for using text and numbers every day. While they are likely to view themselves as unable to read, write and use numbers or computers, they will have their own informal literacy practices. We acknowledge that there are many forms of literacy (Addey, 2018 in Milana et al). The role of the adult educator is to open up new possibilities for the individual, to deconstruct previous negative learning identities and to promote the idea that it is not just the literacy taught in schools that matters.

Impact of adult learning

Participation in adult education programmes shows the following implicit learning as well as the explicit learning.

> Dramatic, positive results in several key areas including income gain, HSE [qualification] acquisition, post-secondary transitions, and overall literacy proficiency development. These findings show clear long-term benefits for individuals who participate in ABS programmes. They further show significant benefit to the communities in which these individuals live and work on a regular and sustained basis. (Morgan et al, 2017, 13)

> The confidence gained through learning one thing can be brought to other parts of life, so the learner starts to ask, 'How can I apply this to everything?'

I can bring the confidence and self-esteem to other areas of my life to help me exist in that room, so the moment I walk in I am already a few steps ahead of where I would be without that confidence and self-esteem. (Galligan, 2021 cited in Bunyan, 2021)

Case study

Paul is an adult-learning worker with a small community-based organisation that supports people over 50 to learn new skills. He himself started off as a volunteer with the project.

> 'We primarily work with over-50s, who seem to be kind of forgotten about with all the changes to digital technology. Everything is going online; you've got your online banking and all these different things, but older people that haven't really been brought up with it, have just been left behind. We found that there is a huge outcry of need for what we're doing. Pretty much no one in the older generation has a knowledge of online banking, even though every bank in Scotland now tells you to go and do online banking.
> And they are like, "how do we do this? We don't even have a device".
> Everyone is, like, "you can't meet in person anymore, so get online", and the older generation is sitting here going like, "how do we do that? We've never done this before!"
> So, we get quite a lot of people coming to us for that specific reason and we've got people that maybe just want to get in contact with the family that have moved abroad. There is a broad spectrum of people that we see. It was good how much time we spent with people [during the COVID-19 pandemic] and how much they learned and it was definitely worthwhile.
> We do have elderly people who come to us for a basic digital skills class at the start, but we do try, for some of them who show an interest, to build them up and eventually they will become volunteers for us. And

a lot of our volunteers have actually come from that route, where they've started just learning how to use the device and then they're actually showing people how to use the device themselves, which is good to see. When you see the kind of change of what they were when they came, and then what they're actually doing now, it's good that you can get volunteers through that route as well.

But it does feel valued and the people that come to tell us that, they are quite happy with what we do. Does it feel valued in terms of the money we get from the government? Maybe not, but it feels valued from the people that come to us.' (Paul McCurdy, 2022, Focus Group)

Epistemologies of adult learning

Bagnall and Hodge (2018) suggest that adult education is predominantly informed by four different epistemologies (ways of knowing), each given dominance according to the cultural context of the time. 'Each draws on historical deep roots in Educational policy, practice, advocacy and theorisation' (Bagnall and Hodge, 2018, 14).

As adult educators, we will have used many of the different epistemologies within our practice at some time or other. All of these are important and valued; they speak to our underlying values about what knowledge is and how it should be created (see Chapter 1). Table 11.1, which draws on Bagnall and Hodge (2018), illustrates the different epistemologies that frequently underpin adult learning.

The influence of the neoliberal movement (see Chapter 2) on the language of adult education and its commodification of educational endeavours has meant that, since the Second World War, instrumental epistemology has come to the fore (Bagnall and Hodge, 2018).

'In the end, how can you prove that somebody is not on drugs or on state benefits at the moment because they had that opportunity five years ago and you helped them along to believe more in themselves and in their ability and gave them a hand up?'

'I think so much of the way education is set up is, like, you have to prove that your education is quality and money dangles. And I mean, in America that stems from "No child left behind" back in 2001. That was the turning point where, all of a sudden, like money is dangled and it's switching to that sort of market system. That's created this sort of thing where you constantly have to prove things that you might not be able to actually prove. Like you said, education is a long game. Like, yeah, like, there's a basic skill set, but the things that we really care about actually take years and years after that.' (Lada Copic and Michael Kengmana, 2022, Focus Group)

It is the neoliberal influence that has led to the transformation of the adult learning sector in many countries, since the Second World War, 'into an extension of the vocational education and training sector' (Bagnall and Hodge, 2018, 25). By focusing on predominantly labour market goals, this neoliberal form of education fails to acknowledge learners' prior skills, knowledge, learning goals and aspirations. Such learning negates the transformative possibilities of education. As community workers, we acknowledge that when we work with adults we are working with people who already have knowledge and build programmes of learning on what they can do, rather than what they cannot do.

However, Bagnall and Hodge (2018) suggest that the dominance of instrumental epistemology is coming to an end and that a new educational epistemology is emerging, one which they name as *situational*. Situational knowledge is derived from context through experiential approaches. It explores complexity and the learning that can be derived from our responses to situations. It values lived experience. 'Situational knowledge might be seen, then, as contributing to human well-being through the situational capability that it would afford individuals and collectivities in responding to their cultural realities' (Bagnall and Hodge, 2018, 29–30). Therefore, we would argue it should be of great interest to those of us working with adult learners within a community-work tradition.

Table 11.1: Epistemologies of adult learning

Disciplinary epistemology understands knowledge as truth and suggests that learning is a process of enlightenment which can occur as a result of following certain rules.	Assessment is 'strongly focused on assessing learners' mastery of the content' (Bagnall and Hodge, 2018, 17). Within this context, teachers are prioritised.	An example from the English for Speakers of Other Languages classroom might be learning that is very focused on the rules of the language, or literacy learning that follows a competence-based reading scheme.
Constructivist epistemology understands knowledge as an active process through which learning is achieved through participation in *authentic experiences*. (Bagnall and Hodge, 2018, 22)	This humanistic approach to education focuses on the development of social practices and values educators as facilitators of learning.	Examples might be the language-experience approach, whereby learning is developed through doing, or literacy that is developed through social practices.
Emancipatory epistemology understands knowledge as power and sees education as a political process.	Education is focused on conscious raising and the self-actualisation of the learner and their situation. The work of Paulo Freire, which we will discuss later, sits within this epistemology.	An adult learning example would be teaching reading and literacy so that adults can vote.
Instrumental epistemology understands knowledge as action. It is focused on the learning which is responsive to and valued by the wider culture at the time.	Learning is responsive to the individual and the cultural context and success is understood as related to the identified tasks and needs.	An example might be contextualised learning that is focused on getting a job in a certain industry.

John Dewey, whose pedagogy influenced many theorists in education, believed that learning is socially constructed and offered this helpful explanation: 'Since life means growth, a living creature lives as truly and positively at one stage as at another, with the same intrinsic fullness and the same absolute claims. Hence education means the enterprise of supplying the conditions which insure growth, or adequacy of life, irrespective of age' (Dewey,

1916, 51). The role of the adult educator, therefore, is to work with learners to create the conditions for growth in all aspects of family, community and vocational life and remove the barriers that stop individuals from fulfilling their potential.

Reading the word to read the world

> 'Students may have a low reading level, but that doesn't mean that they are not intelligent people or they don't come to this class with worlds of experiences and knowledge and wisdom from their own background and history and family and all of those things.
>
> I think the Freirean idea of empowering people is really important, like critical thinking. We're not just trying to bank, right? Like dropping knowledge into students as if that's useful, because it's not, and we know well now, if that method had worked earlier, when they were children, they wouldn't be in the situation that they are in now, right? So, to me, there is an extra importance on bringing those, I guess, more revolutionary sort of theories ... even though, I don't think that's what they should be, because it shouldn't be revolutionary to empower people to think critically about their lives and empower them to feel confident in learning spaces and also provide them with an ownership that they belong here, you know.'
> (Kimiko Petsche, 2022, Focus Group)

Perhaps one of the greatest influences on modern adult learning and community development theory is the Brazilian thinker and educator, Paulo Freire (1921–97). Freire was very critical of both the instrumental and disciplinary epistemologies referred to earlier, describing 'banking' as a process through which the teacher deposits knowledge into the adult learner without acknowledging the learner's social context or prior learning.

In the seminal text *Pedagogy of the Oppressed* (2017), Freire suggests that knowledge and truth are social constructs created by those who hold positions of power and privilege (the oppressors). The Literacy Education that Freire developed questions official truth and privileged forms of knowledge, shining a light on inequalities and power structures. This dialogical methodology encourages participants and workers alike to be critically reflective and develop an analysis of the social context in which they are operating, reclaiming their full humanity and developing literacy in the process. The role of the adult-learning worker is to help build the capacity of individuals to take control of their learning and their lives themselves. Freire called this awakening 'conscientisation', a type of social awareness developed through praxis (reflection and action). This methodology sits within the emancipatory tradition of education. For Freire, education was a political act. For example, through being helped to become literate, the Brazilians with whom he worked were able to participate in the political process, vote and have a stake in decisions which affected them. Indeed, there is evidence to support the impact of literacy on civic participation, voting and volunteerism (Morgan et al, 2017).

We would argue that if education is a political act, then as workers it is essential that we understand how our own political ideology impacts upon our practice. The work we do with adults in communities is about inequalities, poverty and social justice, as examples, and to be effective we must have an analysis of that in our practice.

Freire (2017) describes a process of revolution and awakening of learners to the reality of their own experience under a colonial system. He suggests that we must be cautious of this movement of adult learning being hijacked by any elite. We can see this tendency among actors within communities, including, at times, adult educators themselves, who may claim to liberate but may have a tendency to objectify learners for their own political point of view. All liberatory movements are pedagogical in nature, we propose, and it must be a process of thinking together. We cannot do things *to* others. The following quotation shows ways of doing things *with* not *to*.

> 'And I think that is what I value so much, when decisions are being made about the programme, or I need to do something in the programme, I'm also gonna ask the students in the class. ... What materials

you are interested in learning about? And really trying to incorporate that choice ... making sure that they have a say in what happens and are involved as much as possible in the process; that transparency makes that learning environment feel far more adult than some of the things that we're focusing on, which are pretty elementary. And that can be a difficult line to cross because you don't want to treat someone who is a lot older than I am and could probably be my parent or grandparent ... so showing that ownership, in providing that space for them, I think is really, really important.' (Kimiko Petsche, 2022, Focus Group)

When the learning is placed within an individual's social context, development of functional skills is not the only thing that will happen; when learners can extend these skills, they develop what Freire called critical literacy.

'You say we are teaching people to read and write, but we are actually empowering people to stand more firmly on their two feet and to do critical thinking. When you teach somebody to read, you don't teach them just to decode letters, you teach them critical thinking about that reading that they are doing, and if they're doing writing, how to write and where does that lead?' (Lada Copic, 2022, Focus Group)

We can see the impact of language and literacy on the health and family life of this learner from Scotland:

Slowly, slowly, started to improve my English. ... That made me feel really good. I was able to attend the doctor's myself, the hospital myself and other appointments. [Previously] when I wasn't able to speak or understand English, I had to take my son with me to the doctor's and that caused problems when it was to talk about personal things like periods etc. Then once my son got married, I started to attend my own appointments.

Now I feel very good – it makes me happy. I now have a small granddaughter who speaks [only] English at home, so it helps me to communicate in English with her. I also watch TV to improve my English – I watch cartoons with my grandchildren too! (Dundee City Council, 2019, np)

Transformative learning theory

The American educator Jack Mezirow (1997) developed the concept of 'perspective transformation' to describe the powerful learning that changes the way that people think and feel, making us question our beliefs, assumptions and purpose. Mezirow suggested that everyone has a set of meaning perspectives that develop, through our culture, upbringing and experiences. We are rarely fully conscious of these ways of seeing ourselves and the world and we use them to filter any new learning. Two people can interpret the same information in a completely different way based on these perspectives or worldviews. Much of what we learn takes place in this way; it does not change the way we see the world; it just adds to what Mezirow called our 'existing meaning schemes'. He categorised these schemes in three ways: personal/psychological; sociolinguistic; and epistemic.

The personal schemes describe beliefs about ourselves and what we can or cannot do. For example, 'I am not very good at X or I am really good at Y'. Sociolinguistic or sociocultural schemes are beliefs about the world and society relating to social norms and cultural expectations about race, class and gender. Epistemic schemes relate to how we understand knowledge and our beliefs about how it is made. For example, older people are less likely to trust news that comes from social media, while young people are less likely to trust mainstream media outlets. Perspective transformation happens when we have new experiences that don't fit into our existing meaning perspectives. This often happens at times of transition, but the learner can also be led towards new experiences for pedagogical effect. Mezirow (1997) called these 'disorienting dilemmas'. They challenge our sense of ourselves; what we think about the world; or our understanding of knowledge.

In order to manage these new experiences, we have to reformulate our perspectives and assumptions. This can sometimes be painful, because we have to let go of deeply held underlying beliefs and it can be difficult, because it requires thought and critical reflection. There is no guarantee, of course, that perspective transformation will take place. Adult educators can only offer learners the opportunity to reflect on their learning and behaviour and become aware of and critically analyse underlying assumptions.

> A defining condition of being human is that we have to understand the meaning of our experience. … In contemporary societies we must learn to make our own interpretations rather than act on the purposes, beliefs, judgments, and feelings of others. Facilitating such understandings is the cardinal goal of adult education. Transformative learning develops autonomous thinking. (Mezirow, 1997, 5)

Mezirow describes this as a ten-step process. His ideas have been further developed to accommodate learning in relation to others, feminist perspectives, critical social theory and emotional, affective and subconscious dimensions of learning.

Often referred to as *transformative learning theory*, since it was developed, Mezirow's theory has been a dominant theory in adult learning but has been used in divergent ways. Hoggan (2018) argues that *perspective transformation* relates to Mezirow's original theories and *transformative learning* is a *meta-theory* and should be used to refer to 'a wide range of theories that address learning that results in personal, cultural or social transformation' (Hoggan, 2018, 40). Hoggan (2018) argues that we should focus on the outcomes of transformative learning, rather than the processes, since not all transformations look the same. We find his *typology of transformative learning outcomes* helpful to the community worker. He suggests that we should look for outcomes related to 'changes in worldview, self, epistemology, ontology, behaviour and capacity' (Hoggan, 2018, 43). It is important that we are intentional about the outcomes we seek to achieve through our practice and understand fully the impact that our work can make on individuals and communities.

Analysing or thinking about what is said

As adult-learning workers, it is important to be both reflective and reflexive in our consideration of what is taking or has taken place (McArdle, 2020). Reflexivity is challenging our own taken-for-granted assumptions about the way the world is or should be, challenging features of our 'habitus' or ways of being based on our personal and social histories. Our solution to an individual problem may not be the solution for someone else. As we listen to our learners, we need to pay close attention to who we are and understand the facets of the landscape we are exploring, the context. We do not walk away unchanged and need to deal with our own feelings and thoughts about a session we have had with learners.

Stories and other forms of conversation characteristically have a time sequence, exploring past, present and future. This manifests itself as what happened in the past; what this means to the individual now; and likely future behaviour or feelings, as a consequence of the past and present. Other aspects will be emotions and feelings, hopes and fears. When working with individuals and communities, we can also look for moral dispositions, judgements about the value of ideas or people and rights and wrongs of the world.

Trauma-informed practice (TIP)

Many of the adults with whom we work have been through traumatic experiences in their childhood or adult lives. They may bring this trauma to the adult learning relationship, and as practitioners we must develop an awareness of how to work in a trauma-informed way. We do not seek to dwell on or question the traumatic experience and, therefore, we must assume that all the adults with whom we work have experienced trauma in some way or other at some point in their lives, regardless of whether the adult learner has shared such an experience.

Previous trauma manifests itself in a range of ways such as emotional and psychological reactions including 'depression, low self-esteem, and suicidal ideation; physical problems like chronic pain; psychiatric problems such as anxiety/panic, borderline, post-traumatic stress, and dissociative identity disorders; and behavioural problems including substance abuse, eating disorders, domestic violence, and self-injury' (Knight, 2015, 26). Survivors of trauma may have issues forming positive relationships and may have a deep mistrust of others.

Knight (2015) offers this helpful description of how we should approach trauma:

> Trauma informed practice doesn't mean that the practitioner assumes the client is a survivor. It also doesn't mean that the focus of the intervention will be on the past trauma.
>
> Rather, the practitioner is sensitive to this possibility and to the ways in which the client's current problems can be understood in the context of past victimization. The worker also recognizes the potential implications that being a survivor have for the client's willingness and ability to enter into a working alliance; evidence suggests this may be especially challenging for survivors, given core beliefs characterized by hostility towards others, and their difficulties forming positive attachments. (Knight, 2015, 26)

As discussed earlier, our role is to contribute to Freire's idea of *conscientisation*, which builds the capacity of individuals to take control of their learning and lives. We must be careful, however well intentioned, to not support our learners to the point where we are creating dependencies, rather than emancipation; our practice must promote self-efficacy and independence.

Adult-learning workers are not therapists and, should this be required, our role is to signpost and refer on to qualified professionals. Our role is to be sensitive to the possibility that current challenges experienced by adult learners, whether those be literacy or self-esteem issues, may be the result of past trauma. We must acknowledge that our learners' experiences and understandings are valid, even if they do not match our own, and, through the learning relationship, offer new possibilities for change and growth.

Supporting an adult learning sector

Adult education has a diverse landscape. Job roles may include teachers, educators, practitioners, assessors, specialists, trainers and tutors, who may teach 'foundation skills; core skills; basic skills; language, literacy and numeracy; essential skills; basic education; life skills; and further education' (Medlin, 2016, 15). Furthermore 'adult literacy and numeracy workers might engage with learners in the community, in their homes, in an evening college, in a local health centre, at an educational institution, in a correctional centre, at a registered educational provider, online, in a homeless shelter or refuge, in a workplace' (Medlin, 2016, 16).

How do we support a sector that looks so different, in so many places? The adult educators with whom we spoke expressed frustration that their work was still not well understood, despite campaigns and despite the outcomes of their work being seen and experienced by decision makers, as well as communities. If the work of community-based adult-learning workers is not understood by communities, it is also not understood by other parts of the professional sector. Most of the practitioners we spoke with felt that their work was not valued, particularly by decision makers.

> 'Will we be treated equally, in terms of facilities and where we are offered, you know? We shouldn't be the second cousin. When you walk in, you should have the same vibrancy that you have in another further education establishment. And all the toys … the simple things, you know, how the centre looks, how it's equipped, the furniture, all that is really important. And it puts a value on it and if you're stuck in the back room of a hall and, while it's powerful locally, it's about valuing it.' (Fran Kennedy, 2022, Focus Group)

It is a sad fact that, in many countries, adult-learning workers are often paid little more than the living wage, but organisations expect that they will be highly educated, experienced and agile. In some other countries, adult educators are not required to have a pedagogical background or qualification at all. Research from Austria (Frei, 2022) found that there was a link between how educators work and how learners succeed; where working conditions were precarious, for example, adult-learning tutors employed as sessional staff, success was lower.

We have shown in this chapter that low skills and confidence affect adults, families, communities and national outcomes across health and the economy. Community-based adult educators are committed to creating a society that is more equitable and socially just and they are good at it. Therefore, their work needs to be resourced, celebrated and prioritised as a matter of urgency. We all need to contribute to this goal.

Principles in practice

1. Understand and acknowledge the social context in which your learners are working. Think what this means for your practice.
2. Acknowledge that trauma may affect our learners' abilities to learn and change. What can you do to acknowledge this?
3. Acknowledge the knowledge that already exists among learners. How do you account for this in your practice?
4. Ensure that you design your programmes with flexibility, to ensure that adults with low skills in low-paid jobs have opportunities to engage. This may require you to work in the evenings and at weekends.
5. Ensure that participants are involved in making decisions about the learning and that your practice is responsive to their needs.

Challenge questions

1. What is unique about your practice with adults in communities?
2. How do you create opportunities for experiential learning with the adults you work with?
3. How does your work build the capacity of individuals to take control of their learning and their lives themselves?
4. How do you take account of the culture and social background of your participants as the context for their learning?
5. How do you make learning accessible?
6. How do you contribute to the positive profile of adult learning as a sector?

References

Addey, C. (2018) Assembling literacy as global: the danger of a single story. In M. Milana, S. Webb, J. Holford, R. Waller and P. Jarvis (eds) *The Palgrave International Handbook on Adult and Lifelong Education and Learning.* Palgrave Macmillan, London.

Adult Learning Australia (2021) *Submission to Inquiry into Adult Literacy 2021.* Available at: https://ala.asn.au/wp-content/uploads/2021/03/ALA-submission-into-Parliamentary-Inquiry-into-Adult-Literacy-2021.pdf (Accessed: 3 April 2022).

Bagnall, R.G. and Hodge, S. (2018) Contemporary adult and lifelong education and learning: an epistemological analysis. In M. Milana, S. Webb, J. Holford, R. Waller and P. Jarvis (eds) *The Palgrave International Handbook on Adult and Lifelong Education and Learning.* Palgrave Macmillan, London.

Bunyan, P. (2021) Hallmarks of the political in community organizing: an Arendtian perspective, *VOLUNTAS: International Journal of Voluntary and Nonprofit Organizations* 32(4): 910–20.

Bynner, J. and Parsons, S. (2005) *Does Numeracy Matter More?* University of London, London.

Dewey, J. (1916) *Democracy and Education: An introduction to the philosophy of education.* Macmillan, New York.

Dundee City Council (2019) *Dundee ESOL Learner Voice Project.* Internal report. Dundee.

European Commission/EACEA/Eurydice (2021) *Adult Education and Training in Europe: Building inclusive pathways to skills and qualifications.* Eurydice Report. Publications Office of the European Union, Luxembourg. Available at: https://data.europa.eu/doi/10.2797/898965 (Accessed: 6 March 2022).

Frei, W. (2022) *A Talk on Adult Learning in Europe and the EPALE experience.* Eurydice Network [Facebook] January. Available at: www.facebook.com/EurydiceEU/videos/a-talk-on-adult-learning-in-europe-and-the-epale-experience/618906785835775 (Accessed: 3 April 2022).

Freire, P. (2017) *Pedagogy of the Oppressed.* Penguin Modern Classics, London.

Galligan, A. (2021) featured in K. Bunyan, *Episode 8: Talking with the tutor: Anna Galligan on teaching drama*. [Podcast] Conversations in Adult and Further Education. Available at: https://anchor.fm/karen-bunyan/episodes/Episode-8-Talking-with-the-tutor-Anna-Galligan-on-teaching-drama-euvqnr (Accessed: 6 March 2022).

Grotlüschen, A., Buddeberg, K., Redmer, A., Ansen, H. and Dannath, J. (2019) *Vulnerable subgroups and numeracy practices: how poverty, debt, and unemployment relate to everyday numeracy practices*, Adult Education Quarterly 69(4): 251–70. Available at: https://journals.sagepub.com/doi/full/10.1177/0741713619841132 (Accessed: 18 March 2022).

Gouthro, P. (2019) Taking time to learn: the importance of theory for adult education, *Adult Education Quarterly* 69(1): 60–76.

Hoggan, C. (2018) Exercising clarity with transformative learning theory. In M. Milana, S. Webb, J. Holford, R. Waller and P. Jarvis (eds) *The Palgrave International Handbook on Adult and Lifelong Education and Learning*. Palgrave Macmillan, London.

Knight, C. (2015) Trauma-informed social work practice: practice considerations and challenges, *Clinical Social Work Journal* 43: 25–37. Available at: https://doi.org/10.1007/s10615-014-0481-6 (Accessed: 3 April 2022).

McArdle, K. in McArdle, Briggs, S., Forrester, K., Garrett, E. and McKay, C. (2020) *The Impact of Community Work: How to gather evidence*. Policy Press, Bristol.

Medlin, J. (2016) *The Australian Literacy and Numeracy Workforce: A literature review.* National Centre for Vocational Education Research, Adelaide. Available at: www.ncver.edu.au/__data/assets/pdf_file/0023/83570/The-Australian-literacy-and-numeracy-workforce.pdf (Accessed: 27 February 2022).

Mezirow, J. (1978) Perspective transformation. *Adult Education Quarterly* 28: 100–110. Available at: http://dx.doi.org/10.1177/074171367802800202 (Accessed: 27 February 2022).

Morgan, K., Waite, P. and Diecuch, M. (2017) *The Case for Investment in Adult Basic Education*. Report prepared by ProLiteracy. Available at: www.proliteracy.org/Portals/0/Reder%20Research.pdf?ver=2017-03-24-151533-647 (Accessed: 27 February 2022).

OECD (2019) *Skills Matter: Additional results from the survey of adult skills*, OECD Skills, OECD.

UNESCO Institute for Lifelong Learning (2019) *Fourth Global Report on Adult Learning and Education*. UNESCO Institute for Lifelong Learning, Hamburg.

12

Employability

Kirsty Forrester

Introduction

Employment for many young people and adults can offer a route out of cycles of poverty and disadvantage, and is an important social determinant of health (see Chapter 9). We know that getting a job promotes well-being and discourages negative thoughts and behaviours, offering an opportunity to make new social connections and to widen networks.

Employability covers the range of work done with young people and adults in communities and other educational settings, to help them move into jobs and other meaningful occupations. It is not just for the unemployed, but can also help people move into better, more sustainable employment. Who gets to decide what is a meaningful occupation is a difficult question and one which we feel each of us, as community workers, must pose. There are many tools and frameworks which exist to help individuals identify their ideal job or what skills they need to develop to access their local labour market. There is a great deal of research about the poor outcomes for disadvantaged individuals and communities, but there is little theory which deals specifically with how we might work with these people in relation to their employability goals. In this chapter we will explore this work and the challenges it presents to the community worker and we will identify theory which might help us as practitioners.

Policy context

Allatt and Tett (2019) suggest that employability work is driven by the assumption 'that work of any kind is the solution to poverty' (52). Indeed, policy discourse around getting people into employment is often couched in the language of social justice and is influenced by a human capital perspective. This perspective is focused on measuring a limited number of standardised skills, with a focus on productivity and competition (Allatt and Tett, 2019). The driver behind this type of work is not citizens' well-being, but economic outcomes. We need to think carefully how this driver impacts on our work in communities and the commodification of individuals for economic rather than social motivations, because 'this economic discourse then tends to drive a curriculum that prioritises narrow employment skills-focused learning that neither respects learners' own goals nor values their life experiences' (Allatt and Tett, 2019, 42).

The failure of economic and employment policy has led to a rightward shift towards a more pronounced neoliberalism (see Chapter 2). Stiglitz, Sen and Fitoussi (2010) argue that policy makers must consider the impact on quality of life across different domains when designing policies. We need to 'shift emphasis from measuring economic production to measuring people's well-being (Stiglitz, Sen and Fitoussi, 2010, 10). The community workers we spoke to expressed frustration that employment was prioritised at all costs, regardless of the impact on well-being.

> 'The likelihood is that we'll push people into poverty, because once you start to work, you lose certain benefits. I think that it's quite cruel. We'll get people into a job without the recognition that working costs money; getting a bus to an interview or having the appropriate clothing, it costs them money.' (Nat Wealleans-Turner, 2022, Focus Group)

Purcell (2022, 237) argues that 'the "problem" of worklessness is individualised, but the solutions are system-driven and often exacerbate individuals' marginalisation'. We resist policy initiatives that 'imply the problem of exclusion lies in the deficits of the target population' (Webster et al, 2004, 42); we argue that, unless policies seek to address the causes of systematic injustice and poverty, employability will largely fail as an endeavour for well-being.

> '[Employability] is about that confidence building, team working, turning up on time, being well groomed and all those kind of things, which is obviously really valuable. But there was nothing beyond that in terms of developing the hard skills that are going to give young people a start, a more secure foothold in the labour market. One of the things that gets my back up is this idea that young people just need that foot on the ladder. It sounds right, you know, but more and more research is showing that that's not the case. And certainly, in my own research for young people in Scotland, that wasn't the case. They were caught in the secondary labour market, where they're moving from an employability programme to college, to short-term employability programmes to unemployment, to volunteering and going back into college. But none of it's leading anywhere, to anything sustainable, because they're not developing the hard skills which would give them that foothold on the labour market, that rung on the ladder. This is a phenomenon that moves across not just Scotland and the UK but into Europe as well. And I know research is beginning to find that people are trapped in this secondary labour market, not only from when they leave school but well into people's 30s as well.' (Alan Mackie, 2022, Focus Group)

To be innovative, governments need to create a policy landscape that offers apprenticeships to adults as well as young people; to offer bold wage subsidies for employers willing to take a chance on someone who does not have a usual employment biography; and a skills-recognition process that is accessible to everyone.

Current practice in Europe is focused on supporting unemployed people into work through training and other initiatives. European funding requires European Union member states to register long-term unemployed people with employment services and offer them individual in-depth needs assessment and a tailor-made job integration agreement, which may include mentoring, job search, education and training and support to reduce employment barriers (European Commission, 2022). We suggest that all countries should have a system like this, where individuals have a single point of contact and the individual assessment should take a holistic approach and assess the barriers to employment, skills, experiences and the life situation of long-term unemployed people. This can be done with the help of profiling and segmentation tools.

To access government funding in the UK, common requirements of most employability programmes are:

- Monitoring of attendance, often with targets (for example, an individual must not fall below 80% attendance).
- Monitoring of participants. Training courses completed, progressions into work or training, qualifications achieved.
- Tracking of participants for up to two years after they complete the programme.
- Detailed data gathering about personal and family situations and finances, often used to ensure that participants are getting all to which they are entitled.
- Sanctions for participants who do not engage or whose attendance falls below the target set.

While targets are set in the UK, it is our experience that agencies do have a level of autonomy in how they deliver such programmes, allowing community workers within the sector to design practice around the values and ethics of their profession. However, as community workers we are concerned that the human rights of the people we seek to support are infringed when they are forced to attend employability programmes or risk losing unemployment benefits.

The labour market driven approach

Neoliberal theories suggest that the power to change one's own destiny lies with the individual and that commitment and training are all that is required. However, this, we argue, is in a context – in the UK and other countries where neoliberalism is dominant – of decades of poverty and generations of unemployment. Undoubtedly, globalism, the digital age and the development of the gig economy have helped to advance such ideas and impacted upon how work and workers are valued and understood. Employment in the 21st century is often either fixed term or casual, meaning that 'any foothold in the labour market for the most disadvantaged is often precarious' (Carpenter et al, 2007, 169).

The emphasis on state-funded labour market programmes has, in many places, replaced traditional youth work and adult basic education programmes. In Denmark, for example, the exclusive focus of national strategies of adult education is on labour market skills (Larson and Cort, 2019, 189); and in many countries, only adult education programmes that lead directly to qualifications exist (European Commission/EACEA/Eurydice, 2021). Although innovative publicly subsidised work-based learning (apprenticeship) programmes and flexible, accelerated learning programmes are effective and welcome (European Commission/EACEA/Eurydice, 2021), these should not be the *only* offer available. As community workers, the authors are uncomfortable that some people may be excluded from learning because they do not want to or are not ready for accredited learning or vocational courses.

Michael Kengmana (2022), a Community Worker, told us about new state funding his project had received that will require his adult ESOL learners to find jobs, regardless of their situation or the unpaid domestic work they already carry out. His programme supports many mothers who are not ready for employment because they care for young children and other family members. He expressed a concern that the important work of supporting vulnerable women to develop skills and build relationships to aid their integration would be lost (Michael Kengmana, 2022, Focus Group)

With so much funding targeted at delivering employability projects, many community workers feel that it has changed the nature of their work, with résumés and cover letters becoming the focus of the adult literacy and youth work curriculum space. Purcell (2022, 222) argues that what distinguishes the work done by community workers 'is its focus on wider social and economic outcomes than more "mainstream", curriculum-driven and employment-focussed provision'. The authors of this book on theory into practice believe that voluntarism is integral to all good community work built on trust and mutual respect, and we feel a disquiet at working with clients mandated to attend an employability programme. Although the benefit may be that we can engage learners who may otherwise not have thought about improving their skills through informal learning, if participation remains voluntary, the impact we can make is significant.

Of course, the impact of a human capital approach is that work is focused on a narrow set of outcomes and targets, such as accreditation achieved, courses completed, volunteering placements or employment gained. Other outcomes which are important may be missed; our clients are often far away from the jobs market and, although significant for them, progress can be small and slow and often doesn't seem to be valued. Indeed, research reveals that 'the top-down, target-driven regime, informed by the short-term work-first approach focused on immediate employment, was hampering [employability programmes] from making further progress' (Carpenter et al 2007, 4).

> 'Fundamentally, as community workers we should absolutely be rejecting [targets and outcome-driven employability projects], because we should be working at the starting point of that individual. It should be voluntary participation and it should take that person on a journey, however long it takes them to get there; and it shouldn't be constrained by made-up time frames.' (Richard Bryce, 2022, Focus Group)

This quotation supports the idea that participation in employability programmes should be voluntary and should not be constrained by time frames. Many of the practitioners to whom we spoke were critical of national employment agencies and their approach of 'get a job, any job will do'. Ross told us about his own experience when he was unemployed. Despite starting work part time with the organisation for whom he works now as an adult learning tutor, he was told to quit by the employment agency and find full-time employment.

'Now my hobbies were restoring furniture and rock climbing, so they put this information in a computer and came back and told me that I should be applying to be a lumberjack!
I was like, "what! a lumberjack! I mean, there's no sense there". I was tutoring and beginning to do well at the Workers Educational Association, but "No, no, no, you can't do that. You've got to work full time". So, I saw what a lot of our students are facing.' (Ross Weatherby, 2022, Focus Group)

Unfortunately, many employability programmes make little impact on poverty or the lives of people at whom they are directed (Webster et al, 2004), targeted as they are at the symptoms of an economic problem, rather than the root cause of the problem.

Underpinning this whole approach is a shift from sociological and structural explanations of unemployment and 'worklessness', emphasising the responsibilities of governments, to psychological or cultural explanations, emphasising individual responsibility and personal agency. These can tend to blame the victim by identifying 'welfare dependency' as the cause rather than the symptom of labour market exclusion, thus requiring disciplinary 'welfare reform'. (Carpenter et al, 2007, 5)

Employability assumes that jobs exist for people and that these jobs will enable them to be better off in employment, but in many of our communities this is simply not true. Either these jobs do not exist or the employment available keeps people trapped in low-paid, short-term contracts and insecure employment. We must consider not just the number of jobs but their quality.

Understanding barriers to employment

While many people aspire to get a job (Webster et al, 2004), for some this may be a longer-term goal, rather than an immediate priority, and others will struggle to overcome barriers to entering the labour market.

Those with the highest levels of unemployment and worklessness are often those considered special interest groups, such as the disabled, people identifying as LGBTQ+, ethnic minorities, older workers, younger workers and the poor. For example, research across Europe, Australia and North America revealed that race and gender persistently impact on the ability of women and people of colour to find employment (Riach and Rich [2002], cited in Speeden, 2007, 49). Across the developing world, women, particularly in rural areas, may have very low levels of literacy and, therefore, have little chance of gaining employment (UNESCO, 2019). Issues around literacy and language are often the main barrier to participation in the training and learning which might enable these populations to improve their skills and therefore find employment. Evaluation of national employability programmes across Europe found that skills 'audit' (assessment) is still not a standard practice and, in the majority of cases, it is not used to identify gaps in basic skills such as literacy, numeracy and digital skills. Furthermore, basic skills are not always embedded into support measures for low-skilled adults, while they are fundamental for successful progression towards further learning qualifications (European Commission, 2019).

The practitioners we consulted for this chapter talked about their frustrations that equalities measures were often not embedded or budgeted for in programmes. Carpenter et al (2007) suggest that this is a symptom of the 'human capital or "work-first plus" approach', meaning that 'equalities measures are only seen as justifiable so long as they have an economic rationale consistent with the current government policies' (Carpenter et al, 2007), 160).

Migrant workers and refugees may struggle to have their skills and qualifications recognised in the country in which they are living (UNESCO, 2019), making it harder for them to find employment.

> 'For integration of refugees and asylum seekers as well as other migrants in the labour market, while volunteering is for many a free choice of giving time, often it's the only option. Is it really a free option of volunteering for these people or is it the only way

of building up a British CV to be accepted in terms of employment? For some it was really a free choice, but for some others it was the only choice.' (Francesca Calo, 2022, Focus Group)

Research shows that ethnic minorities tend to be underemployed (Wilson and Darity, 2022; Francis-Devine and Clark, 2022) and, while we welcome the establishment of national qualification frameworks within Europe which allow a broader range of qualifications and learning to be recognised and credit rated (European Commission/EACEA/Eurydice, 2021), we feel that this should go further, allowing for the skills and competencies gained through employment and other ways, such as volunteering, to be recognised. As well as migrants, other groups have also developed skills without having them accredited, or have informally worked their way up through job roles within a company without being certified, keeping them trapped within lower-paid employment. We know that even when people have the right skills, qualifications and experience they may not be able to find work because of more hidden barriers, such as their address, their name or how they look or talk. While employment can help those with addictions to better manage their recovery through positive occupations and increased self-esteem, the demands of a methadone recovery programme can mean that patients have to be late for or absent from work, making sustained employment challenging (Webster et al, 2004, 20).

Case study

A mother whose son was on a methadone programme and making good progress told me that she was delighted when he managed, despite few qualifications, a poor work history and a criminal record, to find employment. Living rurally, there were a limited number of buses he could take to get to work on time, so the mother asked if she would be allowed to administer his methadone at home, but it was refused, which meant he could not continue working, as the pharmacy didn't open till 9:30 and he had to be at work for 9:00. This impacted on both of them, in terms of their mental health, and left them feeling under suspicion and that there was really no point in trying.

Living rurally is often a barrier to employment. A lack of local opportunities can mean that people have to rely on public transport, which is expensive and can be unreliable, to get to work. It can be almost impossible to live and work in the countryside without access to a private vehicle (Piette and McCarthy in Carpenter et al, 2007, 64). It is frustrating that young people are forced to leave these communities to find suitable employment (Carpenter et al, 2007, 64), something that is also felt in more urban settings too; their home, their community is a sense of security to them in a sea of uncertainty. The practitioners we spoke to expressed frustration that often the geographical barriers with communities or for individuals were not understood by employment agencies and training providers.

> 'In Aberdeen, same as any other city, you don't want to venture from one area into another area. ... We've got to think about what we're asking people to do and where we are asking them to go. Or, you know, if they have gone through substance misuse problems and they're known in the community for being like that and then maybe being through criminal justice, they don't feel good about themselves anyway. So, they don't want to come out. They don't want folk from their own community to see them.' (Ross Weatherby, 2022, Focus Group)

We need 'concerted efforts to tackle exclusion and disadvantage in genuinely empowering ways' (Carpenter et al, 2007, 159) that focus on work sustainability addressing cycles of poverty.

Future of work

The community workers we spoke to revealed that many people they knew were working online in ways that were not recognised or understood by national and local skills agencies.

'The school referred a young person who never went to school. So, I met him and discovered that his Instagram's got 420,000 people on it and he's making 800 to 1,200 quid [pounds] a month in sponsorships. Why would he go to school? What are they gonna teach him? He's essentially taught himself this.

The world is continually changing. Young people are finding their own way and we need to do more work around those kinds of broader entrepreneurial and self-management type skills, rather than trying to fit them in boxes that society has decided are proper jobs. I think the structures around employability are way behind where the technology has taken us and I think that that's a very significant issue because a lot of young people just don't believe the stories are being told about what work is these days, because they see that work is a really diverse range of things.' (Richard Bryce, 2022, Focus Group)

Indeed, Cantrell (2021) argues in the same vein as this focus group quotation, that the idea of a job per se is 'increasingly becoming a relic of the industrial era'. She suggests that the future of work is one in which people will demand that work better fits around their lifestyles and families. While the choice and autonomy that the digital age can offer us as employees will be positive for most of us, the authors of this book are concerned about the impact of increasing automation and a lack of investment, stable employment and income for those who are already being left behind in the UK and many other countries. 'Gone are the days when companies' workforce agendas revolved only around hired employees performing work along linear career paths. Today's workforces comprise a range of internal and external players – employees, contractors, gig workers, professional service providers, application developers, crowdsourced contributors, and others' (Kiron et al, 2021).

A capabilities approach

The capabilities approach has emerged as an alternative to common discourses of neoliberalism. At the start of this chapter, we asked who gets to decide what is a meaningful occupation. For many, the answer would undoubtedly be employment, but we would argue that there are other 'occupations' which can be meaningful for individuals and which promote well-being for them, their families and communities.

> 'Folk are going round in circles. I've got folk coming to the project who really enjoyed it a couple of years ago and have gone off to college, they've ended up volunteering somewhere and then within months, they're back to the project again because the work they've been told to do has had a detrimental effect on their mental health.' (Ross Weatherby, 2022, Focus Group)

Sen (1999) argues that happiness and desire fulfilment are indicators of well-being. If someone is unhappy or their desires and aspirations are not fulfilled, we can assume that their well-being is affected (Sen, 1999). Asking someone to do work they do not want or cannot do will not promote well-being and sustainable employment. We argue that current human capital approaches to employability, which suggest that employment is the means to securing well-being, will not result in well-being for all the individuals or our communities.

Carpenter et al (2007, 1) 'advocate an alternative capabilities and human rights approach as the most appropriate way forward beyond both employability and human capital approaches.' Also known as the human development approach, 'it begins with a very simple question: what are people actually able to do and be? What real opportunities are available to them?' (Nussbaum, 2009, x).

People may be argued to have fundamentally similar needs and we are each born with potential. The capabilities approach argues that we have a 'moral and political responsibility on human rights grounds to respect these and actively create the economic, social and political conditions to which people can "flourish" and achieve "personhood"' (Carpenter et al, 2007, 170). It is the opposite of neoliberal approaches which emphasise personal responsibility and is, instead, 'concerned with entrenched social injustice and inequality, especially capability failures that are the result of discrimination or marginalisation' (Nussbaum, 2009, 19).

> This approach conceives a person's life as a combination of various 'doings and beings' (functionings) and of his or her freedom to choose among these functionings (capabilities). Some of these capabilities may be quite elementary, such as being adequately nourished and escaping premature mortality, while others might be more complex, such as having the literacy required to participate actively in political life. (Stiglitz et al, 2010, 63)

Nussbaum (2011) argues that it is the responsibility of governments to ensure that all citizens are able to exercise or engage with a threshold level of ten basic capabilities: life; bodily health; bodily integrity; senses, imagination and thought; emotions; practical reason; affiliation (social interaction); other species; play; and control over one's environment (Nussbaum, 2011, 33–4).

Many of the people with whom we work have all these capabilities, but often the conditions do not exist for them to exercise them. For example, in the UK we have a skills shortage of plasterers and many resettled Syrian refugees with these skills and abilities, but not the recognition to work in their trade in the UK. The basic and internal capabilities are there, but not the combined capabilities, or not the political and social environment for them to thrive. The capabilities approach fits well with community-based programmes, which support individuals to define their own needs and strengths and collaboratively address these. Clients are viewed holistically, within their social context. People are supported to develop their skills, which may help them to find employment, but, in the end, this should be their own decision.

Social practice model

Research in England by Purcell (2022) found that:

> By moving away from provision designed to drive learners towards the jobs market through

participation in large scale and impersonal accredited courses, Community Wise has been able to generate enthusiastic participation and progression (as defined and experienced in their own way) for them. This approach facilitates individuals' choices to engage in meaningful-to-them activities that can accommodate the mental and physical health challenges they face; and, through the development of genuine social relationships with practitioners and peers based on mutuality, care and respect, can go some way towards ameliorating the impact of these on their daily lives. (Purcell, 2022, 236)

A social practice model of learning, influenced by the work of Paulo Freire which we discussed in our chapter on adult learning (Chapter 11), provides a framework to develop this kind of learning.

The social practices approach,

- Recognises, values and validates the range of experiences and skills that people bring to any learning.
- Starts from people's strengths and aspirations, not their weaknesses, or perceived 'needs'.
- Recognises and builds on the ways that people learn.
- Provides learning that develops from, and is embedded in, contexts which are relevant to the learner.
- Recognises the different values, emotions and perspectives that are embedded in learning.
- Is open about the power dimensions of learning and enables learners to exercise power themselves.
- Develops learners' critical capacities.
- Develops learners' abilities to use their learning in other contexts. (Community Learning and Development Managers Scotland, 2014, 3)

The approach to adult learning that recognises the cultural and social context within which the learner operates develops a curriculum around their learning goals and aspirations and, we would argue, is a good starting point for ethical, learner-centred, capabilities-informed practice which leads to positive outcomes for individuals. We do not use 'employability practice' because we acknowledge that employment is not right for everyone.

Other approaches

Carpenter et al (2007) describe three other models of employability which are worth exploring.

(i) 'egalitarian structuralist' approaches prioritising demand-side interventions to promote equality and 'better work' alongside an improved benefits system, within an employment-based society; and

(ii) 'egalitarian utopian' approaches that promote a post-employment society encouraging informal community self-activity, often involving decoupling from the economic system. (Carpenter et al, 2007, 161)

(iii) '*Life-first*' rather than '*work-first*' approach which involves democratic and devolved employment services which respond to the local needs of disadvantaged communities rather than operating on the basis of mandates and sanctions. (Carpenter et al, 2007, 178)

There is much literature about the impact of community-based learning on adults and communities, but less has been written about the impact of this work on practitioners themselves. Engaging in work with communities is a shared endeavour, through which both the participant and the worker are changed. Through empowering practice, we can help communities to understand their rights and to discover our own; to find peace and, in the process, we learn, develop deeper empathy and are empowered. Nearly all the community workers we spoke to, however, felt a sense of uneasiness about engaging in the employability space; it seemed never to be an entirely positive experience for them. Those who had found a way through, such as Ross Weatherby, had managed to achieve a broad range of outcomes with participants, some of which related to employability and employment, but without being bound by specific tied-down outcomes, which would have changed the nature of his flexible and developmental project.

Research has shown that, where employability projects are most successful, it is because they are holistic, focusing on 'the broader needs of clients, rather than focusing only on equipping them for the labour market' and 'the way that they were operating seemed a major reason for the successes made. This derived from the clear values of combined ethics of care, empowerment and social justice, as well as simply providing time for people and "being nice" as one of the clients put it' (Carpenter et al, 2007, 23–4).

We suggest that we can work with people in ways which help them to achieve their goals. Community workers need to focus not on a narrow curriculum of skills for employment, but to look more broadly at developing the skills to engage in life and society within a broader community development framework (Speeden, 2007). "In the end it was about making sure people realise they weren't alone, you know, because I think that's the key thing" (Alan Mackie, 2022, Focus Group).

Principles in practice

1. Analyse the context in which you work. Are the jobs good quality and, if not, what can you do about this to influence change?
2. Develop a social practices model that meets the full range of needs of your participants, if you have not already done so.
3. Ensure that you have the resources to reduce barriers and promote participation before entering into a learning relationship.
4. Ask your participants what a meaningful life means to them and respond accordingly, where this does not impact negatively on them or others.
5. Be willing to push back against pre-determined targets and outcomes. People are different, they learn differently, they have different needs and aspirations.
6. Make sure you capture and celebrate the small steps.

Challenge questions

1. Are the courses that are available to adults in your area of a good enough standard to make a difference to people's lives and prospects? Are there opportunities to learn vocational skills if desired?
2. As community workers, how can we offer choice in progression routes into and out of learning?
3. How do you advocate for the full needs of participants, in the face of labour market-driven practice?
4. Think about times in your career when you have accepted the status quo rather than challenging practice that may have tested your values and ethics. What does this tell you about the quality and relevance of your practice?
5. Thinking about the case study of the mother with a son on methadone. What were her challenges and what needed to be done about them?

References

Allatt, G. and Tett, L. (2019) The employability skills discourse and literacy practitioners. In L. Tett and M. Hamilton (eds) *Resisting Neoliberal Education*. Policy Press, Bristol.

Cantrell, S. (2021) *Beyond the job*. Deloitte. Available at: https://www2.deloitte.com/us/en/insights/topics/talent/new-work-models.html (Accessed: 19 June 2022).

Carpenter, M., Speeden, S., Griffin, C. and Walters, N. (2007) *Beyond the Workfare State: Labour markets, equalities and human rights*. Bristol University Press, Bristol.

Community Learning and Development Managers Scotland (2014) A Social Practice Model for Adult Learning: within a community learning and development context [internal report]. Available at: www.cdn.ac.uk/wp-content/uploads/2016/08/CLDMS-Social-Practice-in-Adult-learning-2014.pdf (Accessed: 20 March 2022).

European Commission (2019) *Report from the Commission to the Council on the Evaluation of the Council Recommendation on the integration of the long-term unemployed into the labour market*. European Commission, Brussels.

European Commission (2022) *Long-term Unemployment*. Available at: https://ec.europa.eu/social/main.jsp?catId=1205&langId=en (Accessed: 17 July 2022). https://researchbriefings.files.parliament.uk/documents/SN06385/SN06385.pdf (Accessed: 17 July 2022).

European Commission/EACEA/Eurydice (2021) *Adult Education and Training in Europe: Building inclusive pathways to skills and qualifications*. Eurydice Report. Publications Office of the European Union, Luxembourg. Available at: https://data.europa.eu/doi/10.2797/898965 (Accessed: 6 March 2022).

Francis-Devine, B., Clark, H., UK Parliament, corp creator (2022) House of Commons Library: Briefing Paper Number 6385 14 July 2022: Unemployment by ethnic background [Briefing paper (House of Commons Library)]. Available at: https://researchbriefings.files.parliament.uk/documents/SN06385/SN06385.pdf (Accessed: 17 July 2022).

Kiron, D., Schwartz, J., Jones, R. and Altman, E.J. (2021) *Driving the Future of Work with Workforce Ecosystems*. Deloitte. Available at: https://www2.deloitte.com/global/en/insights/focus/technology-and-the-future-of-work/future-of-work-workforce-ecosystem.html (Accessed: 19 June 2022).

Larson, A. and Cort, P. (2019) The marginalisation of popular education: 50 years of Danish adult education policy. In L. Tett and M. Hamilton (eds) *Resisting Neoliberal Education*. Policy Press, Bristol.

Nussbaum, M.C.I. (2009) *Creating Capabilities: The human development approach*. Belknap Press of Harvard University Press, Cambridge, MA.

Nussbaum, M. C. 1. (2011). *Creating Capabilities: the human development approach*. Belknap Press of Harvard University Press, Cambridge, MA.

Purcell, M.E. (2022) Hope in 'catastrophic' times: participants' stories of nurture and transformation from an innovative community learning initiative. *Research in Post-compulsory Education* 27(2): 219–41.

Riach, R.A. and Rich, J. (2002) Field experiments of discrimination in the market place. *The Economic Journal* 112(483), 480–518.

Sen, A. (1999) *Commodities and Capabilities.* Oxford University Press, New Delhi.

Speeden, S. (2007) Between work and tradition: minority ethnic women in North West England. In M. Carpenter, S. Speeden, C. Griffin and N. Walters (eds) *Beyond the Workfare State: Labour markets, equalities and human rights.* Bristol University Press, Bristol, pp 43–58.

Sen, A., Fitoussi, J-P. and Stiglitz, J. (2010) *Mismeasuring Our Lives: Why GDP doesn't add up.* The New Press, New York.

UNESCO Institute for Lifelong Learning (2019) *Fourth Global Report on Adult Learning and Education.* UNESCO Institute for Lifelong Learning, Hamburg.

Webster, C., Simpson, D., MacDonald, R., Abbas, A., Cieslik, M., Shildrick, T. and Simpson, M. (2004) *Poor Transitions: Social exclusion and young adults.* Policy Press, Bristol.

Wilson, V. and Darity Jr, W. (2022) *Understanding Black–White Disparities in Labor Market Outcomes Requires Models that Account for Persistent Discrimination and Unequal Bargaining Power.* Economic Policy Institute, Washington, DC. Available at: www.epi.org/unequalpower/publications/understanding-black-white-disparities-in-labor-market-outcomes/ (Accessed: 17 July 2022).

13

The environment

Ed Garrett and Karen McArdle

Introduction

The survival of many people, societies and, of course communities, and the biological support systems of the planet are at risk. It is a mainstream view that the biological systems on which all human life relies are, indeed, at risk (Jickling et al, 2021). With the climate and biodiversity crises, the social impact is apparent from scientific evidence. Environmental issues must now be a priority for community work. There is an urgency and an immediacy that runs counter to the often-long-term nature of much of our work, particularly community development. However, as the community work response to the COVID-19 pandemic has demonstrated in many countries, there is clearly the creativity and resourcefulness in the sector and in communities needed to begin to and contribute to practice, to respond to this urgency.

Engaging with theory is central to understanding this community work and developing and extending our practice. Westoby says: 'Community development practitioners, without being enlivened by renewed theory ... can easily become ossified with auto-pilot practice. Human-induced climate change and species extinction certainly invite new theory or new ideas' (Westoby, 2021, 387).

Engaging with theory is complex. Robinson, for example (2018) introduces, us to the 'Four Phases of Theory Engagement', proposing that a cyclical and systematic way of harnessing theory in our operating contexts is beneficial. We are led from phase 1, with a focus on identification of the problem to be solved, through identification of relevant theory or theories of action and evaluation of success, to potential new theories of action. Robinson is accentuating the importance of theory to practice, and alerting us to the need for reflection around what works best. If community workers are to be fully effective, we suggest, they need to be fleet of foot and connected to current and emerging sources of impact of the climate crisis on those with whom we work.

This chapter is divided into two main parts. Firstly, we look at the theory of how we can link what we do as community workers to the environment, and secondly, we engage in more focused discussion on what this means in some key areas of practice.

Social justice and the environment

We need firstly to think about the links between social justice and the environment and what these links mean. For us as community workers, social justice has surely to be our motivation (see Chapter 2). Westoby (2021) stresses our need to work for social justice. 'If we are not haunted by the spectre of justice, then it would be best to walk away from community development, to leave it alone, to do no more damage' (Westoby, 2021, 380).

It is quite clear to us that the environment and social justice are closely linked. As Harley and Scandrett (2019) argue, the natural resources of the environment are a critical part of community development. They form part of the assets of communities. Impacts on environment are, therefore, impacts on communities and impacts on what we can do as community workers. It is also clear that the climate crisis is affecting poorer and more vulnerable people the most. There is a grim logic here, as Harley and Scandrett make clear: 'Economic decision making in the interests of capital accumulation leads to cost shifting onto the environments of those with least economic or political leverage' (Harley and Scandrett, 2019, 8). Accordingly, if we are serious as community workers about social justice, we also then need to be serious about the environment. We look at this sense of the environment as the site of social justice in the next section.

We may, however, want to extend this link between the environment and social justice to something more fundamental. A colleague who works with an organisation with an ecological focus made the following claim about ideology and a political viewpoint: "I would say that as an organisation, we see them as fundamentally linked. One is actually not possible without the other. Yes, whichever way you look at it, I do actually think it's worth seeing that, not necessarily as objective fact, but as an ideological or political viewpoint" (Matthew Evans, 2022, Focus Group).

The environment as the site for social justice

Before we consider what the closer connection between the environment and social justice might be, we need to consider how the environment can be the site for social justice. In terms of the environment, communities can be seen as the most effective way of bringing about sustainable change. Agenda 21, coming out of the United Nations Rio Earth Summit in 1992, recognised the key importance of community-led change. More recently, for example, the Transition Towns movement in the UK is another example of communities taking action into their own hands and on their own terms. This community-led participatory network aims to work from the bottom up for a socially just low carbon future (Transition Network, 2023).

It is important to distinguish community work, and community development, in particular, from much sustainable development. Harley and Scandrett (2019) argue that the sustainable development agenda has been co-opted by capital stakeholders and that the community participatory processes in this agenda have in fact largely been a cover for the neoliberal agenda (see Chapter 2) to cut public services. If this is indeed the case, as community workers it is vital that we are mindful of the values which underpin our work.

A focus group participant outlined clearly how working with communities on environmental issues based on values of social justice, respect, inclusion and empowerment can have positive social and environmental impacts which reinforce each other:

> 'If we can look after and respect our green and local community areas, by involving the communities themselves, then this breeds respect and understanding within the community and leads to increased confidence, self-esteem, self-respect and respect for others. This then leads to a better community, where everyone feels that their voice is heard. They are respected and as a result we will find the community grows in strength. The areas become more environmentally friendly, therefore leading to more green areas hosting lots of new plant life and animal life, allowing for a more natural nature connection between individuals and their own local areas. We can also look at growing food in newly created community gardens.' (Ross Weatherby, 2022, Focus Group)

The environment can also be the site for more direct social and political struggles and, in terms of community development, often the site of struggle between local concerns and other stakeholders. In terms of theory, these struggles are often informed by and understood through critical academic theory, engaging with neoliberalism, alongside reflections and understandings of activists and workers. Harley and Scandrett (2019, 8) attempt to 'draw on all these in order to assist those engaged in struggles for environmental justice – as community workers or social activists, environmentalists or community mobilisers – to address the difficult questions about praxis in the face of the neoliberal onslaught'. As community workers engaged with theory to develop practice, it is important that we also ask questions about praxis (see Chapter 11) and what is driving our efforts.

Our relations with nature, extending community

So far, we have been talking about the environment insofar as it is important for human beings. However, there are other ways to think of the link between the social and the environmental (or natural), which can involve a valuing of the environment in itself. If we make the argument that the environment is part of social justice, then we might also say that the environment is part of the community as the site of social justice. This is a possible opening up of the ambit of community that, Westoby (2021) argues, we need to consider as part of our practice.

A colleague described an example from her practice which illustrates this.

> 'It makes me think of the garden project that we've got going on at the minute with Lindy, a really amazing gardener. She really wants that project to think about, about caring for the garden and who cares for the garden. So, it's not just her and it's not just us. It's also like the cat that comes in and keeps the mice away from the compost, it's the worms, it's the wasps.' (Jess Carnegie, 2022, Focus Group)

This opening up of community as a site of social justice has difficulties, certainly. Benson explores what it means to be in a community, arguing that it involves at least a mutual awareness and interests, as well as some sense of mutual obligations. So, in what sense, he asks, can the non-human be part of such a community? He argues that respect for nature can be based not on a sense of community with it but on its very otherness (Benson, 1999). Although many Indigenous cultures recognise non-humans as part of the community, from the perspective of Western thought, particularly, any deeper identification with nature may be difficult. Kate Soper points out: 'An opposition between the natural and the human has been axiomatic to Western thought, and remains a presupposition of all its philosophical, scientific, moral and aesthetic discourse' (Soper, 1995, 38).

This is an opposition which has its roots in the dualism of Descartes and other philosophical thinkers. Deep green ecology, which is an environmental philosophy which argues nature has inherent value rather than just instrumental value for human beings, proposes an identification with nature, but this philosophy relies on problematic notions of an expanded self (Benson, 1999). An openness towards the possibility of extending community is important if we are to move away from what one focus group participant described as "a world created by capitalism, as a resource to be exploited, rather than a home to live in".

Nature as discursive

Just as we need to be aware of and open to shifting meanings of community and social justice, so too we need to be mindful of how the language of the environment, and its connection to the natural, can be controversial. Soper discusses, 'the semiotics of "nature", which would recall us to the role of the concept in mediating access to the "reality" it names, and whose political critique is directed at the oppressive use of the idea to legitimate social and sexual hierarchies and cultural norms' (Soper, 1995, 3). Soper suggests that an appeal to some way of life being natural can be used as a powerful form of putting that natural way of life beyond political critique. It is important to question critically such uses of the language of nature and how they can embody power. This can be contrasted with the ecological approach to nature 'that has emerged in response to ecological crisis, is critically targeted on its human plunder and destruction, and politically directed at correcting that abuse' (Soper, 1995, 3).

As workers who are perhaps committed to this ecological understanding of nature, we need awareness of how the language we use can mediate or construct the 'reality it names'. For example, McGregor and Scandrett (2022) talk about the dangers of the construction of the climate emergency by those in power. A focus on emergency rather than transition can legitimise an ignoring of justice in transition. As community workers supporting environmental projects, we need to be critically aware of such legitimising actions.

Working with communities

The critical awareness mentioned earlier is not of course to deny the reality of the emergency situation in which we find ourselves. In political terms it means, as McGregor and Scandrett (2022, 12) argue, that 'a left populist politics of climate emergency is one that articulates the connections between lived experiences of social and economic injustice and climate change'. Community workers have an important role to play in supporting the articulation of this connection in terms of local communities. As ever, with community work, this process needs to take place according to the needs and interests of those involved, as the following case study demonstrates.

Case study

> Kevin was working with communities to prioritise actions for a region-wide plan to support eating well and keeping active. At a day-long event involving service representatives and community members, it was suggested early on by a service representative that some environmental principles should underpin the action plan. Most community members were not, however, interested in this suggestion. Understandably, their priorities were more about affordable transport and the food they could put on their children's plates. Through the discussions of the day, connections were made between the economic circumstances in which people found themselves and climate change, putting pressure on prices and other resources. In the end, priorities with a green focus, such as active travel and sustainable local food systems, received support.

Working with communities: voice

Another key role of the community worker will be engaging with communities on environmental issues and, in particular, ensuring that local and marginalised communities are properly heard. Not only is this engagement important in terms of social justice, it is also, as McGregor and Scandrett (2022) point out, these communities that are often first and worst affected by environmental change and have the best understanding of what it means to address this change at a local level. Addressing change can be difficult work and the stakes can often be high, as Butler (2019) describes in an account of community resistance to a mining development in South Africa. Voice can be obstructed not only by threats and persuasion but also by the internalisation of an ideology of respect and knowing your place and by a civil society and its organisations who want to speak for rather than with the communities they support.

It is also the case that environmental issues may attract activists from outside the local community in a way that can challenge the way we work within the community. It can lead to tensions between local communities and environmental activists, as well as complicating or obscuring the voice of the community. For example, Ed was involved in some of the environmental protests in the 1990s, particularly around road building. Ed remembers one occasion when busloads of people descended on a quiet village in Surrey, in England, to occupy some land. There was little local involvement with the community and he spent a lot of time trying to placate local residents. Darcy and Cox (2019) outline the more constructive role that these outside activists can play in a community-led response in a discussion of local opposition to a new gas pipeline from Shell in rural Ireland, bringing new and relevant knowledge, skills and experience.

The following case study illustrates the some of the difficulties associated with supporting the genuine voice of communities.

Case study

> Jess is a community worker with a community arts organisation in North East Scotland. As part of a project called 'The World Is Ours, in Spite of All', with artist and educator Hussein Mitha, she helped to set up the Huntly Youth Climate Warriors, a group of young people interested in climate justice. When the project working with young people ended, the young people were keen to continue and the group has since become independent. Although no longer supporting the group, Jess has remained in touch. She stresses how the group's becoming independent has proved to be an important model for change, creating an autonomous space for young people to discuss and

work together on issues that are pressing to them. The group are developing a highly political voice. Jess also says, however, that the young people have struggled initially with some of the practicalities of running their own group. It would be great if there were other similar groups locally that they could share with and learn from. (Jess Carnegie, 2022, Focus Group)

On a practical level, resources are important for this process. As community workers, we may have access to these resources, such as spaces to meet as well as networks and contacts to bring people together. Funding, including for paid staff, can also be crucial, and the short-term funding of projects, particularly in the third sector, can often be a barrier to effective longer-term engagement. The role of paid staff, particularly if they are paid by the state or through corporate money, can also sometimes be ambiguous, as highlighted by Darcy and Cox (2019) in relation to opposition to the Shell pipeline in Ireland. The ambiguity raises questions about the need for the central role of unpaid community activists and the how communities might employ staff without reliance on state or corporate funding.

Thinking about the practice of community workers, and their pedagogies for educational practice in particular, Jickling et al (2021) explore the complex area of study of environmental ethics, in a sourcebook for educators. They discuss pedagogies that explore, *inter alia*, values and what they term the 'moral impulse'.

- Etiquettes of daily living (what we do in personal and professional lives) are ways of generating the knowledge people need to grapple with the socio-environmental challenges.
- Where value conflicts arise, reflection is a useful tool.
- Ethics do not begin and end with humans, and developing strong moral impulses to the more-than-human world is dependent on having experiences of this. (Derived from Jickling et al, 2021, 270)

Jickling et al (2021) also discuss practical pedagogies that stimulate ethical environmental action. Considering ethics is not just an intellectual exercise, but is deeply rooted in practice and lived experience. Effective learning and teaching help to connect intellectual and emotional aspects of the environment and can bring ethical thinking and feeling into practice. Critique, which Jickling et al (2021) define as naming of problems and resisting ethical injustices, is linked to reimagining, seeing beyond problems, turning problems upside down and inside out to view situations in a new manner. An example is reimagining futures through ways of revealing social structures that are in plain sight and may be fault lines that could be reimagined. For example, they propose, in groups, looking at possibilities for a different future focusing on:

- Language: how to reclaim or reinvent language to express values;
- Social practices: reinventing or redesigning prevailing social practices that shape the environment;
- Images: what new metaphors do we need? (Derived from Jickling et al, 2021, 188)

Jickling et al pose four elemental questions for thinking about environmental ethics:

> What is 'right' and what is not 'right'?
> What could be different?
> What should be (taking a holistic vision of self and others)?
> What realistic concrete action can we take? (Derived from Jickling et al, 2021, 271)

This chapter has emphasised the need for community work to engage with theory so as to develop practice in relation to environmental ethical and practical challenges. It has explored this theory in terms of how we understand the link between the environment and social justice, different discourses of the environment and how we need to be critically aware of how these discourses may impact on our roles as community workers.

Principles in practice

1. There is no social justice without environmental justice.
2. An extended sense of community can be part of the connection between social justice and the environment.
3. Discourses of the environment can be oppressive as well as liberating. Think about the discourses you hear and use.
4. If you are a paid community worker, think about how these discourses might affect how you can support communities taking on environmental issues.
5. As community workers we need to be working with the most marginalised communities, supporting connections between disadvantage and environmental change.
6. Consider your role in learning and teaching for environmental visioning.

Challenge questions

1. How do you see the links between social justice and environmental justice in your work?
2. What is valuable about addressing environmental issues from a community work perspective? What is distinctive about this?
3. Do we need an extended sense of community as part of this work? What might this look like?
4. How have you supported engagement around environmental issues? What challenges have you found?
5. What is your vision for an environmental future thinking about social practices?
6. Thinking of the case studies of Kevin and Jess, what were the strong points of their work, and what were any limitations, in your opinion?

References

Benson, J. (1999) *Environments, Ethics and Human Concern*. Open University Press, Milton Keynes.

Butler, M. (2019) 'Mines come to bring poverty': extractive industry in the life of the people in KwaZulu-Natal, South Africa. In A. Harley and E. Scandrett (eds) *Environmental Justice, Popular Struggle and Community Development*. Policy Press, Bristol, pp 101–16.

Darcy, H. and Cox, L. (2019) Resisting Shell in Ireland: making and remaking alliances between communities, movements and activists. In A. Harley and E. Scandrett (eds) *Environmental Justice, Popular Struggle and Community Development*. Policy Press, Bristol, pp 15–28.

Harley, A. and Scandrett, E. (eds) (2019) *Environmental Justice, Popular Struggle and Community Development*. Policy Press, Bristol.

Jickling, B., Lotz-Sisitka, H., Olvitt, L., O'Donoghue, R., Schudel, I., McGarry, D. and Niblett, B. (2021) *Environmental Ethics: A sourcebook for educators*. Sun Press, Zambia.

McGregor, C. and Scandrett, E, (2022) Framing climate emergency: community development, populism and just transition. *Community Development Journal*, 57(1) 1–16.

Robinson, V. (2018) *Reduce Change to Increase Improvement*. Corwin Sage Publishing Company, California.

Soper, K. (1995) *What Is Nature?* Blackwell, Oxford.

Transition Network (2023) *A movement of communities coming together to reimagine and rebuild our world*. Available at: https://transitionnetwork.org (Accessed: 30 March 2023)

Westoby, P. (2021) 'A community development yet to come': Jacques Derrida and reconstructing community development practice. *Community Development Journal* 56(3): 375–90.

14

Community arts

Sue Briggs and Karen McArdle

'Arts approaches can open a door for people such that, once they go through it, you know they're on a pathway which they can continue on. It's very, very transformative in a way that other things might not be. And it's kind of on the community's level. It's non-judgemental. So, you can go at your own pace and it's non-elitist, but it's just so valuable I think, because you're creating community through the activities that you're doing anyway because you're bringing all these people together.' (Belona Greenwood, 2022, Focus Group)

Introduction

The opening quotation expresses some of the potential of community arts. How often do we come across colleagues who have personal skills and talents which accentuate their ability to practise as community workers? From our perspective, these talents are often woven into practice. We are not only the community worker, but often also a musician, a storyteller, a photographer, an artist, a dancer, a reader. How often do we find colleagues where the delineation between personal and professional activities in our own communities is blurred? We are all residents of a community somewhere. We would argue that we are all participants at some point in our daily lives in the arts. This allows for increased perception and understanding of issues for us as workers, while it can clearly also require us to be vigilant in any misunderstanding of our aligned roles.

The communities and individuals with whom we work are diverse, with multifaceted strengths and challenges. Community workers bring a range of acquired specialist skills and knowledge to their operational work and, when working in partnership with artists, we can call on a wide variety of approaches to strengthen our capacity to deliver successful programmes. Indeed, to build vibrant, resilient, responsive, healthy and well-anchored communities, we must use every tool in our toolbox. In this chapter we will explore what value and results can be brought about through creative and arts-focused interventions.

Community arts in context

The term 'community arts' is often used in a generic way to signify arts or cultural practice undertaken with and by communities and which uses a range of media and artistic practices (Meade and Shaw, 2021). Meade and Shaw discuss collaboration with artists and cite Matarasso (1997), who says 'Community art is the creation of art as a human right, by professional artists, co-operating as equals for purposes and to standards they set together' (Matarasso, 1997, 51). Meade and Shaw also suggest, again from the perspective of the artist, that they may be committed to 'the creation of work that is socially engaged, participatory, situated and in dialogue with its environment' (Meade and Shaw, 2021, 6). The next quotation illustrates the relationship between arts and culture and the link to community identity.

> 'Arts and culture are important in helping to build and sustain a community's identity and can impart a sense of belonging to that community. We can all see the effect of various pop music styles on the generations over the decades in the UK from Mods and Rockers, Teddy Boys, Grunge, Goths, New Romantics etc. The fans of each style form distinctive groups or communities

and are fiercely (quite literally with the Mods and Rockers) protective of their identity.' (Charlie West and Martin Kasprowicz, 2023, Interview)

Looking at arts and culture Meade and Shaw mention how arts practices can 'assume an "activist" character, moving into public realms and mobilising groups of people around issues that shape their lives' (Meade and Shaw, 2021, 10).

Through dialogue with current practitioners, the authors have identified the following messages:

- Community arts can give voice and visibility and capture lived experience.
- Arts initiatives linked to social enterprise practice can be valuable to sustainability.
- Arts initiatives can tackle social injustice.
- Arts activity can be a core element of change.
- Arts activity encourages transformation of the individual and the community.
- Arts activity supports people to work at their own level.
- Arts initiatives can engage participants in setting outcomes and contributing to bigger plans.
- Arts work can be important in creating celebration in community contexts.
- Arts work is always *with* people rather than doing things *to*.
- Filmmaking, for example, and other arts forms can be emotionally resonant and persuasive.
- The use of banner making, for example, and the written word can create links to local heritage, culture and politics.

Arts and well-being

Practice, reflection and evaluation of the role of the arts in health promotion is growing (Clift and Camic, 2016); this is where health is a state of complete physical, mental and social well-being and not merely an absence of disease or infirmity (World Health Organization, 1946). Health interventions have been increasingly driven by scientific evidence, which is of course important, but there is a dimension to human life of aesthetics, with its concerns of pleasure, enjoyment and beauty (Clift, 2012). The arts are about creativity and problem solving; they are also about helping to create meaning and a sense of beauty in our lives (Clift and Camic, 2016). Clift and Camic (2016) discusses how culture gives us identity and takes many forms, including, *inter alia*, how we adapt our natural environment; the institutions we create to express our social and political beliefs; and forms through which we express our beliefs.

The following case study shows the blending of arts and culture for the purpose of enhancing mental health and well-being

Case study

> Dr Hills' Casebook is a project in the UK that combines archives, history and research; approaches to mental health and well-being that include creative writing, film and theatre. The project seeks to provide safe spaces for people to connect, socialise, make friends, share experiences, express themselves, grow their confidence, connect to hope and realise improved well-being. The participants are people living with mental health challenges. The project supports people through the arts to explore and research the archives of a progressive mental health institution from the Victorian period. A film and theatre production have been produced, a book and regular blogs.

An evaluation of the project found the following contributions to promoting well-being through:

- Forging a link between the current identity of participants with mental health issues and historical archives;
- Developing social relationships between participants, a learned capacity;
- Facilitating learning across complex transformational dimensions of mental well-being and learning;
- Promoting key factors that contribute to resilience;
- Developing creativity as a contribution to social and emotional well-being;

- Developing the empowerment and critical energy of participants, linked to mental health and well-being;
- Promoting voice for vulnerable people, in relation to issues associated with mental health and well-being and making that voice heard. (McArdle, 2021)

Sonke et al (2016) describe neurological impacts, as well as qualitative impacts, of the arts across the life span. They cite how research shows that when jazz musicians improvise, their brains turn off areas linked to self-censoring and inhibition and turn on those that let self-expression flow (Limb and Braun, 2008). They also describe Cohen's (2006) study of the impact of cultural programmes on the physical, mental and social health of older adults, which showed that those assigned to choral groups reported higher physical health ratings and fewer medications, doctor visits, falls and other health problems than did those in a control group. Sonke et al (2016) also refer to palliative care settings being able to focus on existential meaning-making through self-expression to ease the suffering of body, mind and spirt.

Matarasso published a seminal study, in 1997, on the link between participating in arts activities and public health. He said of the impact of the arts on health that, 'Rather than the cherry on the policy cake, to which they are so often compared, they should be seen as the yeast, without which it fails to rise to expectations' (Matarasso, 1997, 10). Sonke et al (2016) conclude, looking at the workplace, that repeated research has shown the value of the arts to:

1. Ably complement conventional medical treatment of chronic physical and psychological health conditions;
2. improve physical environments and reduce workplace stress and burnout;
3. enhance relationships in diverse work settings, with higher employee retention;
4. reduce reliance on pharmaceutical medicines;
5. measurably improve workplace performance, cooperation, and mutual support, notably in healthcare settings; and

6. accelerate recovery from many illnesses, with consequently reduced strain on the healthcare system. (Sonke et al, 2016, 119)

Arts and engagement

Early concerns involved discussions about artists being parachuted into communities with the attendant implications of power imbalances between artists and communities. If artists were to work closely with participants, it was felt that there needed to be time to build relationships and mutual understanding in order to create work that was balanced between the needs of the community and the artists involved. (Jeffers, 2017, 155)

Thinking about community arts, as described here, time to build relationships and understand community needs is always essential to secure equitable and productive working relationships between artists and community organisations or initiatives. While any initial community engagement activity must be absolutely engaging, tailored to the needs of potential participants, longer-term engagement is dependent on trust, good communication and built relationships. The community workers with whom we talked described how the arts can be used to minimise power imbalances, which can stifle relationships and dialogue.

'If you're all engaged in an art activity together, you're no longer the teacher, you're no longer the student. You are people, who are inquiring together. Nothing is ever equal, but you can look to structurally make it more equal. That effort is always worthwhile in terms of building the transformative power of art.' (Iain Shaw, 2022, Focus Group)

Words can be very powerful and can release an emotional connection which can be shared in a trust setting. The use of poetry to engage vulnerable older people in expressing themselves during the COVID-19 pandemic period was shared with the authors. Poetry used as an engagement tool in communities where children and families could identify their priority concerns was an example of creative practice shared with us also, as described here.

> 'I personally think you're creating friendships and groups through the activities that you're doing and you're creating trust and you're empowering people to then carry on. But you're also opening up a new view to a new adventure. That will just go on and last for the rest of, sometimes for the rest of someone's lives. I've just seen it over and over again.' (Belona Greenwood, 2022, Focus Group)

Resourcing the arts

Funding and policy background can influence the shape of arts interventions in community settings, sometimes stimulating and sometimes curtailing them.

> 'I personally think the value of using arts and working in communities is so immense, it really, really does matter and there's never enough money that's made available for that work and neither is there the time that should be invested in these projects. It's no good. Are you doing something for five weeks, opening the door for people and then, just leaving them and going on?' (Belona Greenwood, 2022, Focus Group)

> 'Community workers share a passion for making a difference in people's lives, but we also often are at the mercy of grants and people to help support what we do. And they're still rooted in, well, "what can you tell us quantitatively about your work?" You know, they want to see results. They wanna see results that are immediate, which isn't the way it works.' (Joan Harrison, 2022, Focus Group)

Belona Greenwood describes in the next quote how the parameters of projects can sometimes be limiting, and participants setting outcomes can be empowering.

> 'Sometimes, you have a project that you're going to do and it might have its parameters and its final outcomes set in advance [by funders], but actually it is better to have a kind of fluidity, to have the space where you can have the fluidity of just embarking on a journey with your participants on an equal level, you are going towards somewhere that you're working out with them. So, there isn't an imposition of this is the end of the road and that and that – and each step of the way is sort of just taking people with you. And it's so much more empowering sometimes for them to have to decide on the outcomes, on what they end up with and how it surprises, you know? There's a whole surprise element. So, then nothing is being done *to* them, but it is *with*.' (Belona Greenwood, 2022, Focus Group)

We have heard descriptions of restricted practice and 'bending of the rules' of funded projects to achieve a better purpose, also termed 'congruent duplicity' (Mark Richardson, 2022, Focus Group). The notion that arts work can be both dangerous and provocative in a good and creative way is one which we find quite inspiring.

Arts and empowerment

> 'In my music development work and studies in Ottawa, we talk about three aspects of citizenship in terms of aspiration – the responsible citizen, the participatory citizen and the justice-orientated citizen. The fourth and underpinning aspect is the right to well-being. I wanted to encourage this in my practice so that it not only became habit but also empowering.' (Joan Harrison, 2022, Focus Group)

> 'Social justice fires me up – people should have the freedom and the right to express themselves. I can't tell you the number of, especially women, I've worked with who believe that they have no valid story, that

they have no value, and it makes me really cross. I also come across people who actually think they have no confidence, but my God, they do. They are full of value.' (Belona Greenwood, 2022, Focus Group)

Reflecting on the quotations already presented, it is clear that the value base of the community worker is crucial to successful work in unlocking community potential and empowering individuals.

Coyle (2018) describes the importance of building a sense of belonging as an important hook in terms of collective action and cementing community activity in the world of community work.

> I'm giving you these comments because I have very high expectations and I know that you can reach them. That's it – just 19 words. None of these words contain any information on how to improve. Yet they are powerful because they deliver a burst of belonging cues. Actually, when you look more closely at the sentence it contains three separate cues:
> 1 – you are part of this group. 2 – this group is special: we have high standards here. 3 – I believe you can reach those standards. (Coyle, 2018, 56)

Arts to support social change

For the community worker, the arts are about social change as a major priority, and often we take advantage of opportunities that emerge to facilitate social change, as the following case study illustrates. It also illustrates the passion and commitment that often accompany our work.

Case study

> 'When I became a citizen in Canada the citizenship judge said, "Now everyone of you go out and do something to make a difference in your community!" And so I went to the National Arts Centre director as I had already been playing there [as a musician] and I said, "How about if I do a quilt project?" I developed

a project and it took over three years. There were eight quilt shops in the city at that time and we put out publicity that anybody could pick up a square of fabric: it came in a plastic bag with a permanent marker and some directions that you could write, draw, paint anything that you want to depict the importance of the arts in society or in education. And we ended up with so many blocks and we did it by hand and the quilts hung in the lobby of the National Arts Centre for three years.

I got the Prime Minister involved and I started calling celebrities and saying "would you be part of this?" And most of them were incredibly wonderful. Like Ben Heppner – I don't know if you know, if you're an opera fan at all ,but he's an incredible tenor – and he got his whole family involved and our Minister of Heritage got involved and prima ballerina Karen Kane. I mean it was amazing. So anyway, that's what started it. I did it as a volunteer but I kind of got addicted because of the letters that came in. People were writing saying how much it meant to them and I had thought I would have to beg people to do this! But people were writing and saying thank you because the arts has meant so much to me. One woman said that she had cancer. She was in stage four of her cancer and that she wanted to be able to say thank you to the arts for giving her pleasure at the end of her life. I still have that letter. But it was the first time I started really seeing the arts as a way to make social change.' (Joan Harrison, 2022, Focus Group)

What do successful arts-related interventions look like in community-work contexts? Mark Richardson describes how the creative process can be a planning tool:

> 'I'm just thinking about all these sort of different planning tools – frameworks for planning, workstream planning, project management documents and so on. But should the creative process itself be being advocated for, as being the appropriate and planning

tool? Or are we trying to knock square pegs into round holes here, in a sense? It seems like we're using inappropriate frameworks to capture and push through a process here. But success does need to be articulated.'
(Mark Richardson, 2022, Focus Group)

Another participant in one of our focus groups described an arts project in Ottawa, Canada, which used doormats purchased from a large supermarket to capture the words for welcome in a large number of languages, in order to support integration and to build initial relationships in a community-based project. This also highlighted the need to build trust when working with others, in particular those who may be more vulnerable, and we agreed that this could take a long time and needed to be seen as a valuable asset worth persevering for.

Where does our influence in community arts come from?

The community workers with whom we spoke highlighted the importance of nurturing our own creative forces to sustain self. We recharge our batteries in those things which feed us as human beings: in reading, watching, listening, telling, drawing, sharing and other avenues which sustain and develop us. At times, we use our personal skills and talents in vibrant ways in our workplace. An important factor is to know ourselves and our skills through self-reflection against the backdrop of the activities we work through, whatever the vehicle for delivery in our setting. We have found the self-evaluation framework *How Good Is Our Culture and Sport? 2* (Education Scotland and VoCAL, 2022) valuable in focusing attention on what is working well, what tells us this and what could be done next.

This chapter has alluded to important messages about the role of creative approaches and arts interventions in community-based work. Like the threads running through a woven blanket, they illuminate the importance of values, which chimes with all other practices described in this book. Intention is described as everything; the clarity of purpose when setting out. The validity and importance of arts work as a community engagement tool, has been emphasised. The danger of short-term funding creating pressure and untrustworthy outcomes has been raised as a flag of concern which can limit and inhibit practice. The importance of case studies to capture successful outcomes with an arts and community focus is something we would like to register in the reader's thinking. "I just thought there's one word that should always be there with community arts working anywhere, and that's *connection*. Whether it's helping people to connect with themselves or with wider society. But connection is a keyword" (Belona Greenwood, 2022, Focus Group).

We conclude with a reflection from two colleagues about the project Vox Liminis in Scotland. Vox Liminis is a community development and arts organisation working to effect change in and around the criminal justice system. William, from the Unbound Community, which is at the centre of Vox's work, relates that:

'Before I was invited to Unbound, I had never really created anything apart from learning a few chords on a guitar and practising Bob Dylan songs in my prison cell.

'The space at Unbound – and the people there, who in various ways have been involved in the criminal justice system – was vibrant, alive; there was a creative energy which thrilled me. I suddenly felt "Hey ... I have something here, there's something in me screaming to be expressed and this feels like a place it can be expressed in". But having been in prison 20 or 30 times over a period of 25 years of heroin addiction, it had been lying dormant in me, which is a horrible thing really.

'I kept writing and came up with a song called "Caged Bird" which I played and sang at the Solas Festival last June. We all performed there, and it was an amazing experience. Then it was played on BBC Radio Scotland's Roddy Hart Show along with other songs from Unbound people. Roddy called the song "Thought provoking and powerful". Amazing stuff!

I've also been going with Vox into HMP Castle Huntly to do song-writing workshops. It is a powerful experience for someone who was in prison so many times to go back in and just be there.

> All this has given me great encouragement, even though I can still only play a few chords, to start a guitar group in the town I live in. It's going great – it's a community thing and brings people together. It helps me. And hopefully other people see that, even though I was hopelessly lost. Somehow we can go beyond an old life to a new freedom ... not just getting out the prison gate but getting out of habitual ways of life that trap us.' (William Clelland and Alison Urie, 2023, the Unbound Community, Vox Liminis, www.voxliminis.co.uk)

A community that 'makes' things together can spark positive and generative change for individuals, the wider community (in Unbound, in William's town and in HMP Castle Huntly) and wider society (through radio play). We hope that this case study might provoke dialogue about our approach to social justice issues and suggest how creative approaches to community practice can help us to explore links between personal troubles and public issues.

Principles in practice

1. Understand the core purposes of organisations and individuals with whom you work in partnership, becoming familiar with the practice of others.
2. Consider the wide range of skills you have in your practice toolbox; revisit those from the perspective of community empowerment.
3. Harness opportunities for peer review across practice which includes creative and arts-based work in community settings.
4. Consider ways in which to further develop your own practice in engagement; are there ways in which creative and arts-based approaches could enhance this?
5. Look at ways in which different approaches could unlock doors with some of the more vulnerable people we work with.
6. Identify an example of success where creative and arts-related approaches have been instrumental.
7. Follow up on some of the writers referenced in this chapter; explore their thinking further.

Challenge questions

1. Reflect on creative and arts-based approaches used in your work or by colleagues you may work with. What makes them distinctive?
2. Can you think of an example where the use of creative and arts-based approaches has been successful in engaging hard-to-reach individuals/groups?
3. How do we know that creative and arts-based approaches underpin impacts that we seek?
4. Reflect upon the involvement of creative and arts-based workers/organisations in partnerships you may be involved with. Consider the impact of their interventions.
5. Do you think that there is enough emphasis on the incorporation of creative and arts-based technique and skills in training programmes for community workers?
6. How does the Vox Liminis example make you feel about the arts in community work? Why is this so?

References

Clift, S. (2012) Creative arts as a public health resource: moving from practice-based research to evidence-based practice. *Perspectives in Public Health*, 132(3): 120–7.

Clift, S. and Camic, P. (eds) (2016) *Oxford Textbook of Creative Arts, Health and Well-being*. Oxford University Press, Oxford.

Cohen, G.D., Perlstein, S., Chapline, J., Kelly, J., Firth, K.M. and Simmens, S. (2006) The impact of professionally conducted cultural programs on the physical health, mental health, and social functioning of older adults. *Gerontologist* 46(6): 726–34. DOI: 10.1093/geront/46.6.726. PMID: 17169928.

Coyle, D. (2018) *The Culture Code: The secrets of highly successful groups*. Penguin Random House, London.

Education Scotland and VoCAL (2022) Self-Evaluation Framework: How good is our culture and sport? 2. Available at: https://education.gov.scot/media/ufyd0lyg/frwk13-hgiocs-080916.pdf (Accessed: 10 October 2022).

Jeffers, A. and Moriarty, G. (2017) *Culture, Democracy and the Right to Make Art*. Edited for the British Community Arts Movement. Bloomsbury Publishing, London.

Lim, D. and Braun, A. (2008) *Neural substrates of spontaneous musical performance: an fMRI study of jazz improvisation*. PloS ONE 3(2): e1679, DOI: 10.1371/journal.pone0001679.

Matarasso, F. (1997) *Use or Ornament? The social impact of participation in the arts*. Available at: https://arestlessart.files.wordpress.com/2015/09/1997-use-or-ornament.pdf (Accessed: 23 February 2023)

McArdle, K. (2021) *I Saw How Far We've Come, in Other Ways, We Haven't: Evaluation report of Dr Hills' Casebook*. Change Minds, Norfolk, UK.

Meade, R. and Shaw, M. (2021) *Arts, Culture and Community Development*. Bristol University Press, Bristol.

Sonek, J., Rollins, J. and Graham-Pole, J. (2016) Arts in healthcare settings in the United States, in Clift, S. and Camic, P. (eds) *Oxford Textbook of Creative Arts, Health and Well-being*, Oxford University Press, Oxford.

World Health Organization (1946) *Constitution*. Available at: www.who.int/about/governance/constitution (Accessed: 23 February 2023).

15

Digital community work

Kirsty Forrester

Introduction

The world is changing significantly, with digital technology and the internet a significant part of all our lives. Worldwide, 4.65 billion people (58.7%) use social media, with 63% of the world's population using the internet; on average, adults spend almost seven hours per day online (Datareportal, 2022). In the 21st century, it is often online and in the digital space that many people find and build community. Indeed, 'few would argue that traditional, in-person, pedagogical practices are ideal for everyone' (NovoEd, 2020, 10). With so much of our lives taking place online, opportunities and community spaces in which to connect have invariably reduced. Even prior to the COVID-19 pandemic, almost half of Americans (47 per cent) said they did not have meaningful in-person social interactions on a daily basis (Cigna, 2018). Community work seeks to engage people where they are and, as practitioners who build our practice on relationships, traditionally built on the streets and in community venues, we need to consider how to use digital tools to expand our reach and support with communities, to address the barriers to their full participation. This will include 'those who may be geographically and socially isolated' (European Commission, 2018, 2), as described in the following quote.

'It's not just about access to devices or technology. It's a more complex challenge. We need to try to help people understand that it's not enough just to be able to build a Facebook post. In the 21st century there are a range of competences needed in order to be considered basically digitally competent. ... All jobs [will] require digital skills of some sort. So, we're still going to see a lot of people and face challenges in the coming years with automation and machine learning and all that kind of thing, starting to impact manual and unskilled work. It's a lot of work trying to reach those furthest behind and ensure we leave no one behind ... it's still a huge uphill battle.' (Mark Kelly, 2022, Focus Group)

Digital tools such as social media, online forms and e-mail offer a quick and easy way to target our engagements, to create rich learning experiences, increase participation, enhance community work outcomes, overcome barriers and provide high-quality data about the impact of our interventions. If our job as community workers is to work with people to enable their full participation in community, society and family life, then we must consider what our responsibility is to support them to be digital citizens, able to engage fully online with digital content and services.

In community work we often talk about our role in promoting active citizenship. In this chapter we explore our responsibility to help communities become active digital citizens. If our work is truly about addressing social exclusion, given that modern life and our participation in society requires digital competence, community workers in the 21st century must have the digital skills and knowledge to train, and proactively use digital media and technology. This will deliver better outcomes for communities, but community workers must also advocate for their own digital entitlements. To aid communities to become digitally literate, it is therefore essential that we are digitally literate ourselves. Pawluczuk et al (2019) define digital literacy 'as the ability to use information technology for both information sharing and information creation practices' (Pawluczuk et al, 2019, 59).

Digital empowerment

Case study

Sonia Garcha is a community worker supporting women entrepreneurs living in slums in Pune and Pimpri Chinchwad and 5,000 women fish vendors in Mumbai, India. Mobile data is inexpensive and affordable in India, allowing all sections of society to get online. Support from central government to link smartphone technology with financial inclusion programmes aims to ensure that no one is left behind.

Despite innovative government programmes and cutting-edge technology, Sonia says that the lack of financial, digital and basic literacy among women and limited access to mobile technology pose a major challenge and, as a result, digitisation has widened the gender gap. India's use of digital platforms for everyday tasks has meant that many women who do not have digital confidence have to rely on children or male relatives to access their children's school results, to register children for school, order gas, pay for electricity or book transport.

> 'Even when we started working in this particular area, everybody was working for digital literacy, so they said "Oh we can give you two laptops, why do you need funding for digital empowerment? What are you trying to do with phones? Let's set up a bus with multiple laptops and they can learn computers". That's not digital empowerment, right? They don't have access to that kind of technology. It was also difficult to explain to people why digital empowerment was required, because people could not understand, because they think digital empowerment is equal to digital literacy, right, which is not true.' (Sonia Garcha, 2022, Focus Group)

'DigiShakti', the digital empowerment of women, is a process designed to overcome the digital gender gap, to provide an opportunity to the women to access financial services and information and to use digital technology to improve their daily lives. Through the programme, women learn about their digital rights and safety, increase their awareness, become independent digital citizens and build community networks to share information and support each other.

> 'If you look at our community women, the bank account is in the name of the mother, but in most cases the children are operating it, because the woman fears the ATM [automatic teller machine]. We are empowering her about why it is important to track your bank account, not simply teaching her to track her bank account, so she will understand.
>
> In our training programmes we are building in these kind of checks. So, that's why I was saying that digital empowerment is very different from digital literacy, right? It's about teaching people why it matters and that it's not just about the skills.' (Sonia Garcha, 2022, Focus Group)

Since the programme was founded in 2018, Sonia and her team have trained over 200,000 women living in both urban and rural areas. During the COVID-19 pandemic, when the government used digital platforms and technology to disseminate information and distribute aid, by translating messages into their local language and using WhatsApp and text messaging (SMS), these digitally empowered women were able to share information with their communities. They could ensure that women were getting the aid to which they were entitled; those who were employed as domestic workers were able to track their wages, which had been moved online during the pandemic. Likewise, they could ensure that women were receiving government COVID-19 relief payments and could use digital payments to buy food for their families, during a time when they could not go to the bank to withdraw cash. Rural women previously had to take a day off work to walk 10–15 kilometres to go to the bank; they now were able to track their bank transactions on their smartphones. Mothers registered their mobile numbers with their schools, to receive messages about the children, and small vendors and store owners were able to use online payments, which has reportedly strengthened their businesses and increased their turnover.

All the community workers we spoke with told us that digital literacy alone was not enough to ensure active participation. We agree with Stommel (2022), who encourages educators to 'approach (digital) tools from a critical pedagogical perspective: it is as much about using digital tools thoughtfully, as it is about deciding when not to use digital tools, it is also about paying attention to the impact of digital tools on learning' (Stommel, 2022).

> 'We've created a generation of young people who are consumers of digital content and not creators and contributors of digital content. We're now moving to such a digitised society through hybrid and mobile or remote working that a lot of the jobs that are going to be created don't exist right now. So how do we prepare them? How do we use these technologies for campaigning? How do we use these in terms of true empowerment?' (Darran Gillan, 2022, Focus Group)

The questions raised by Darran Gillan in this quotation are important to us all as community workers. The idea of digital hybrid pedagogy focuses on 'digital fluency' needs rather than 'digital literacy' needs. Being fluent requires competencies and capabilities that go beyond a basic skills level. Sonia's work with disadvantaged women is an excellent example of why this matters. If a citizen is digitally literate, they can follow guidance about using a specific application, platform or program and use it effectively. If they are digitally fluent, they can seek, find and select an appropriate application, platform or program from a range of tools and can use it effectively, but can also navigate and share the outcomes collaboratively, confidently, appropriately and safely with others.

As our profession tries to establish how to develop digitally fluent citizens and explores what our role is within the digital space, theories of learning can help us better understand how knowledge is developed in the digital age. Digital learning can help learners to become independent learners, help them to develop resilience and become more self-sufficient. These are abilities which are transferable into real-world situations and, therefore, we argue that community workers should consider how digital learning can help to enhance participation.

Connectivism

In Chapter 8, on networking and partnership, we explored the importance of supporting the community to build networks. We argue, as community workers, that we must not neglect the digital space where communities spend so much of their time. Chapter 8 proposed that the strength of participants' networks is one of our strongest assets. If we are to serve vulnerable communities well, it is therefore essential, in the 21st century, that community workers build networks of connections and information online. Siemens (2005) calls such well-connected groups of people 'hubs', who are able to 'foster and maintain knowledge flow. Their interdependence results in effective knowledge flow, enabling the personal understanding of the state of activities organizationally' (Siemens, 2005, 6).

Connectivism, first introduced in 2005 by George Siemens and Stephen Downes, relies heavily on technology and building the capacity of individuals to find information and develop their own learning. It is collaborative, empowering, and it supports individual perspectives and the diversity of opinions, theoretically providing for no hierarchy in the value of knowledge. These underlying principles are congruent with community work values and it should, therefore, be of interest to the community worker. Connectivism emphasises that it is not what you know that is important, but knowing what you will need to know in the future, and having the capacity and the networks to find that information. It is up to the learner to create their own learning experience, engage in decision making and enhance their learning networks. It is our role, as educators, to support them to become active 21st-century citizens. 'When knowledge … is needed, but not known, the ability to plug into sources to meet the requirements becomes a vital skill. As knowledge continues to grow and evolve, access to what is needed is more important than what the learner currently possesses' (Siemens, 2005, 7).

Connectivism suggests that learners should combine thoughts, theories and information to build new learning. It suggests that technology is changing what, how and where we learn, with digital connectedness offering unlimited opportunities to expand and make choices about our own learning. Connectivism promotes collaboration and discussion, allowing for different viewpoints and perspectives concerning decision making, problem solving and making sense of information. Connectivism promotes learning that happens in online spaces, such as through social media, online networks, blogs or information databases.

Connectivism says that 'we can no longer personally experience and acquire learning that we need to act' (Siemens, 2005, 4). Learning is, therefore, more than our own internal construction of knowledge; rather, our external networks allow us to gain and connect information in a network, thus expanding our learning and helping us to derive our competence from forming connections (Siemens, 2005, 4). Connectivism is based on the theory that we learn when we make connections, or links, between various sources, or nodes, of information, and we continue to make and maintain connections to form knowledge.

The main principles of connectivism are:

- Learning and knowledge rests in the diversity of opinions.
- Learning is a process of connecting specialized nodes or information sources.
- Learning may reside in non-human appliances.
- Capacity to know more is more critical than what is currently known.
- Nurturing and maintaining connections is needed to facilitate continual learning.
- Ability to see connections between fields, ideas, and concepts is a core skill.
- Currency (accurate, up-to-date knowledge) is the intent of all connectivist learning activities.
- Decision-making is itself a learning process. Choosing what to learn and the meaning of incoming information is seen through the lens of a shifting reality. While there is a right answer now, it may be wrong tomorrow due to alterations

in the information climate affecting the decision. (Siemens, 2005, 5–6)

The responsibility for developing new learning lies with the learners, rather than the educator, whose job it is, instead, to help learners take control of their own learning and development.

Creating digital transformation

During the COVID-19 pandemic, the digital divide exacerbated other issues related to poverty and exclusion. Those with access to digital equipment and an internet connection were able to shop, learn and access healthcare online. Those without a device or the skills to utilise them were made more vulnerable and were further excluded, and this exclusion 'further emphasised the need for social fairness in access to lifelong learning' (European Commission/EACEA/Eurydice, 2021, 25). Even within local community work teams, digital responses can lead to further inequalities, with disjointed delivery and different tools used by different staff. Responding to learners' individual needs is important and this can be challenging for service users, who have to navigate from one platform to another.

> 'Community workers need to be empowered. They need to be told that they are the front line. They are the ones that are connecting to the furthest behind. ... We need people, the community organisations, those at the front line of this challenge to be able to be brave and provide digital literacy, digital inclusion and safe spaces for people to acquire the skills. The European Commission calls digital competence a survival skill; it is a critical life skill in the 21st century. Invariably, the community sector is where people will need to come for that support, so we must have digitally enabled workers. The skills that you have now will not be the skills you need in five years. So continuous professional development is going to be absolutely critical.' (Mark Kelly, 2022, Focus Group)

As Mark Kelly indicates in the quotation, many community workers themselves do not yet have the equipment, skills or confidence to succeed in a digital environment; they themselves need to be empowered. While our organisations have responsibility to provide devices and invest in staff and client training, we must also recognise that the onus is on us, as community workers, to recognise that promoting digital skills is not someone else's job but, rather, underpins everything that we do with communities now and in the future. We need to ensure we have 'an agile mind-set, being willing to try new things and learn from both success and failure, and [need to] be supported to do so' (Pawluczuk et al, 2019, 61).

We agree with Frankiewicz and Chamorro-Premuzic (2020), who argue that 'digital transformation is less about technology and more about people'. Mezirow's (1978) *Transformative Learning Theory*, which we discussed in Chapter 11 on adult learning, may be helpful for us as educators seeking to support communities and, even, colleagues. Our personal beliefs can limit our ability to embrace change and learn new things, by telling us that we are good at some things and not at others. By providing community work participants with a safe and supported opportunity to engage and reflect on new learning and critically analyse underlying assumptions about themselves and their ability to engage with technology, we can transform their perspectives.

> 'What happens when we have pretty much covered everything in terms of digital equality? Where, as we go on through the years, eventually everybody will pretty much have 90% equal access to connectivity and devices? It then becomes more about digital equity. It's not about everybody having a pair of trainers, but everybody having a pair of trainers that fit, because right now it's "let's get everybody out there a laptop and a Wi-Fi device and then we will teach them some digital skills and we're off to the races!" But as we start to refine these things more and more, it's about tailor-making the response and that's where you're starting to see an issue about

confidence and motivation now.' (Darran Gillan, 2022, Focus Group)

Darran Gillan describes the importance of tailor-made responses. If people develop their own responses, then those responses will likely fit better and help them to develop their capabilities. To offer a service for a digital age, we need to engage fully with all stakeholders to identify what change should look like. Community workers need to have a broad analysis of how digital transformation affects lives and an understanding of the needs of individuals, grounded within the wider social context in which communities are living and working.

The community workers in our focus group described the rapid digital transformation that took place as a result of the COVID-19 pandemic, but also a culture of risk aversion and boundaries put in place by organisations once they began to catch up. Some organisations, for example, specified that only certain digital platforms could be used, even if that platform was not what people were already using, or was unfamiliar. Unless learners in these organisations were willing to move onto these new platforms, they were sometimes excluded from the informal learning opportunities that had been such a support to them in the early days of the pandemic. "It was basically like disregarding all our community work values, our practices about meeting where people were at" (Darran Gillan, 2022, Focus Group).

The desired outcomes and underpinning value base for community work should be the same, whether online or delivered face to face, and therefore should not be considered as a separate methodology (European Commission, 2018; Pawluczuk et al, 2019). Rather, digital skills should be seen as an additional set of tools to be used. The community workers we spoke to in our focus group described the bravery of some community workers, who 'broke away' and started to explore other platforms and technologies better suited for digital community engagement. "As we started to understand these platforms better, you then started to see organisations taking it one step further, where they were not just meeting in Teams anymore or Zoom, and that was because they started to get a new language" (Darran Gillan 2022, Focus Group).

Different forms of digital learning

During the pandemic, digital conferencing platforms such as Zoom, Google-Meet and Microsoft Teams all gained a popularity in the UK, which has continued as institutions seek to rationalise the physical space they manage and increase their capacity. Many found that the experiences of online learning compounded the isolation they were already experiencing because of lockdown.

Salmon's (2014) five-stage model focuses on how we can keep participants engaged in digital experiences or online learning environments and fits well within community-work practices. The five stages, described by Salmon are:

Access and motivation: In the first stage, we focus on welcoming and encouraging learners into the digital environment. We need to consider access; do the people with whom we are working have the ability, technology and motivation to access digital learning? Often in online or digital environments this stage is forgotten, as very basic skills and confidence are assumed. Learners can disengage. Our role is to support the learner to engage, access and take the first steps on their digital journey.

Online socialisation: In the second stage, we focus on building our community, what Salmon describes as 'online socialisation or culture building' (Salmon, 2014). It is about encouraging our learners to send and receive messages and take part and navigate the digital environment. Here our role is to help our learners make connections with other learners, to communicate why we are doing what we are doing and to ensure that all their needs are met.

Information exchange: In the third stage we focus on encouraging learners to begin to exchange information with one another and practise learning. It is here that we must try to 'shift the paradigm ... from individual consumption to social participation' (NovoEd, 2020, 3).

Knowledge construction: In the fourth stage we begin to construct new knowledge with our learners and introduce an element

of challenge to digital learning. Here the community worker is less active in developing the learning; instead, the learners are beginning to function within the digital environment independently. We continue to support and provide feedback.
Development: In the fifth stage our learners reflect on their learning and begin to look towards their next steps.

Salmon's model focuses on building and maintaining connections between participants and workers, at all stages of the model, and reducing isolation, even within online learning environments. It should be of interest to community workers because of its focus on the participant experience of learning rather than ticking-off learning outcomes, which can sometimes be the case. We agree with Walker and Warner (2021, 8) that it provides 'an effective architecture for creating meaningful learning, on the proviso that learning is developed in a participatory manner with students and that outcomes are not predetermined'.

Case study

In the following example, Michael, a community worker in the US, describes how online learning has removed barriers for the adult learners with whom he was working.

> 'We just did a wave of recruitment and overwhelmingly everyone wanted online. The first year of COVID everyone was like, "I wanna get back in person", including myself. I still miss teaching in person, because there are dynamics that you can't have. But for the population of immigrant parents that we're working with, it actually has worked really, really well to the point that they desire it, because it's allowing them to learn. They have so many things going on. If they have a new-born, they can't leave the house to go to class, but now, all of a sudden, they're able to be in class. I have a lot of students who get a new job in the middle of the semester, and it used to be those students – they're gone – because they're like, "I got a job. I wanna stay, but it conflicts with time". Now I have students who

are at their job on headphones listening in. And it's not perfect, but it's something that never would have been possible.' (Michael Kengmana, 2022, Focus Group)

Digital well-being

Digital resilience is defined as an individual's ability to 'understand when one is at risk online and make informed decisions about the digital space they are in', to 'know when to seek help', to be able to 'recover when things go wrong online by receiving the appropriate level of support' and to 'learn from ... experiences and ... [be] able to adapt future choices' (UKCIS, 2019, 5). The UK Council for Internet Safety (UKCIS) say that digital resilience 'is primarily built through experience rather than learnt, fostered by opportunities to confide in trusted others and later reflect upon online challenges' (UKCIS, 2019, 6).

Making participants aware of their rights online is an important part of digital community work. The human rights approach, developed by Baroness Beeban Kidron into the *5 Rights Framework* (5 Rights, 2022), may be helpful.

The 5 Rights are:

- *The Right to Remove* 'what you yourself have put up. It doesn't challenge Freedom of Speech, but the first rule of conscious use is being able to control what your history will look like online, in the space you curate'.
- *The Right to Know* 'who and what and why and for what purposes, your data is being exchanged. And a meaningful choice about whether to engage in that exchange'.
- *The Right to Safety and Support.* This right includes protection from illegal practices, but also acknowledges that what can be upsetting online is often not illegal and that 'support is sparse, fragmented and largely invisible to those ... when they need it most'.
- *The Right to Informed and Conscious Use.* This right says that people 'should be empowered to reach

into creative places online, but at the same time have the capacity and support to easily disengage.
- *The Right to Digital Literacy.* 'To access the knowledge that the internet can deliver, [people] need to be taught the skills to use, create and critique digital technologies, and given the tools to negotiate changing social norms.' (5Rights, 2022)

As workers and organisations, we need to apply a digital rights-based approach to our work with communities. We can use it as a tool to assess how we are doing and where we need to make progress. We have a responsibility to the communities we serve to ensure they can realise all of their rights.

We would like to finish this chapter with the wisdom of the community workers with whom we spoke in preparing this chapter.

> 'We have to remember that we have to go to the space the learner is at and that doesn't change. It will evolve, but it doesn't change our core objective of trying to facilitate where they are and understand where they're at and respond to them in a way that is useful, effective and supports. Our core mission is about the furthest-behind first; making sure that how we respond … is continuing to evolve. We can't just stick-in in terms of the practice we have done or the way things used to be done. Our continuous professional development and being responsive, changing people from digital consumers to digital creators, is our huge objective over the next decade … [we need to] remain committed to the furthest-behind first, but really understand where the people are at and be responsive to them. And again, it's the confidence piece, it is being able to ensure people have at least the basic competences in order to be digitally active and included. It's still a very complex task and there's a lot of work still to be done.' (Mark Kelly, 2022, Focus Group)

'This is here to stay, we're not going to be able to wish it away. We have to look at the horizon. We have to prepare our communities, prepare our community workers.' (Sonia Garcha, 2022, Focus Group)

Principles in practice

1. Community work seeks to support individuals and communities to manage change, and digital transformation is undoubtedly the biggest change affecting society. Think about your responsibilities in this regard to the communities with which you are working.
2. Rather than digital skills, focus on digital empowerment; that is, helping communities to understand when and why they should use digital tools and how to find information if they do not already have it.
3. In an ever-changing world, often we will be finding out together. As community workers we can provide the resources to do this. By involving communities as partners in our digital learning journey, our practice will be more authentic.
4. Ensure that your work seeks to help communities realise their digital rights.
5. Remember that literacy needs can be masked through online communication such as social media; this can then become a barrier to further learning, although digital tools can help alleviate problems.
6. Do not assume any level of digital skill when working with communities.

Challenge questions

1. Our field of practice seeks to reduce barriers to individuals' full participation in family, community and society – how does your practice seek to overcome barriers arising from an increasingly digital age?
2. How can you employ digital approaches to enhance your practice and expand your reach?
3. How can you use digital tools and assistive technologies to promote inclusion?

4. What could you do to upskill, so that you can better support the communities with which you are working in this regard?
5. What is your opinion of Sonia Garcha's case study? Was this good work, and if so, why?

References

5rights (2022) *The 5Rights Framework*. Available at: https://5rightsframework.com/ (Accessed: 13 November 2022).

Cigna (2018) *Cigna 2018 U.S. Loneliness Index*. Available at: www.cigna.com/assets/docs/newsroom/loneliness-survey-2018-updated-fact-sheet.pdf (Accessed: 26 October 2022).

Datareportal (2022) *Digital 2022 April Global Statshot Report*. Available at: https://datareportal.com/reports/digital-2022-april-global-statshot (Accessed: 26 October 2022).

European Commission (2018) *European Guidelines for Digital Youth Work*. Available at: www.digitalyouthwork.eu/wp-content/uploads/2019/09/european-guidelines-for-digital-youth-work-web.pdf (Accessed: 26 July 2022).

European Commission/EACEA/Eurydice (2021) *Adult Education and Training in Europe: Building inclusive pathways to skills and qualifications*. Eurydice Report. Publications Office of the European Union, Luxembourg. Available at: https://data.europa.eu/doi/10.2797/898965 (Accessed: 6 March 2022).

Frankiewicz, B. and Chamorro-Premuzic, T. (2020) Digital transformation is about talent, not technology. *Harvard Business Review*. Available at: https://hbr.org/2020/05/digital-transformation-is-about-talent-not-technology (Accessed: 23 February 2023).

Mezirow, J. (2018 [1978]) Transformative learning theory. In *Contemporary Theories of Learning*. Routledge. London, pp 114–28.

NovoEd (2020) *The Guide to Design for Learning: Overcoming digital fatigue and creating engagement*. NovoEd, Inc, San Francisco, CA.

Pawluczuk, A., Webster, G., Smith, C. and Hall, H. (2019) The social impact of digital youth work: what are we looking for? *Media and Communication* 7(2): 59–68.

Salmon, G. (2014) *Scaffolding for Learning*. Available at: https://youtu.be/4pKsZ6dVhlI (Accessed: 11 November 2022).

Siemens, G. (2005) Connectivism: a learning theory for the digital age. *International Journal of Instructional Technology and Distance Learning (ITDL)*, January. Pittsburgh, Duquesne University, USA. Available at: https://jotamac.typepad.com/jotamacs_weblog/files/Connectivism.pdf (Accessed: 5 December 2022).

Stommel, J. (2022) *What Is Digital Pedagogy?* Available at: https://hybridpedagogy.org/tag/what-is-digital-pedagogy/ (Accessed: 13 November 2022).

UKCIS (UK Council for Internet Safety) (2019) *The Digital Resilience Framework*. Available at: www.drwg.org.uk/the-framework (Accessed: 13 November 2022).

Walker, J. and Warner, D. (2021) Transformative digital communities through participatory pedagogy. Conference paper. International Conference for Media in Education (ICoME), August. Available at: www.researchgate.net/publication/354552492_Transformative_Digital_Communities_through_Participatory_Pedagogy (Accessed: 26 July 2022).

16

Community research

Karen McArdle

'I was probably apprehensive at the start. I think because we were new workers going into an area where there was a history of a kind of lack of engagement; a sense of a community that had been neglected and abandoned; that priorities had always lain elsewhere apart from that community. And then to come in with something that's a bit different, that's involved in using video cameras and getting people to really trust us and open up, I was kind of apprehensive "Is this going to work? Are we actually going to be able to build the relationships quickly enough that are going to allow people to trust us and kind of go through this process with us?" And so that was just a learning curve because I really didn't know how that was going to go.

'I think typically and historically, if we were asked to go and consult on an issue around why poverty persists, it would have probably been a lot more traditional methods used, purely around questionnaires and focus groups, without maybe having that more robust kind of creative way of actually capturing what people are saying. So, I think we do have experience about that. But I think what came out of it just felt like this was something different, even to us who were community engagement workers, it just feels, it just feels meaningful.

It was a process, and it took months. We are just at the end of it now and it started in the summer, we're talking six months. I think it was about giving yourself time, you know, and permission to take the time, to really explore it. Whereas before, you know, we might say right, we'll have a one-off session or we'll do a one-off consultation event about an issue or a theme and that would kind of be the stop and start of it, but this has just been a much more kind of flowing process where there's been different parts of that and it's been allowed to go back and sense-check and revisit and change how we were asking people things as we're learning more as we go. So, I think that's been something that's probably been different about it and something that, you know, going forward I think giving us that, that's maybe something I would take, would give ourselves permission to actually take the time to explore things in more detail. And using different ways of doing it as well.

I think that the crux of the whole thing is that, is that participant voice, that's the difference, that's why we are invited to all these conferences, now the government are interested, funders are interested and it's not because of what's been written, it's because of what's been said by people living there. And I think that's a really important part of this, because it's like when it comes to what next, what do we do next with this? That's the greatest tool that we've got in terms of driving change in terms of engaging with funders, in terms of engaging with other services.

And people have been involved; I think what's been good about it is that people have been able to be involved in small parts or have more involvement, you know, more significant involvement with it. Some people have just, you know, have just taken photos and that was the extent of their involvement, or some people have done an interview. Some people have been part of the process right through and the filming and being part of the filming events and kind of engaging with services.

And I think that's definitely something that the team feel: that there's a danger that this is just held up as something that's a really good piece of work, but actually, if nothing happens with it, if we don't do anything with it, then it's not really achieved anything other than, you know, participation. And so, I think there's a sense of, yeah, responsibility, and going forward, think there's and ... always a sense of expectation, I think, because we value it so much, we think there's going to be change on the back of this.' (Alan Gunn, 2022, Interview)

Introduction

In the quotation that opens this chapter, Alan Gunn reports on an action research project which was participatory and used filming to engage people in the research process. It is clear from his description that the project was dynamic and mattered because the participants' voices were being heard. It is this approach to research that we value highly in our practice.

This chapter focuses on only two approaches to research in the community. These are narrative inquiry and action research, the latter including participatory action research (PAR). These have been selected as they are considered by the authors to be of most use to practitioners, as both are consistent with the values of community work (see Chapter 2). Also, in the case of action research, it has a developmental and change focus as well as one of inquiry. We can provide only an introduction to the two approaches here. Further reading is required if they are new to you and you decide to use them. Here we just hope to whet your appetite for research.

Research in the community is frequently closely linked to community engagement (see Chapter 7), with needs assessment and consultation being important dimensions. Getting to know your community is important as the first step towards finding the community you wish to research; understanding, for example, the community's demographic but also social, economic and political features or trends and, of course, key relationships in the community (Tinglin and Joyette, 2020). Building relationships is important to both narrative inquiry and action research, which seek to work with people at a deeper level than, say, being respondents in interviews or questionnaires. It is important to build trust, share power and control and create reciprocity (Tinglin and Joyette, 2020).

Finding a suitable space and time for conducting your research is important so as to make it accessible for participants, as it can often be a 'big ask' to get people involved in research. Finally in engagement, Tinglin and Joyette (2020) discuss equity, and this is of significance in both research and engagement to ensure a good sample and effective participation in your research. It is about diversity and avoiding tokenism in participation by avoiding unilateralism and by adopting engagement processes relevant to different segments of the community.

Narrative inquiry

People are storytellers by nature, we suggest. Stories provide coherence and continuity to an individual's experience and have a central role in our communication with others (Lieblich et al, 1998). Stories assist us to explore and understand the inner world of the individual and his or her identity. Narrative inquiry looks at the past (the story); the present (how it is framed now) and the future (what this means for future identity and behaviour). It is not the same as interviewing people; rather, it sees people as individual case studies of self-narrative. We know or discover ourselves and reveal ourselves to others by the stories we tell (Lieblich et al, 1998).

> People shape their daily lives by stories of who they and others are and as they interpret their past in terms of these stories. Story, in the current idiom, is a portal through which a person enters the world and by which their experience of the world is interpreted and made personally meaningful. Narrative inquiry, the study of experience as story, then, is first and foremost a way of thinking about experience. Narrative inquiry as a methodology entails a view of the phenomenon. To use narrative inquiry methodology is to adopt a

> particular view of experience as phenomenon under study. (Connelly and Clandinin, 2006, 479)

The usual interview, in which a person asks another person questions, is replaced in narrative inquiry by active participation of two people who co-construct a narrative and the meaning behind it. We aim in narrative inquiry to get detailed case-study accounts of life rather than brief answers to pre-set questions. Narrative inquiry's main strength, in our opinion, is that it does not frame with a set of questions the answers that the individual will provide. Nor does it frame directly what they will be thinking about when they answer. The participant decides what is worth talking about. If you are discussing an adult learning event, for example, and you ask a question about confidence building, you are framing what the person will mention or think about. If, on the other hand, you ask them to tell you about the first time they heard about the event, and then prompt and probe until they tell you what it meant for them, you will find out about what the impact of the event was. It is quite common to conduct a narrative interview with only one question, which invites a story to be told.

Case study

> Karen was asked to do research on the impact of COVID-19 in a local government area to identify what was needed to support people post the COVID-19 pandemic. She chose to start with the invitation, 'Can you tell me about the first time you heard about the COVID virus?' She then prompted people to talk about their experiences of COVID-19 and lockdown by simply asking them to say what happened next. She chose not to ask about mental and physical health or social well-being, even though this was her interest, but all participants talked about these topics. They talked about the past and their experience of COVID-19, how they felt now, and from this Karen could deduce how they would feel if the virus were to re-emerge and how they were likely to cope in the future. All the issues raised were from the participants. No prejudged

issues were imposed on the participants. The purpose was to get detailed accounts, not brief answers.

When conducting narrative interviews, it is a much more natural conversation than the more traditional, brief, predetermined questions followed by equally brief sometimes anodyne answers. Interviews have implicit rules, such as turn taking; only one person asking; and only one person answering; sticking to the point; and not speaking for too long. Instead, we aim for a dialogue, in which the participant becomes at ease and tells us about an experience and all that goes with it, including emotions, feelings and sense of self, along with the meanings the individual has made of the experience. Often artefacts can be used to prompt memories, such as asking people to draw pictures or the researcher providing pictures to prompt memories. Narrative inquiry is a highly accessible way of interviewing people, in that it is more natural than a traditional research interview and people generally find it easy to tell stories of their own experience.

> As we enter into narrative inquiry relationships, we begin the ongoing negotiations that are part of engaging in a narrative inquiry. We negotiate relationships, research purposes, transitions, as well as how we are going to be useful in those relationships. These negotiations occur moment by moment, within each encounter, sometimes in ways that we are not awake to. The negotiations also occur in intentional, wide awake ways as we work with our participants throughout the inquiry. (Clandinin, 2006, 47).

It is important to think about the audience for the narrative. People turn to narrative to remember, justify, argue, persuade, engage, entertain and even mislead an audience (Riessman, 2008). There is also the question of the truth of what is said. Stories can change over time and be embellished or toned down, but we would argue that they are still true. At the time of a serious accident, for example, a person may tell what happened with sharpness of detail and emotions of fear and distress. Later the story may become one of relief at recovery and be less accurate, but both, we argue, are true at the time of telling. Accordingly, when analysing data, you need to have been responsive to the demeanour and perceived intentions of your participant and need to consider if your own demeanour and characteristics affected the process. Did your own gender or age or background affect the story told?

As narrative studies are usually case studies, they can be conducted with smaller samples than other forms of interview inquiry. As case studies, it is usual when reporting to include lengthy quotations so that the person who has given the case study is not lost in snippets of their experience.

Participatory action research (PAR)

'Action Research is universally acknowledged as about change, collaborative and democratic practices, and a commitment towards humans' and other entities' well-being, including animals and the living planet' (McNiff, 2014, 14). McNiff goes on to say that the fact that action research is about collaborative and democratic practices makes it political. It is also about change to the status quo, which is why we propose that it is so relevant to community work. McNiff (2014) also describes how it is self-reflective and is goal orientated towards social action and is both evolutionary and transformational. All these characteristics of action research make it relevant to community work, we suggest.

Participatory researchers have in common the desire to leverage knowledge in a participatory way to support meaningful change (Ortiz Aragon and Brydon-Miller, (2022). Ortiz Aragon and Brydon-Miller suggest, drawing on Stringer and Ortiz Aragon (2021), that there are three core elements in action research:

learning through and for action;
action informed by learning;
participation by those who know, that is, knowledge or experience owners.

Acting to learn and learning to act are at the core of all action research cycles of inquiry. Ortiz Aragon and Brydon-Miller state that action researchers believe traditional researchers and academics do not take enough action and practitioners do not do enough reflection and leveraging of knowledge. This may result in the dilemma of the ungrounded academic versus the unthinking practitioner (Reeler, 2007).

PAR is not just doing research projects as a practitioner. It is more a philosophical stance that enables people to question and improve taken-for-granted ways of thinking and acting (McNiff and Whitehead, 2009). Doing action research involves several things:

1. Taking action: what you do in your practice to improve something.
2. Doing research: how you find out about and analyse what you do in practice, to see.
3. Telling the story and sharing your findings: telling others what you have done and how you have done it and why it is important. You make a claim to knowledge that you have done or learned something that has influenced processes of improvement. (McNiff and Whitehead, 2009, 11)

There are many perspectives on PAR. It has no single inventor; rather, it was the result of a clash between traditional scientific explanations and rough reality (Swantz, 2008). Action research traditionally follows cycles of action and reflection. Cycles of inquiry may be multiple, interrelated and frequently last beyond the course of an inquiry, as the development work that goes with the inquiry is often long standing.

Case study

Kirsty and Karen were involved in a participatory action research project, which explored ways in which communication between the police force in Scotland and Black, Asian and minority ethnic (BAME) communities could be improved. We undertook three cycles of inquiry, engaging police officers as co-inquirers in the action research with us.

Cycle One was primarily about engagement with BAME communities, benchmarking their understanding of the role of the police and raising issues from life stories. We explored previous experiences of crime, policing and barriers to communication and how to tackle these barriers. Meetings with the BAME participants took place over lunch or dinner, because of the social importance of food as a bridge for the initiation and development of relationships.

In Cycle Two, three focus groups were held; one with community workers; one with co-inquiring police officers; and one with the project's Steering Group, which included senior police officers, to assist with data analysis; to process experiences of the project; and to triangulate data.

In Cycle Three, exemplar information films and flyers were developed. This cycle of inquiry sought the opinion of three groups of BAME community members and police officers on these materials, as exemplars for Police Scotland on how the research findings might influence practice. The notion of developing films was derived from the findings of Cycles One and Two, in an iterative process – a characteristic of action research, whereby impact exists beyond the bounds and conclusion of any project.

The case study shows how the processes of PAR can be implemented. The criteria selected for validity are important in PAR. Swantz (2008) quotes Moser (1975), saying the first criterion is transparency, that is, all participants are able to trace the process of the PAR, its functions, aims and methods. The second criterion is compatibility of the aims with the methods and means by which the aims are reached. We would add to this, congruence of values of the domain of practice and the methods used. Third, the participatory researcher should be able to claim that they know the situation better than any outside observer and that they have honestly set out all the aspects of the PAR they had become aware of.

Narrative and participatory action research

Wheeler and Bivens (2022) discuss storytelling as participatory research. They discuss how storytelling shifts the action and knowledge discussion in two ways. Firstly, storytelling moves away from seeing action and knowing as separate and it encourages us to work at the intersection of these. Also, storytelling challenges the distinction between personal and political forms of knowing and action. It prompts us to think how action may be taken to change wider systems and structures derived from individual experience (Wheeler and Bivens, 2022).

Ethics

We cannot discuss research without reference to ethics. Ethical guidelines usually refer to avoidance of harm; no deception; informed consent; and unrecognisability and confidentiality. If you are using PAR, then thinking differently and more broadly is important. Durham University (2022) has published an excellent guide to community-based participatory research (CBPR). They cite the ethical principles in Table 16.1, pointing out that this is not an exhaustive list.

Kemmis and McTaggart (2000) argue how practice may be viewed as either objective (an outsider's view) or subjective (a participant's view), or indeed dialectically in terms of both. Accordingly, dialectically means an attempt to understand practice in terms of the mutual-constitution, tensions and connections between the outside and inside; between researcher and participant (Kemmis, 2008). In action research and in the social and educational domains, we are normally concerned not only with practices as the behaviour or intentional actions of individuals, but also with the ways those practices are socially constructed by systems and policies that precede and shape the conduct of practice/praxis.

As community workers we have usually learned significantly about our practice and about our local communities. Engaging in community research is to engage in active learning and reflection to deepen, or even to begin, this process of inquiry, and it is in our opinion an exciting way to experience praxis.

Principles in practice

1. When selecting methods, do a lot of reading about research to ensure your approach and methods are consistent with the values

of community work, as expressed by professional bodies such as International Association for Community Development (IACD).
2. Consider how you will engage with participants who may become co-inquirers or the sample of participants with whom you will work.
3. If using narrative inquiry, consider how you will conduct a natural conversion without asking leading questions that frame the answers for participants.
4. Consider how you will assess the 'truth' or authenticity of the story if you are using narrative inquiry.
5. Think about how your characteristics (gender, age, ethnicity and so on) will affect a narrative inquiry interview.
6. If you are doing PAR, think about how you will plan your cycles of inquiry, but be aware that these are emergent and build on each other as the research proceeds.
7. Read the chapter on participation (Chapter 5) and think about how this applies to your action research.
8. Think about both the personal and political in both narrative inquiry and PAR, thinking about the individual and systems and structures.
9. Consider the ethical principles that will apply to your research and make sure these are accounted for in your process.

Table 16.1: Community based participatory research: a guide to principles and practice

---

1. **Mutual respect:** developing research relationships based on mutual respect, including a commitment to:
    - agreeing what counts as mutual respect in particular contexts;
    - everyone involved being prepared to listen to the voices of others;
    - accepting that people have diverse perspectives, different forms of expertise and ways of knowing that may be equally valuable in the research process.
2. **Equity and inclusion:** encouraging and enabling people from a range of backgrounds and identities (for example, ethnicity, faith, class, education, gender, sexual orientation, (dis)ability, age to lead, design and take part in the research, including a commitment to:
    - seeking actively to include people whose voices are often ignored;
    - challenging discriminatory and oppressive attitudes and behaviours;
    - ensuring information, venues and formats for meetings are accessible to all.

Table 16.1: Community Based Participatory Research: a guide to principles and practice (continued)

3. **Democratic participation:** encouraging and enabling those involved in the research to contribute meaningfully to decision-making and other aspects of the research process according to skill, interest and collective need, including a commitment to:
    - acknowledging and discussing differences in the status and power of people involved in the research and working towards sharing power more equally;
    - communicating in language everyone can understand, including arranging translation or interpretation if required;
    - using participatory research methods that build on, share and develop different skills and expertise.
4. **Active learning:** seeing research collaboration and the process of research as providing opportunities to learn from each other, including a commitment to:
    - ensuring there is time to identify and reflect on learning during the research, and on ways people learn, both together and individually;
    - offering all those involved the chance to learn from each other and share their learning with wider audiences;
    - sharing responsibility for interpreting the research findings and their implications for practice.
5. **Making a difference:** promoting research that creates positive change for communities of place, interest or identity, including by:
    - engaging in debates about what counts as 'positive' change, including broader environmental sustainability as well as human needs or spiritual development, and being open to the possibility of not knowing in advance what making a 'positive difference' might mean;
    - valuing the learning and other benefits for individuals and groups from the research process as well as the outputs and outcomes of the research;
    - building a goal of positive change into every stage of the research.
6. **Collective action:** individuals and groups working together to achieve change through the research, including a commitment to:
    - identifying common and complementary goals that meet partners' differing needs for the research;
    - working for agreed visions of how to share knowledge and power more equitably and promote social change and social justice;
    - recognising and working with conflicting rights and interests expressed by different interest groups, communities of practice or place.
7. **Personal integrity:** people conducting the research behaving reliably, honestly and in a transparent and trustworthy fashion, including a commitment to:
    - working within the principles of CBPR;
    - ensuring accurate and honest analysis and reporting of research;
    - being open to challenge and change, recognising and reflecting on one's own privileges and prejudices and being flexible and prepared to work with conflict.

(Durham University, 2022, 10–11)

Challenge questions

1. When thinking about research approaches and methods, do you take into account the values that underpin your work and choose consistent methods?
2. When undertaking research or evaluation do you consider the best ways to engage your participants, so they have genuine power in the processes you are using?
3. When conducting interviews do you consider the impact you are having on the participants' answers, from the method you are using to frame the answers, to your own character and profile as the interviewer?
4. Critical reflection is crucial to PAR. How will you manage this?
5. When doing research or evaluation do you routinely think of the impact on systems and structures, as well as the individual perspective?
6. Thinking about Karen's research post COVID-19, have you ever done anything similar? If so, what were the outcomes and was the research framed by you or the participants?

References

Clandinin, D.J. (2006) Narrative inquiry: a methodology for studying lived experience. *Research Studies in Music Education* 27: 44–54.

Connelly, F.M. and Clandinin, D.J. (2006) Narrative inquiry. In J.L. Green, G. Camilli and P. Elmore (eds) *Handbook of Complementary Methods in Education Research*, 3rd edn. Lawrence Erlbaum, Mahwah, NJ, pp 477–87.

Durham University (2022) *Community-based Participatory Research: A guide to ethical principles and practice*, 2nd edn. Centre for Social Justice and Community Action, Durham. Available at: www.durham.ac.uk/media/durham-university/departments-/sociology/Ethical-guidance,-final-version,-Dec-2022.pdf (Accessed: 16 July 2023).

Kemmis, S. (2008) Critical theory in participatory action research. In P. Reason and H. Bradbury (eds) *The Sage Handbook Book of Action Research*, 2nd edn. Sage, London.

Kemmis, S. and McTaggart, R. (2000) Participatory action research. In. N. Denzin and Y. Lincoln (eds) *Handbook of Qualitative Research*, 2nd edn. Sage, Thousand Oaks, CA, pp 567–605.

Lieblich, A., Tuval-Mashiach, R. and Zilber, T. (1998) *Narrative Research: Reading, Analysis, and Interpretation*, Vol. 47. Sage, London.

McNiff, J. (2014) *Writing and Doing Action Research*. Sage, London.

McNiff, J. and Whitehead, J. (2009) *Doing and Writing Action Research*. Sage, London.

Moser, H. (1975) *Aktions forschung als kritische Theorie der Sozialwissenschaft*. Kos Verlag, Munich.

Ortiz Aragon, A. and Brydon-Miller, M. (2022) Section introduction: Show me the action! Understanding action as a way of knowing in participatory research. In D. Burns, J. Howard and S.M. Ospina (eds) *The SAGE Handbook of Participatory Research and Inquiry*. Sage, London.

Reeler, D. (2007) *A Three-fold Theory of Social Change and Implications for Practice, Planning, Monitoring and Evaluation*. The Community Development Resource Association, Cape Town.

Riessman, C.K. (2008) *Narrative Methods for the Human Sciences*. Sage, Thousand Oaks, CA.

Stringer, E. and Ortiz Aragon, A. (2021) *Action Research*, 5th edn. Sage, Thousand Oaks, CA.

Swantz, M.L. (2008) Participatory action research as practice. In *The Sage Handbook of Action Research: Participative inquiry and practice*. Sage, London, pp 31–48.

Tinglin, W. and Joyette, D. (2020) *Community Engagement in a Changing Social Landscape*. Friesen Press, Vancouver, BC.

Wheeler, J. and Bivens, F. (2022) Storytelling as participatory research. In D. Burns, J. Howard, and S. Ospina (eds) (2022) *The Sage Handbook of Participatory Research and Inquiry*. Sage, London, pp 649–62.

17

Leadership in community work

Kirsty Forrester and Sue Briggs

Introduction

Our starting point in this chapter is a question: who are the leaders when we consider community work practice; and this is followed by a second important question: where are they? We argue that they are at all levels in our work. Every community worker provides a leadership role at some level and function of society and the organisation. Leadership as a subject and a focus is important in the challenging world of tackling poverty, of seeking social justice and of harnessing learning to effect change.

We would argue that such a world of practice requires courage and values in action and that leadership needs to be seen, at all levels, to succeed; essentially, in public and voluntary sector organisations, in higher and further education institutions, in government, in community-based endeavours. Some of the most enduring and admirable leadership qualities encountered by the authors have been in community-based practice and by those in voluntary roles.

Transformational leadership

> 'Leadership shows up at all these different levels, and in some cases you are the leader; in another case, somebody else is. I had this wonderful mentor and he said "You know, if you're going on a trek but if you don't know

how to read a map, you're going to talk to the guy with a map behind you, and that person's going to become the leader. And then when it comes time to eat, the person who can cook is going to be the person who takes the lead". So, this idea of always kind of moving to the head of the line, depending on what was needed. So, leadership has to do with what the challenge is, you know?' (Lynn Clark, 2022, Focus Group)

This focus group quotation illustrates how we all have the potential to take the lead at different times in our career. The authors believe that many of the best leaders see themselves not as experts but as facilitators who can motivate others and develop talent within a team. This resonates with the concept of transformational leadership, a leadership approach defined by James MacGregor Burns in 1978. 'The result of transformational leadership is a relationship of mutual stimulation and elevation that converts followers into leaders and may convert leaders into moral agents' (Burns, 1978, 40). Burns (1978) describes how leaders can shape, alter and elevate the motives, value and goals of followers through the vital teaching role of leadership. This, he asserts, is transforming leadership; it is concerned with end values such as liberty, justice and equality. Transforming leaders raise their followers up through levels of morality. The following quotation illustrates the importance of trust in leadership.

'I think it's about trust and promoting their ownership. Being new to being a manager, you know, I tend to step in quite a bit and try and sort things and, sometimes, that can be the easier option, just sorting it out, especially if they find things difficult, but I think taking the time to support them to look at solutions themselves and kind of trusting themselves a bit.' (Alan Gunn, 2022, Interview)

Ethical leaders

Ethical leaders live and work to achieve the common good. Their practice is underpinned by a set of principles and values, such as integrity, respect, trust, fairness, transparency and honesty. As a value-based profession, ethical leadership should therefore be the norm for community work practitioners. Our work should inspire those around us to behave ethically but, on a personal level, it should improve our self-esteem and sense of worth. Kathleen Johnston (Focus Group, 2022) says that good leadership is about having an emotional connection with others.

Cunliffe (2016, xvii) suggests that 'managing is a relational, reflexive and ethical activity. It is not just something one does but is more crucially who one is and how we relate to others'. This is also true of the leadership explored in this chapter, and this description acknowledges that people, relationships and critical dialogue build strength within teams and that, as leaders, we need to be aware of our wider impact, not just on the immediate task but also on a range of stakeholders.

Hadjieva (2021) suggests that 'the roles senior leaders play are many and complex, but in today's environment they all need to be able to inspire, support and lead through change and transformation'. If public services are to meet their challenges, then good leadership is vital. Leaders need to be open to new ideas and be strategic in their thinking. Youngs and Evans (2021, 211) suggest that 'Leadership rather than being a constant, is temporal in nature ... and [a] possible outcome of practice, rather than an expected prerequisite'.

Separating terminology: leadership and management

The authors recognise that leadership and management are often interrelated; however, we have chosen in this chapter to focus our attention on our particular exploration of leadership, leaving the reader to find elsewhere further detail of concepts of management. However, we find Fullan's observation worthy of attention:

> I have never been fond of distinguishing between leadership and management. They overlap and you need both qualities. But here is one difference that it makes sense to highlight: Leadership is needed for problems that do not have easy answers. The big problems of the day are complex, rife with paradoxes

and dilemmas. Yet we expect our leaders to provide solutions. We place leaders in untenable positions (or, alternatively, our system produces leaders who try to carry the day with populist, one-sided solutions that are as clear as they are over simplified). (Fullan, 2020, 1)

The future of our work in communities

The communities with whom we work and how our work is understood by stakeholders have, for many years now, been in an ongoing process of change. Migration resulting from war and climate change, the impact of fluctuating financial markets and the resulting poverty, and increasing digitisation mean the profile and needs of our clients continues to change and we must adapt our services in response. As our work is about addressing systemic issues of poverty and exclusion, promoting well-being and supporting progression into work, education, family and community life, we ask how to do that effectively in uncertain times. For too long our sector has kept doing what it always has without engaging with the future of work and education. 'Future of Work' (FoW) describes the rapidly changing environment, underpinned by exponential advances in technology, demographic and economic shifts, resulting in the need for businesses to better engage with their workers to truly understand their motivations and expectations at work' (Deloitte, 2020, 3).

Good leadership is of critical importance if our sector is to support communities to engage with an ever-changing world. Thurman (2021) says there is much to be learnt from how organisations navigated the COVID-19 pandemic.

> Changes that 'would have taken years' had suddenly become possible because of the scale and immediacy of the crisis. Organisations were forced to adapt at pace … staff were given time and permission to listen to individuals and given trust and autonomy to act flexibly and responsively according to need. And we heard about the difference that this was making for the well-being of staff and communities alike.

> However, this sudden shift in approach was only possible because organisations stopped doing certain things, and in that space allowed something else to emerge: in essence, the balance shifted to rely less on tried and trusted processes and more on the skill and intuition of people. (Thurman, 2021, 10)

Like many other sectors, we were open to new ideas and different ways of doing things and we stopped doing what we normally do, allowing time and space for new ways of working to emerge. Individual staff and teams were given room to be creative. We must ask ourselves what we can learn from this as leaders seeking to support communities and teams to move forward. It is essential to give ourselves permission to stop and ensure that as we introduce new ways of working we build strong foundations across the organisations and teams in which we are working. Kathleen Johnston (2022, Focus Group) suggests that leadership is about 'bringing people together and being clear about the direction of travel and then harnessing that collective energy and potential to drive improvement forward'. Deloitte (2020) describe this as a human-centric approach which focuses on positive employee experiences.

Against a backdrop of incessant change in our personal and professional lives and with an invisible thread of pressure and urgency, it is worth thinking about the importance of values and principles in our ways of working. Munby (2019) gives us an opportunity to think about this in his discussion of ethical leadership within school communities. His reflections are relevant to us, working in community contexts, as he advocates a focus on moral purpose and social justice. He asks us to 'be constantly aware of the power of leadership, for good or ill' (Munby, 2019, 245). He proposes that, in the style of moral compass reflection, we ask ourselves:

> What is the best recent example we have seen of our values in action?
>
> Is there anything we have seen or done recently which contradicts our values?
>
> What more could we do to use our values to promote better outcomes for all children? (Munby, 2019, 244–50)

Human-centred organisations

Community work is a field of professional practice which is underpinned by a strong value base and a commitment to ethical practice. As a sector that seeks to address inequalities and support people to make change for themselves and their communities, we should give particular notice to ethical and social perspectives of human-centred management (Burdon, 2019), considering 'the consequences of the decisions of leadership on society, both inside the company and externally including on partners, customers, investors, and the community' and making decisions 'based on personal moral codes of ethics and conduct' (Burdon, 2019).

A human-centred organisation is focused on creating better experiences for staff and the communities it serves, 'builds resilience and de-risks innovation through continuous iteration and learning, cares as much about the experience of its diverse, empowered teams as it does about its customers and intentionally, actively embeds these principles into the fabric of the organisation' (IBM, 2022).

The human-centred organisation is very focused on fulfilling its mission for the communities it serves. This focus also benefits those within the organisation: a sense of purpose is one of the most significant motivators for work (Pink, 2010) and, as community workers who are motivated by a commitment to social justice, feeling that our work is worthwhile develops a commitment which can sustain us through periods of great change and challenge. As leaders, we need to further develop this sense of purpose within teams by creating a shared understanding about priorities, moving forward.

IBM suggests that three forms of transformation are required to build human-centred organisations: they are agile transformation, design thinking and digital transformation.

Agile transformation: We feel that as a sector we often demonstrate our ability to respond quickly to emerging challenges effectively. We are good at developing new work streams and creative learning responses. But we must take care not to spread ourselves too thinly or to navigate too far from our core purpose and values as practitioners working with communities.

Indeed, understanding our purpose and being able to describe our impact well is essential if we are to address the inequality that exists within the communities in which we are working.

Design thinking: Many community workers will be familiar with outcome-focused planning models, but such models are often rigid and used as a linear process. In contrast, design thinking (Design Council, 2019) has divergent thinking built in, and when interventions seemingly don't work it is 'an opportunity to reflect and to discover new innovative ways to face the challenges ahead' (Hadjieva, 2021). Design thinking, sometimes called service design, encourages us to welcome these insights and promotes iteration. As leaders we can learn from design thinking as we seek to adapt services and ways of working for a digital age.

Digital transformation: Kane et al (2019) say that 'a leader who is not digitally literate will struggle to keep abreast of emerging trends and developments and will fail to grasp how those trends can bring new value or represent a threat to the organisation'. It is our experience that when new systems have not been implemented well, it is because managing change has been outsourced to those with no authority or understanding of the complexity of the work and the specialist needs of community-work teams. There is an onus on all of us, starting at the top, to ensure that we keep abreast of and up-skilled in, digital trends (see Chapter 15).

It is increasingly evident that relationships are at the heart of improving outcomes for organisations and improving well-being for individuals and communities. There is a growing recognition that it is often not what we do but how we do it that matters to people. For organisations of all types, approaching this understanding through the lens of kindness could radically change the things that they prioritise and the way that they operate (Thurman, 2021, 3). Carnegie UK's Kindness Leadership Network developed a set of principles that offer a framework through which to do this:

1. Listening – We will create time and space to listen, to understand what kindness means for everyone in our community.

2. Understanding – We will build a shared understanding of what kindness means within our organisations, and consider how to use recruitment, appraisal and other HR [human resources] processes to promote the types of attitudes, behaviours and culture that we want to see.
3. Permissive – We will give people in our organisations the permission to put kindness at the heart of their everyday practice, recognising that this often requires acting flexibly and responsively.
4. Systemic – We will identify where systems and processes (our own and those we work with) get in the way of kindness – and we will work collaboratively to change these.
5. Reflective – We will create time and space for reflection: to share challenges and celebrate successes, but also to reflect on how we are, because we know that a culture of kindness is built on the well-being of the people in our organisations.
6. Learning – We will develop ways to measure the difference we are making and tell an authentic story of change. (Thurman, 2021, 15)

Diversity in practice and the organisation

To address the wicked problems that community work seeks to tackle, diversity in our teams and organisations is very important. As Chambers (2009, 8) says, 'we cannot be successful – or even human – without other people. We can't grow or develop without the diversity offered by other viewpoints, other life experiences, other value systems'. Syed (2019, 23) says that 'teams that are diverse in personal experiences tend to have a richer, more nuanced understanding of their fellow human beings. They have a wider array of perspectives – fewer blind spots. They bridge between frames of reference'. By diversity we do not only mean demographic differences of age, gender, race and religion; it is also about cognitive diversity and 'differences in perspective, insights, experiences and thinking styles'. As Syed says, 'intelligence ... is built upon collective diversity ... innovation is about ... the networks that permit their recombination' (Syed, 2019, 15).

As leaders, we suggest, we should seek to bring together people from diverse backgrounds, with diverse experiences and education, and those who think differently who will challenge our perspectives, assumptions and beliefs, because when we surround ourselves with people who share the same ideas and background as ourselves we may be unaware of other ways of doing things and we may miss something important. This is called 'perspective blindness' (Syed, 2019, 21). One of our sector's greatest strengths is our workforce, and the many different routes that people have taken to become community workers provide much diversity. Diversity can enhance collective intelligence and encourage innovation and creativity. This is one of the reasons why we often have a greater impact when we work in partnership and bring together the skills and specialities of other disciplines to make an impact on the lives of the most vulnerable in our communities (see Chapter 8).

We all come to work with families, histories, cultures, interests and experiences which affect our approach to our work and how we feel about ourselves when we are at work. Many staff talk about the positive impact on relationships and the support offered by colleagues during the COVID-19 pandemic, when we shared our homes and lives with each other online in ways we had not done before. Team members thrive when allowed to approach problems differently and work towards their strengths. Acknowledging and celebrating their diversity builds the team.

Collaboration

Positive collaboration, which we discussed briefly in Chapter 8, is key to successful, ethical organisations (Collins et al, 2020). Collaboration ensures that our services are efficient and effective and our working environment is a supportive one where team members can develop their practice. In many ways collaboration is linked to leadership, with those in leadership roles creating the collaborative culture within the organisation.

According to Archer and Cameron (2013), to encourage effective collaboration, leaders need to be able to:

- build relationships
- handle conflict
- delegate responsibility when necessary.

> The need for leaders to work together across organisational and cultural divides is a growing phenomenon in all industries and is arguably even more of an imperative in the delivery of public services, particularly since the advent of the financial and economic crisis. Often the requirement is to be able to quickly mobilise a team, harnessing resources from several disciplines to find a solution. While technology helps, it is the attitude of the individuals, their willingness and ability to collaborate that determines that speed of response and the capacity to resolve the problem. (Archer and Cameron, 2013)

One of the leaders we spoke to talked about the importance of collaboration when developing organisational leadership and capacity:

> 'Do we know how to meaningfully collaborate? Do we know how to hook people in and connect with people and then build those relationships? Sometimes we assume that people know how to do that, but it is important to actually take the time to build that shared understanding of meaningful collaboration and go back to create the conditions for building collective responsibility. So, a key part of being a leader must be to pay attention to how we're collaborating and who we're collaborating with and ensuring that we are connecting and collaborating with all the different parts of the system, because if we don't, you know, it's just, it's just talking it. It doesn't actually mean that we're going to do it.' (Kathleen Johnston, 2022, Focus Group)

The Collaboration Framework designed by the Northern Alliance Improvement Collaborative, Scotland, is a tool worth sharing and allows for further attention to collaboration in practice for education (Northern Alliance Collaboration Framework, 2022). It has been designed by practitioners, managers and leaders from a range of learning-focused professional backgrounds. It provides a framework to examine the success of collaborative intentions and approaches allowing greater confidence and understanding to develop. It supports leadership in collaboration in a tangible way.

We often focus on developing collaboration between people and organisations, but according to Deloitte LLP (2020), successful outcomes depend on effective collaboration between the work that needs to be delivered, the people who actually do it and the places where work is conducted. As Kathleen Johnston said in the Focus Group, we need to be 'ensuring that we are connecting and collaborating with all the different parts of the system'. Collaboration is not just about the who and the how, but also about what and where and how all those things interact. Many of us have experienced the challenges of this type of collaboration as we try to bring community work into the digital age or navigate the COVID-19 pandemic. While the people and the work may remain the same, the places where we work, both real and virtual, may no longer work and, as leaders, we must have an awareness of the whole system and what is required for it to flourish.

Kathleen Johnston also suggested that leadership is about developing a sense of collective responsibility across the system so that it is not just about managers and strategic leaders. She says that our practice must seek to strengthen those voices of not just the learners and communities with whom we are working but the practitioners who are influencing and driving forward policy. As leaders, our role is to ensure that our policy reflects all the people in the system.

> 'I think, in the work they do, they all have to display that leadership approach and hopefully that then filters into them developing leadership approaches in the people that they are supporting as well. I don't think that always happens organically. And maybe that's something that we need to reinforce – that there can be challenges and some of those power

relationships, and power dynamics and stuff.' (Alan Gunn, 2022, Interview)

The issues that community workers seek to address are complex, systemic issues of inequality and injustice, and often we need to collaborate with colleagues across organisational and professional divides to ensure that we achieve transformational change.

> Working and leading in complex systems means that we can never fully know what the impact of an intervention in one part of the system will be on other parts, or where we can find a new connection ... there is a high level of interest and demand for our work to support the development of Collective Leadership and ... this can take many different forms.
>
> - Practices that support self-reflection – pausing, journaling
> - Understanding complexity – systems leadership, wicked issues
> - Curiosity and inquiring stance
> - Relational – listening, asking 'good' questions, building relationships, surfacing diversity, working more comfortably with emergence – not knowing, taking action in uncertainty. (Collective Leadership for Scotland, 2020)

We are mindful of the valuable links between practice and professional learning as emphasised in Chapter 1. We find Fullan and Quinn's (2016) descriptions of the links between collaboration and learning helpful:

> Improving whole systems requires that everyone shift their practice ... leaping from the current fishbowl to the new bowl of innovation requires new skill and knowledge (capacity building) but is accelerated when we combine it with deep collaborative work (finding other fish to learn and travel with on the journey). People are motivated to change through meaningful

work done in collaboration with others. If we want to shift the organisation, we need to pay attention to both the quality of the capacity building and the degree of collaborative learning. (Fullan and Quinn, 2016, 60–2)

Leadership in community contexts and developing community leaders

As community workers who seek to increase the capacity of communities to respond to future challenges and build resources, part of our role is to support and develop community leaders. Community organising (see Chapter 6) is an approach which focuses on building power by identifying and developing community leaders. We agree with Gilchrist (2019) that effective leaders can often be identified by their ability to build networks within communities.

> In community development, effective networkers exhibit many of the attributes that predict transformational leadership: self-esteem, consideration for others and intuitive thinking. They provide leadership and show entrepreneurial flair, but without (apparently) the drive for personal ambition or profit. Networkers need to be able and willing to defy conventions, break bureaucratic rules, operate effectively in unfamiliar (social) territory and establish personal connections swiftly and smoothly. (Gilchrist, 2019, 117)

Bacon (2009) provides insightful advice and thinking in relation to building leadership within communities. He talks about leading by example and encourages those who are active in communities to claim their role positively. This view was shared by volunteers involved in a successful community music festival:

> 'Leadership is important in any organisation. Leaders in community organisations are often champions of the cause and inspire action in others in the group.

They delegate tasks to individuals and recognise the importance of working together to achieve the goal. They often fulfil figurehead roles – sometimes being the public face of the organisation. Leaders are also the ones that should keep the organisation on track, nurturing the organisation's internal culture and ensuring everyone is involved.' (Martin Kasprowicz, 2023, Interview)

And, while supporting and developing community leaders can be rewarding, it can also be challenging at times, as described in the following case study. Alan leads a team of community workers in the north-east of Scotland.

'Sometimes it is about challenging leadership as well, because sometimes it can be leadership that's not inclusive. And I don't think that will be unique to any one area, I think it's probably quite a common issue when you are supporting community groups. And that's not even a criticism of individuals, but sometimes it is just about trying to really foster that sense that the things that they're doing are about the wider community and not just one particular set of people or one particular agenda. And it's really challenging, especially when, you know, you think people are giving up their own time to do these things, and we always have to be respectful of that. But I think that's something I'm learning more as I go, that there needs to be scope for being able to challenge and discuss approaches and inclusivity. And I think part of that is about an attempt to create that culture as well, that the work that you're doing together is about inequality and the way it affects the wider community. It's a silly thing, but anything that I get that's positive and that's had an impact on the wider community, I share it amongst all those volunteers and congratulate everybody for having a wider impact on the community and, you know, really try to celebrate that. (Alan Gunn, 2022, Interview)

Case study

Challenging inequality and promoting inclusion was fundamental to the practice of all the community workers with whom we have spoken in writing this book. In the following case study, Lynn Clark, an educator working in the north-east of the US, describes the steps she takes to ensure that the organisations in which she works promote inclusion and develop community leaders.

'In the US, we are really struggling with having leadership that is representative of the communities we serve and I am incredibly mindful of that as we move forward, and so we have created these leadership pipelines within organisations and so much of that is making sure that the vision is something that is really synthesised from collective expertise and lived experiences. So much of my leadership is making sure that I've got those voices in the room, whether they be stakeholders or whether they be staff or whether they be proxy representatives of communities that for whatever reason are not feeling comfortable at the table. So that goes hand in hand with accountability or responsibility. But I think that it's very important that you are not only accountable to your funders or governing organisations, but you're also accountable to those people that you serve.

So, when I think about community representation, it's really about being able to create as many access points as possible and to make sure those access points are equitable. We do a lot with parent advocates because we were working with educating parents. When we brought them in we really thought about how we could move beyond diversity to equity. From just simply having that person sitting at the table to making sure that they were talking as much as the person next to them and maybe saying very different things. And then working towards inclusion so that they really felt like they were part of planning the meeting and then belonging so that it was their table.

As we started to think about it, we went to them instead of them coming to us. And it's just those lenses that deepens my understanding and helps me check my own power at the door because, you know, we walk in with tremendous positional power, you know. I self-identify White.

We show up and it might have nothing to do with who we are, but it's how we're perceived in the communities that we're working in. So, to be able to mediate that as much as possible and then to meet our communities where they are. And then once again, having some sort of structure or framework that's going to help you to neutralise some of the power relations that are already in the room.' (Lynn Clark, 2022, Focus Group)

In this chapter we have confronted some of the challenges and interpretations around the concept of leaders and leadership; this has to be resolved by the individual themselves, wherever they are positioned in their organisation and whether a paid worker or volunteer organiser. The authors of this book strongly believe that workers in community contexts are *all* capable of influential and appropriate leadership activity if they unlock this potential.

We share this reflection: best practice is not a full stop; best practice is the current best practice until someone comes up with something better. We must, as practitioners and leaders, embrace change, even if we find it difficult. Our work should constantly be evolving, breaking boundaries and testing new ideas. Individuals, communities and indeed society depend on this.

Principles in practice

1. Ensure that you are clear about your organisation's mission and the purpose of your intervention.
2. In your practice ensure that you invite, consider and seek to understand new ideas and ways of working.
3. Use reflection well to ensure that we build our own leadership qualities and practice.

4. Work with others to strengthen the leadership practice of those around you, including clients, learners, participants and community groups.
5. Consider with care the role which leadership plays in building capacity to improve services and activity, including within communities themselves.
6. Participate as fully as possible in both supporting and challenging change.
7. Explore the nuances and differences between leadership and management in your role.
8. Be sure to recognise yourself as a learner in leadership contexts. There is always much to learn in this regard.

Challenge questions

1. What do users, customers and the community say about your organisation? What do employees and shareholders say about your organisation?
2. How has your organisation's purpose changed over the years? What triggered those changes?
3. To what extent does leadership run through our organisations and practice?
4. Why and how do we value leadership in our operating contexts? How does leadership feature when working in community settings?
5. Why is leadership important in our everyday practice? What barriers can there be?
6. How effective are we in identifying and responding to new and emerging needs? How well do we take others along with us in improvement action?
7. How well do we attend to our own learning needs in relation to good leadership practice?
8. How equipped are we to respond to changing policy or guidance? How well do we respond to and meet new and rapid societal, legislative and community-based changes?

References

Archer, D. and Cameron, A. (2013) *Collaborative Leadership: Building relationships, handling conflict and sharing control*, 2nd edn. Routledge, London.

Bacon, J. (2009) *The Art of Community*. O'Reilly Media Inc, Sebastopol, CA.

Burdon, M. (2019) The rise of human-centred management. *Business Relationship Management Institute*. Available at: https://brm.institute/rise-human-centered-management/ (Accessed: 18 September 2021).

Burns, J.M. (1978) *Leadership*. Harper and Row, New York.

Chambers, E.T. (2009) *The Power of Relational Action*. ACTA, Skokie, IL. Available at: Collective-Leadership-Brochure-2020_Re-Design_Final-Edits.pdf (Accessed: 18 February 2023).

Collins, H. et al (2020) *Collaboration in Action (2)* (Step 2.14). BZFM802: Management of Change: Organisation Development and Design. Available at: www.futurelearn.com/courses/management-of-change-organisation-development-design/1/steps/1185807 (Accessed: 17 September 2021).

Cunliffe, A.L. (2016) *A Very Short, Fairly Interesting and Reasonably Cheap Book about Management*. SAGE, Thousand Oaks, CA.

Deloitte LLP (2020) *The Future of Work: A perfect opportunity for global mobility*. Available at: https://www2.deloitte.com/content/dam/Deloitte/uk/Documents/tax/deloitte-uk-the--future-of-work.pdf (Accessed: 17 September 2021).

The Design Council (2019) *Framework for Innovation*. Available at: www.designcouncil.org.uk/sites/default/files/asset/document/Double%20Diamond%20Model%202019.pdf (Accessed: 18 September 2021)

Fullan, M. (2020) *Leading in a Culture of Change*, 2nd edn. Jossey-Bass, New Jersey.

Fullan, M. and Quinn, J. (2016) *Coherence: The right drivers in action for schools, districts and systems*. CORWIN California and Ontario Principals' Council.

Gilchrist, A. (2019) *The Well-connected Community: A networking approach to community development*, 2nd edn. Policy Press, Bristol.

Hadjieva, J. (2021) *Leading through Transformation: What can business leaders learn from competitive sport?* Deloitte. Available at: https://www2.deloitte.com/uk/en/blog/future-of-work/2021/leading-through-transformation-what-can-business-leaders-learn-from-competitive-sport.html (Accessed: 17 September 2021).

International Business Machines (IBM) (2022) *Building a Human Centred Organisation*. IBM. Available at: www.ibm.com/design/thinking/page/hco (Accessed: 2 January 2023).

Kane, G.C., Nguyen Phillips, A., Copulsky, J. and Andrus, G. (2019) How digital leadership is(n't) different, *MIT Sloan Management Review* 60(3): 34–9. Available at: https://sloanreview.mit.edu/article/how-digital-leadership-isnt-different/ (Accessed: 18 September 2021).

Munby, S. (2019) *Imperfect Leadership: A book for leaders who know they don't know it all*, Crown House Publishing Ltd, Carmarthen, UK.

Northern Alliance (2022) Collaboration Framework: How well are you collaborating in your context? Available at: https://northernalliance.scot/wp-content/uploads/2022/11/NA-Collaboration-Framework.updated.pdf (Accessed: 18 November 2022).

Pink, D. (2010) Drive: The surprising truth about what motivates us. Presentation to the Royal Society of Arts. Available at: www.thersa.org/video/events/2010/01/drive (Accessed: 16 September 2021).

Syed, M. (2019) *Rebel Ideas: The power of diverse thinking*. John Murray Publishers Ltd., London.

Thurman, B. (2021) *Leading with Kindness: A report on the learning from the Kindness Leadership Network*. Carnegie UK, Dunfermline.

Conclusion and celebration

Karen McArdle, Sue Briggs, Ed Garrett and Kirsty Forrester

Prominent throughout this book has been social justice and the need to challenge neoliberalism. One takeaway thought is that we all need to be political. As Freire said in the 1970s (Freire, 2018), education is, in itself, political, and we must allow people to set their own agenda for their learning and development. Being political is not easy and we do a disservice to our communities if we do not engage with theory and make the links. To support this work, we need community workers who are brave and politically engaged themselves.

During the Black lives Matter racial protests in the UK, Charis Robertson (2022) was in agreement with the authors about being politically aware:

> 'You know, this [community work] isn't formal education; we respond to whatever is in the news, in the headlines, and this is going to be in the young people's radar. And our team were incredibly reluctant to go anywhere near it and put anything out online. They were concerned about opening up cans of worms and how to manage it online during lockdown. … And so I think the safety question is valid, but one of the questions is around whose needs is this about and how are we supporting every party's needs in this? Because they're all valid, but we shouldn't shy away from stuff because it's hard.' (Charis Robertson, 2022, Focus Group)

This is a profession that asks a lot of us. Our work is about identifying needs, co-designing programmes of learning, reducing barriers and addressing power imbalances. Research by McArdle et al (2013) showed that good professional educators are born, not made. To understand why what we do matters, as community workers we need empathy, something which arguably cannot be taught. The work we do is complex and we are frequently asked to step outside our comfort zone and engage across differences; it is demanding as we seek to engage with communities at times and in places that reduce the barriers for them; it can be heartbreaking as we see the discrimination faced by the communities we serve and the trauma that they carry with them; it is sometimes risky, and we often find ourselves working against the desired outcome of our employer or funder. But the work we do is rewarding and life changing for the communities we serve and for us as workers. We do not engage in a programme of learning with communities and leave unchanged; as community workers, sometimes we facilitate learning, but we always offer something of ourselves to build trust and, in this way, workers and communities are invested in each other.

As we reviewed what we had written in this book, we considered that we had not discussed poverty enough. It may be argued that the focus in public discourse on poverty may limit change. Poverty, for example, can seem too far away and something out there not to do with us. But poverty, as Lister (2021, 9) describes, includes 'lack of voice; disrespect, humiliation and an assault on dignity and self-esteem; shame and stigma; powerlessness; denial of rights and diminished citizenship'. These aspects of poverty are well within our ambit as community workers. There needs to be discussion of hunger, for example, instead of poverty, and a renewed focus on inequality alongside poverty. It needs to be clear that poverty is about systems, structures and relationships, in which we are all involved and complicit. We can work to change these systems politically. Being political does not mean, necessarily, the need to join political parties. It means being able to effect change in systems and structures that disadvantage people. It is no good just being a sticking plaster on the wound of poverty. We need to effect change where we can. Leaders in community work settings need to model appropriate political activity and support others

Conclusion and celebration

to engage with this. There is a strong need for political literacy education for community workers. Community workers can support others to seek change; they can also adopt an advocacy role, enabling and supporting other services and professions to empower participants, to consult them and to listen to them, for example. Similarly, working from within, community workers can ensure that policy, plans and services are inclusive and consistent with a community work value base.

Celebration is a term used in the title of this chapter and we refer to the need to celebrate what we do as a profession and the important impact of this community work. Valuing the role of theory in our practice to keep it fresh and informed is also important, especially as we work in a profession which has a wide range of associated disciplines. We need to take responsibility for our own learning as well as the learning of others. We need to be interdisciplinary, as has been evidenced by this book, drawing on health, the environment, as well as youth and adult learning, for example. Writing this book has been a challenge for us, as authors, but we have learnt tremendously from others – from academic books, papers, focus groups and interviews, and we are delighted with the strength, robustness and authenticity of the knowledge base that influences our practice. The knowledge base is highly interdisciplinary, reflecting the complexity of our role mentioned earlier. It is also quite idiosyncratic, drawing on such a wide range of activity, which is synthesised into professional domains in some countries, including Scotland. This has contributed to our learning about practice; and we hope it will contribute to yours.

References

Freire, P. (2018) *Pedagogy of the Oppressed.* Bloomsbury Publishing, USA.

Lister, R. (2021) *Poverty.* Polity Press, Cambridge.

McArdle, K., Hurrell, A. and Muñoz Martinez, Y. (2013) What makes teachers good at what they do? The axiological model. In J. McNiff (ed) *Value and Virtue in Practice-based Research.* September Books, Poole, pp 79–92.

Index

A
abuse 38
accountability 86, 112, 270
action research 242–4, 248–51
active citizenship 18
active learning 8–9, 12
activism 41, 62, 86–7, 99, 107–8, 201, 205–6, 212
Adams, Janine 34, 38, 44, 82
Adorno, T. 128
Adult Basic Education (ABE) 158, 162, 183
adult learning 157–78, 192–3
advocacy 108, 130
Advocates for Youth 116
affirmative action 42
Age Scotland 133
agency 36, 37, 73
Agenda 21 200
agile transformation 261–2
Alinsky, S. 84, 101
Allatt, G. 180
Anderson, E.S. 19
anomie 22
anti-racist work 31–2
anxiety 22, 65
apoliticism 64
appreciative inquiry (AI) 84–5
apprenticeships 181, 183
Archer, D. 264–5
Arendt, H. 125, 133
arts
  citizenship 217
  community arts 210–24
  measuring impact of arts projects 53
  as participation tool 70, 71
  and quality of life 83
asset-based community development (ABCD) 84–6, 108, 199
Australia 158, 159
Austria 175
authenticity 71, 109, 151
autonomy 124, 171, 189

B
Bacon, J. 268
Bagnall, R.G. 164, 165, 166
Bauman, Z. 21–2, 27
Beck, D. 18, 23, 25, 26, 52, 79, 81
belonging 83, 218
Benson, J. 202
best practice standards 11–12, 271
Bhopal, K. 35, 41, 42
bias 32–3, 145
Bifulco, L. 73, 74
Bivens, F. 250–1
Black Lives Matter 26, 275
Blickem, C. 84
Bonvin, J.-M. 73
Boothroyd, P. 82
bottom-up 78
bottom-up processes 68
Bowling, A. 124, 126
Braun, A. 214
Brierley, A. 139, 144–5
Brunton, G. 93
Bryce, Richard 184, 189
Brydon-Miller, M. 248
Buchroth, I. 147
bullying 31, 32
Bunyan, P. 163
Burdon, M. 261
Burkeman, O. 7
Burns, J.M. 257
Butler, M. 204
Bynner, J. 159

C
Calo, Francesca 186–7
Cameron, A. 264–5
Camic, P. 212, 213
Canada 91, 217, 218–19, 220

278

Index

Cantrell, S. 189
capabilities approach 189–91
capacity building 69, 85, 96, 125, 131, 134, 268–9
carbon emissions 200
Carnegie, Jess 202, 205–6
Carnegie UK 262–3
Carpenter, M. 138, 140, 183, 184, 185, 186, 188, 190, 193, 194
case study methods 248
Chambers, E.T. 101, 102–3, 263
Chamorro-Premuzic, T. 233
Chanan, G. 77, 78
change/transformation
  agile transformation 261–2
  community arts 218–20
  digital transformation 262
  education 165
  encouraging participation 71
  future of work 259–60
  impact 51–3
  leadership 267
  perspective transformation 170, 171
  social change 81–2
  theory of change 114
  three-step process 99
  transformational leadership 256–7
  youth work 152
choirs 128–30
Cigna 225
citizenship
  active citizenship 18
  community arts 217
  democratic citizenship 37
  rights 67
  youth work 144
civil liberties 65
civil society 68
Clandinin, D.J. 245–6, 247
Clark, H. 187
Clark, Lynn 52–3, 58–9, 116–17, 161–2, 256–7, 270–1
class consciousness 26
Cleaver, F. 63, 69, 70
Clelland, William 221–2
Clift, S. 212, 213
climate crisis 77, 198, 200, 203, 204
coaching 13
co-creation of knowledge 72, 95
co-design 148, 152, 276
code-switching 109
Cohen, G.D. 214

Collaboration Framework 265–6
collaborative working
  across whole system 266
  community arts 215, 222
  connectivism 231
  leadership 264–8
  participatory action research (PAR) 248
  partnership working 112–13, 114, 115, 117
Collective Leadership for Scotland 267
collective responsibility 266
Collins, H. 264
communication
  collaborative working 115
  community arts 215
  networking and partnership working 108–9
community
  brokering trust between communities 31
  concealing power relations 62
  engagement 90–105
  liquid modernity 21–2
  networking 106–7
  politics 64–5
  resilience 77, 82–3
  values 79–81
  who speaks for 73
  why community matters 77
  working with a community despite not being a member 41
  working with communities 41, 77–89
community development
  asset-based community development (ABCD) 84–6
  core principles 80–1
  environment 201
  leadership 268
  networking 107, 108
  strategic public investment 78
Community Development and Health Network 11
community forums 98–9
community larders 49–51
Community Learning and Development (CLD) Standards Council 12
community organising 101–2, 268
community research methods 97–8, 242–55

competition for resources 63
'congruent duplicity' 217
connection 34, 91, 101–2, 106–8, 221, 236, 258
connectivism 230–2
Connelly, F.M. 245–6
conscientisation 168, 173
consciousness 24–5
constructivism 85, 166
consultation 96, 99, 243, 244
Cooke, B. 62
Copic, Lada 9, 161, 165, 169
corruption 65
Cort, P. 183
cost-benefit ratios 56–7
counter-hegemony 23, 25–6
COVID-19
  community arts 215–16
  community resilience 77
  digital community work 228, 232–5
  digital literacy 163
  health and well-being 121
  impact on social interactions 225, 264
  leadership 259
  loneliness 132
  models of health 123
  narrative inquiry 246–8
  professional learning 13
  solidarity 107
Cox, L. 205, 206
Coyle, D. 218
Crenshaw, K. 35
critical literacy 124, 169
critical pedagogy 229
critical reflection 25, 26, 33, 35, 79, 80
critical thinking 26, 33, 35, 169, 171
Cunliffe, A.L. 258

D

Darcy, H. 205, 206
Darity Jr, W. 187
de St Croix, T. 152
Deloitte 259, 260, 266
democracy 37, 65, 67–9, 73, 81
Denmark 183
deprived areas
  engagement 94
  equality and inclusion 33
  health inequalities 122–3

partnership working 111
youth work 139
Descartes, R. 124, 202
design thinking 262
development projects 63
see also community development
Dewey, J. 166
dialogue and deliberation 100
DigiShakti 227–8
digital community work 225–41
digital competence 232
digital conferencing platforms 235
digital exclusions 158, 163
digital fluency 229
digital learning 13
digital literacy 226, 227, 229, 232–3, 238
digital networks 108
digital transformation 262
digital well-being 237–9
digital work 188–9
dignity 18, 71
disability 31, 160, 186
disadvantage
  asset-based community development (ABCD) 85
  equality and inclusion 31, 38–9, 42
  health inequalities 131
  participatory budgeting 63
  prejudice 21
  'seldom heard' groups 73
  social impact assessments (SIAs) 54
  values and community work 79
  youth work 139
discourse 24, 35, 36, 125, 139
diversity 263–4
Doherty, L. 152
doormats project 220
Dorling, D. 20, 23
Downes, S. 230
Dr Hill's Casebook 213
dualism 124, 202
Durham University 251, 252–3
Dworkin, R. 19

E

Eberle, M. 82
economic justice 81
education
  adult learning 157–78
  educational attainment 159–60
  emancipatory tradition 168

Index

environment projects 206
political nature of 275
professional learning 5–16, 267–8, 276–7
youth work 138–9, 142–5, 147, 149
see also learning
Edwards, B. 110
efficiency 63
Elden, S. 129, 130
electoral politics 68, 108
elitism 20–1, 210
Emejulu, A. 36, 37
emotional capital 83
employability 179–97
empowerment
  community arts 216–18
  core principles of community development 81
  digital empowerment 227–30
  employability 193
  environment 201
  health and well-being 129
  participation 61, 70
engagement
  barriers to engagement with adult learning 160–2
  community arts 215–16
  community engagement 90–105
  community research methods 242–55
  versus connection 145
  digital community work 226, 232–5
  environment 198–209
environmental justice 201, 203
epistemic meaning schemes 170
equality
  asset-based community development (ABCD) 86
  core principles of community development 81
  employability 186
  equality and inclusion 30–47
  social justice 19, 26
  see also inequality
Equality and Human Rights Commission 31, 32, 39
Equality Impact Assessment (EIA) 39–40
Eraut, M. 6–7
Escobar, O. 100
Esteves, A.M. 54

ethics 71, 206–7, 251, 257–8, 261
ethnic minorities 33–4, 160, 186, 187, 249–50
European Commission 182, 183, 186, 187, 225, 232, 234
European Union 181
evaluation of impact 48–60
Evans, L. 258
Evans, Matthew 200
evidence of impact 49–51, 53–9
experiential knowledge/lived experience 7, 41, 70, 143, 203–4, 207

F

fairness 17, 21
false consciousness 24–5
'false partnerships' 110
family learning contexts 32
family-learning work 159
fear 22, 65
feminism 35–8
financial literacy 228
Fitoussi, J.-P. 180
Fleurbaey, M. 18
focus groups for community engagement 97–8
food larders 125–6
Fook, J. 25
forums 98–9
Foucault, M. 9, 24, 25, 52, 62, 92, 129, 130
'Four Phases of Theory Engagement' 199
Francis-Devine, B. 187
Frankiewicz, B. 233
Freda, B. 138, 140
Frei, W. 175
Freire, P. 10, 25, 26, 39, 52, 101, 131, 166, 167–8, 169, 173, 192, 275
Fullan, M. 258–9, 267–8
funding
  adult learning 160–1
  community arts 216–17, 220–1
  community organising 102
  community research methods 243
  competition for resources 63
  environment projects 206
  equality and inclusion 39, 40
  evidence of impact 50
  participatory budgeting 63–4
  partnership working 111
  youth work 149

Fung, A. 68
Furlong, A. 143–4
future of work 188–9, 259–60
Fyfe, I. 147, 151

G

Garcha, Sonia 227, 228, 239
garden projects 202
Gaventa, J. 67, 68, 69
gender equality 32
gig economy 183, 189
Gilchrist, A. 102, 106, 107, 108, 112, 115, 268
Gillan, Darran 229, 233–4, 235
Giroux, H.A. 138, 139, 145, 150, 151
Glasby, J. 108, 110, 114
globalisation 21–2, 26, 183
good life 22
Gouthro, P. 157–78
governance 67–9, 109
Gramsci, A. 23, 26, 103
Graney, A. 126
greed 21
Greenwood, Belona 210, 216, 217–18, 221
Grotlüschen, A. 159
Gudykunst, W.B. 109
Gunn, Alan 49–50, 70, 79–80, 110–11, 112, 242–4, 257, 266–7, 269

H

habitus 172
Hadjieva, J. 258, 262
Hall, S. 82, 83
Hancock, B. 129, 130
'hard to reach' groups 73
Harley, A. 199, 200, 201
Harrison, Joan 57, 216, 217, 219
Harrison, R. 84
Harvey, D. 21
Haugen, E. 109
health and social care partnerships 114, 127
health and well-being 72–3, 82–3, 121–37, 204, 212–14
  see also mental health
Health Issues in Communities 131
health literacy 123–4
health service policy 72–3
healthy communities 82–3
hegemony 23, 25, 27, 103

heuristics 32
Hoare, G. 23, 26
Hodge, S. 164, 165, 166
Hoggan, C. 171
homophobia 33
hope 49
Hothi, M. 102
Howitt, R. 54
human capital 83, 180, 184, 186, 190
human flourishing 190
human rights
  capabilities approach 190
  core principles of community development 81
  employability programmes 182
  equality 31–3
  online rights 237–8
  participation 65
  social justice 18–19, 21
human-centred organisations 261–3
Hung, K. 70
hunger 26, 276
Hunter, Susan 138, 141, 146, 149, 150, 151–2, 153
Huntly Youth Climate Warriors 205–6

I

identity 22, 211–12
impact
  adult learning 162–3
  equality and inclusion 39–43
  evaluation of impact 48–60
  and the role of theory 7
  youth work 148–9
inclusion 18, 26, 30–47, 86
India 227
Indigenous cultures 202
Indigo Valley, Australia 107–8
Industrial Areas Foundation (IAF) 101
inequality
  adult learning 160, 168
  equality and inclusion 30–47
  health inequalities 122–3, 130–4
  neoliberalism 20–1
  participation 64
informal learning 142–5, 150, 184, 234
informal literacy practices 162
instrumentalism 164–5

Index

International Association for Community Development (IACD) 12, 80
intersectionality 35, 36
interview methods 101, 245–6, 247
Ireland 152
Israel, B. 126

J

Jarvis, P. 51
Jeffers, A. 215
Jeffs, T. 143, 150, 151
Jepson, A. 70
Jickling, B. 198, 206, 207
Johnston, Kathleen 113, 258, 260, 265, 266
Jones, J. 131, 132
Jones, O. 109, 110, 112, 117
Joseph Rowntree Foundation 123
journals, access to 8
Joyette, D. 91, 245

K

Kane, G.C. 262
Kasprowicz, Martin 212, 268–9
Kelly, Mark 226, 232, 233, 238
Kemmis, S. 251
Kengmana, Michael 165, 183, 236–7
Kennedy, Fran 116, 174
key texts 10
Kidron, Beeban 237–8
kindness in leadership 262–3
Kiron, D. 189
Knight, C. 173
knowledge
 action research 248–9
 community engagement 100
 construction of knowledge in online learning 235–6
 epistemologies of adult learning 164–7
 experiential knowledge 7
 knowledge flow hubs 230
 lay knowledge 72, 126
 lived experience 7, 41, 70, 143, 203–4, 207
 local expertise 117
 for partnership working 117
 professional knowledge 126–7
 professional learning 5–16, 267–8, 276–7
 situational knowledge 165
triangulation 93
valuing knowledge 92–4
Kothari, U. 62

L

labour market programmes 182–5
language, importance of 26, 109, 117, 203, 207
language barriers to employment 186
Larson, A. 183
Lawson, E. 14
lay knowledge 72, 126
leadership 256–74
learning
 action research 248
 adult learning 157–78
 community arts 213
 community-based learning 112–13
 connectivism 230–2
 CPD for community workers' digital literacy 232–3, 238
 digital literacy 227–9
 family learning contexts 32
 family-learning work 159
 health education 131–2
 informal learning 142–5, 150, 184, 234
 kindness in leadership 262
 measuring 49–50
 models of learning 51–2
 and participation 71–2
 professional learning 5–16, 267–8, 276–7
 skills-focused 180
 social construction of 166
 social practice model of learning 191–3
 transformative learning theory 170–1
 workplace as a learning environment 6–8, 11–12
 youth work 142–5, 147
 see also education
Ledwith, M. 20, 24, 25, 39, 71
Lewin, K. 99
LGBT 31, 186
libraries, access to 8
Lieblich, A. 245
Limb, D. 214
Lindsjö, C. 131
liquid modernity 21–2
Lister, R. 276

literacy 158, 161–2, 167–70, 183, 186
Little, J. 109, 110, 112, 117
lived experience 7, 41, 70, 143, 203–4, 207
Lloyd, J.E. 124
lobbying 65
local leadership 85
local place-based approaches 85, 205
local politics 65–6, 67–9
loneliness 125, 132–4, 235
long-term impact, measuring 50
long-term investment in communities 78

M

MacGregor Burns, J. 257
Mackie, Alan 147, 151, 181, 194
management (versus leadership) 258–9
Mansfield, S. 92
Marmot Review 122–3
Matarasso, F. 211, 214
Maxwell, Connor 141–2, 148
Maynard, L. 142–3, 149
McArdle, K. 7, 33, 35, 49, 58, 73, 80, 92, 100, 110, 112, 114, 172, 214, 276
McCurdy, Paul 164
McGregor, C. 203, 204
McIntosh, P. 42
McNiff, J. 248, 249
McTaggart, R. 251
Meade, R. 211, 212
media coverage 23–4, 65, 70, 139, 145
medical model of health 124, 126
medicalisation 129
Medlin, J. 174
mental health 132, 188, 190, 213, 214
mentoring 13
meritocracy 41–2
methadone programmes 187
Mezirow, J. 170, 171, 233
migration 158, 186, 259
Milana, M. 162
Milroy, Ken 90–1
mini publics 100–1
Mitchell, Jane 121, 127
models of health 123–5
models of youth work 143–4
Moon, J. 10, 11

morality 71–2, 79, 206
  see also ethics; values
Morgan, K. 158, 159, 162
Moser, H. 250
Motivation, Opportunity, Ability (MOA) model 70–1
Moyn, S. 18
multidisciplinary partnerships 113
Munby, S. 260
mutuality 202

N

Naidoo, J. 126–7
narrative inquiry 244, 245–8, 250–1
National Health Service (NHS) 122
National Occupational Standards in Community Development 11, 80
National Standards for Community Engagement 91, 96
National Youth Work Agency 145
nature, role in community 202–3
needs assessment 128, 182, 244, 276
neoliberalism
  adult learning 164–5
  capabilities approach as alternative to 189–91
  effect on community workers 27
  employability programmes 180, 182–5
  environment 199, 201
  and human rights 18
  ideology of 19–22
  loneliness 134
  meritocracy 41–2
  participation 64–5
  social justice 275
  sustainability 200
  wellness discourses 125
networking 106–9, 230–2, 268
non-human members of community 202, 206
Northern Alliance Improvement Collaborative 265–6
'Nothing about us, without us' 41
NovoEd 225, 235
Nussbaum, M. 190, 191
Nutbeam, D. 124

O

obesity 126
OECD 158, 159

Index

older people
  adult learning 163
  employability 186
  online banking 228
  online learning 235–6
  see also digital literacy
  online work 188–9
Ortiz Aragon, A. 248
othering 65, 139
outdoor gyms 94

P

PACT (presence, attunement, connection and trust) 144–5
Parkin, C. 147
Parsons, S. 159
participation 61–76
  in best practice standards 11–12
  as core theme of social progress 51
  empowerment 61–3
  encouraging 69–72
  participative democracy 81
  social impact assessments (SIAs) 54
  youth work 145
participatory action research (PAR) 242–4, 248–51
participatory budgeting 63–4
participatory governance 68
participatory research 130
partnership working 109–16, 127, 131, 264
passive objects of community development 36–7
patriarchy 35
Pawluczuk, A. 226, 233, 234
Payne, M. 86, 87
Perlman, D. 133
personal meaning schemes 170
perspective blindness 264
perspective transformation 170, 171
Petsche, Kimiko 159, 161, 168–9
physical capital 83
Pickett, K. 64
Pink, D. 261
planning tools 219–20
policing 249–50
politics
  education as political act 168
  electoral politics 68, 108
  environment 203–4
  local politics 65–6, 67–9
  need to be political 275
  participation 64–5

political literacy 26, 277
political representation 108
populism 203–4
positivism 126
poststucturalism 35, 36
poverty
  barriers to engagement with adult learning 160–1
  community research methods 242–3
  digital divide 232
  employability 188
  employment as solution to 180, 181
  and health 123
  literacy 159
  neoliberalism 26–7
  political activism 276–7
  varied aspects of 276
power relationships
  code-switching 109
  community arts 215
  community engagement 93, 94–5, 99–100
  community organising 101–2
  empowerment 61–3
  feminist theory 36
  health and control 125–30
  hegemony 23, 25, 27, 103
  leadership 271
  neoliberalism 21–2
  partnership working 111
  power as discipline 129
  privilege 42
  resistance 52
  shifting power from 'users' of a service 132
  social justice 24–5
  theory of 9
  valuing knowledge 93
  voice 92
  young people 149–50
powerlessness 22, 24, 87
praxis 168, 201, 251
precarious work 161, 183, 185, 189
prejudice 21, 33
privilege, people with 38, 41–3
professional knowledge 126–7
professional learning 5–16, 267–8, 276–7
protected characteristics 30–47
psychiatry 129
public health 130, 214

public sector 73
public services 68
public transport 99, 188
Purcell, M.E. 180, 183, 191
Purcell, R. 18, 23, 25, 26, 52, 79, 81
purpose, sense of 261
Putnam, R. 83, 133

Q

quilt project 219
Quinn, J. 267–8

R

race 26, 33, 35, 186, 275
  see also ethnic minorities
radical theory 39
Rawls, J. 17
Reeler, D. 249
reflective practice
  action research 249
  adult learning 172
  in best practice standards 11–12
  community arts 220
  critical reflection 25, 26, 33, 35, 79, 80
  digital community work 236
  kindness in leadership 262
  leadership 267
  participation 71
  professional reflections on theory tool 14
  theoretical grounding 10–11
  values and community work 79, 80
reflexivity 33, 79, 80, 172, 258
refugees and asylum seekers 186–7
Reich, J.A. 82, 84
relational meetings 102–3
relationship building
  community arts 213, 215
  community engagement 95–6
  digital community work 225, 230–2
  leadership 262, 264–8
  networking 106–8, 230–2, 268
  youth work 143, 150–1
  see also social capital
reproductive justice 116
resilience 77, 82–3, 213, 237, 261
resistance 35, 52, 130, 204
respect 19, 71, 114, 115, 151, 184, 201, 205

Rettie, Pauline 152
Richardson, Mark 50, 217, 219–20
Riessman, C.K. 247
right-wing populism 20
Roberts, H. 139
Robertson, Charis 127–8, 138, 142, 147, 150, 275
Robinson, V. 9, 199
Robson, S. 37–8
Rocco, M. 132
Roche, J. 150
Rose Hill, S. 133
Roseter, B. 150
Ruggieri, K. 124, 125
rural areas 33–4, 112, 187–8, 228
Ryan, A. 35, 36

S

Sacheder, D. 139
Sadker, D. 32
Salmon, G. 235, 236
Saxena, N. 61, 69, 71
scale of impact 53, 58
Scandrett, E. 199, 200, 201, 203, 204
science 126, 128
Scottish Human Rights Commission 32
Scottish National Occupational Standards for Community Development 80
Seighart, M. 32
'seldom heard' groups 73
self-determination, in best practice standards 11–12
self-evaluation 54, 55, 220
self-organised movements 141
Sen, A. 107, 180, 190
service design/design thinking 262
sexual harassment 32
Shaw, Iain 50–1, 215
Shaw, M. 211, 212
short-termism 22, 40, 78
Siemens, G. 230, 231–2
situational knowledge 165
Smith, A. 19
Smith, M. 143, 150, 151
social accounting 57
social capital
  engagement 91, 95–6
  and health 125, 132
  loneliness 133–4
  working with communities 82, 83

Index

social change 52, 81–2
social determinants of health 122
social enterprise 212
social exclusion 80, 81, 139, 226
  see also disadvantage
social impact assessments (SIAs) 54–6
social justice 17–29
  adult learning 160
  in best practice standards 11–12
  capabilities approach 190
  community arts 217–18
  core principles of community
    development 81
  as core theme of social progress 51
  employability 194
  employment 180
  environment 199–201, 202
  and health 123
  leadership 260
  and the need to be political 275
  values 79
  valuing knowledge 93
  youth work 147
social media 65, 95, 170, 189, 225,
  226, 231
social model of health 127–9
social practice model of
  learning 191–3
social progress, core themes of 51
social return on investment
  (SROI) 56–7
socialist theory 39
sociolinguistic meaning schemes 170
Socrates 8
solidarity 51, 107
Sonke, J. 214–15
Soper, K. 202, 203
special interest groups 40–1
Speeden, S. 186, 194
Spence, J. 37–8
Sperber, N. 23, 26
Springett, J. 20, 24, 25
stakeholder perspectives, gathering
  56–7, 112, 201, 234, 270
stereotyping 21, 24, 32
Stiefel, M. 62
Stiglitz, J. 180, 191
stigmatisation 44, 161, 276
Stommel, J. 229
storytelling 245–8
strengths-based approaches 85,
  191, 211
Stringer, E. 248

Stuart, K. 142–3, 149
Stuart, Nadia 13
substance misuse 187–8
surveys 94, 97
sustainability
  in best practice standards 11–12
  core principles of community
    development 81
  environment 198–209
  neoliberalism 200
  partnership working 109–10, 117
Swantz, M.L. 249, 250
Syed, M. 263–4

T

'tall poppy syndrome' 27
Tam, H. 77, 78
Tattersall, A. 108
Tawney, R.H. 40–1
Taylor, M. 109, 112, 115, 117
Taylor, P. 71, 72, 122, 126, 128
Tett, L. 64, 180
Thelen, L. 73
theory (generally) 6–16
Thin, N. 51
third sector 73, 113, 116, 127,
  133, 256
Thompson, N. 17, 21
Thurman, B. 259–60, 262–3
Tinglin, W. 91, 245
tokenism 103, 111, 245
top-down processes 78, 84, 184
totalitarianism 133
transformation *see* change/
  transformation
transformational leadership 256–7
transformative learning
  theory 170–1
Transition Towns 200
transparency 86, 250, 258
trauma-informed practice
  (TIP) 172–3
Traveller communities 33
trust
  community arts 215
  engagement 90, 114
  ethical leaders 258
  mutual investment 276
  participation 71, 73
  voluntarism 184
  youth work 145, 150
Tuckwood, Dawn 125, 128
Tyler, I. 20, 21, 22, 64–5

U

UK Council for Internet Safety (UKCIS) 237
UN (United Nations)
  Agenda 21 200
  Convention on the Rights of the Child 149
  Global Goals 109–10
  UNESCO 159–60, 186
Unbound Community 221–2
unconscious bias 32–3, 145
unemployment 180, 181–2, 184–5, 186
unpaid care work 183
Urie, Alison 221–2
US
  leadership 270–1
  literacy 158
  No child left behind 165
  online learning 236–7

V

values
  action research 250
  community arts 218, 220–1
  community work 79–81
  diversity 263
  environment projects 206
  ethical leaders 257–8
  impact evaluation 58
  leadership 260, 261
  networking 107
  practice compass 11–13
  science 128
valuing knowledge 92–4
vernacular language 109
Visioning Outcomes in Community Engagement (VOiCE) 96
voice
  agency 36, 37, 73
  community arts 214
  community engagement 92, 96
  community research methods 243
  empowerment 65–7, 68, 82
  environment 204–5
  participation 72–4
  poverty as lack of 276
  reaching the excluded 97
  youth voice 151–2
Voices for Indi campaign 107–8
voluntarism/voluntary participation in community work 143, 149, 161, 184
voluntary sector 73, 113, 116, 127, 133, 256
Vox Liminis 221–2
vulnerable communities 79
  see also disadvantage

W

Walker, J. 236
Warner, D. 236
Wealleans-Turner, Nat 8–9, 34, 39, 44, 146–7, 180
Weatherby, Ross 67, 184–5, 188, 190, 194, 201
Webster, C. 181, 185, 187
welfare system 31, 185
well-being
  and community arts 212–13
  community resilience 83
  definition of 124–5
  digital well-being 237–9
  employment policies 179, 180
  impact evaluation 48–9
  meaningful occupation 190
  participation 73
  values 80
  see also health and well-being
West, Charlie 211–12
Westoby, P. 198, 199, 202
Wheeler, J. 250–1
Whelan, Aine 48
Whitehead, J. 249
wicked problems 78, 263, 267
Wilkinson, R. 64
Williamson, T. 72, 73
Wilson, V. 187
wisdom 72
Wolfe, M. 62
women and girls
  digital literacy 227–8
  employability 186
  feminist theory 35–8
  gender equality 32
  health and well-being 130–2
  literacy 186
  unconscious bias 32
  unpaid care work 183
work placements 10
worker rights 65
workplace as a learning environment 6–8, 11–12

Index

'workplace readiness' 7
World Health Organization 122, 124, 212
Wright, E. 68
Wyler, S. 78

Y

young people
  definition of youth 140
  employability 181
  youth community engagement 95
  youth work 138–56, 183
Youngs, H. 258
youth justice system 144

Z

Zautra, A. 82, 83

www.ingramcontent.com/pod-product-compliance
Lightning Source LLC
Chambersburg PA
CBHW051530020426
42333CB00016B/1852